BERGSON AND
PHILOSOPHY

BERGSON AND PHILOSOPHY

John Mullarkey

University of Notre Dame Press
Notre Dame, Indiana

Published in the United States in 2000 by
University of Notre Dame Press
Notre Dame, Indiana 46556

ISBN 0-268-02161-9

© John Mullarkey, 1999

Edinburgh University Press Ltd
22 George Square, Edinburgh

Library of Congress Cataloging-in-Publication Data
A catalog record for this book is available
from the Library of Congress

Contents

Contents

Acknowledgements

I would like to express my appreciation to all those who have had to read various versions of this book, in particular, John Chisholm, Sebastien Gardner, Sarah Richmond, David Wood, Peter Poellner, Leszek Kolakowski and Keith Ansell Pearson. Amongst those who have either commented on my work or whose conversation has inspired it, I would especially like to thank Owen White, Brian O'Connor, Brendan Guilfoyle and Pete Gunter. I must equally record my debt to Betty whose intervention in July 1993 was a great influence on Chapter Six. The Philosophy Department at Middlesex University as well as Geoff and Mary Midgeley's APIS group in Newcastle were also kind enough to invite me to speak to them about this work on Bergson.

The generosity of various funding bodies has helped to keep this project afloat over the years; they include The British Academy, The University of Warwick and the Philosophy Department at University College London. I also benefited from a sabbatical granted to me in 1997 by my colleagues at the University of Sunderland, for which I am grateful.

Earlier drafts of some of the material in this book have appeared previously, contained in the following articles by the author: 'La Philosophie Nouvelle, or Change in Philosophy', in John Mullarkey (ed.), *The New Bergson* (Manchester: Manchester University Press, 1999), pp.1–16; 'Bergson and the Language of Process', in *Process Studies*, pp. 44–58, vol. XXIV, Spring 1997; 'Bergson: The Philosophy of *Durée-différence*', in *Philosophy Today*, pp. 367–80 vol. XL, Autumn 1996; 'Bergson's Method of Multiplicity', in *Metaphilosophy*, pp. 230–59, vol. XXVI, July 1995; and 'Duplicity in the Flesh: Bergson and Current Philosophy of the Body', in *Philosophy*

Today, pp. 339–55, vol. XXXVIII, Winter 1994–95. I gratefully acknowledge the permissions granted by these journals to use this material.

Finally, I would like to acknowledge the support of my wife, Annalaura, whose patience and love deserve my warmest thanks. I dedicate this book to the memory of my mother, Peggy Mullarkey.

Abbreviations

The page references to the published English translation(s) are given first, followed by those to the French original in either *Oeuvres* or *Mélanges* as appropriate.

CE   Henri Bergson, *Creative Evolutions*, London, Macmillan, 1911. Translated by Arthur Mitchell from *L'Evolution créatrice* (1907), in *Oeuvres*, pp. 487–809.

CM   Henri Bergson, *The Creative Mind: An Introduction to Metaphysics*, New York, Philosophical Library, 1946. Translated by Mabelle L. Andison from *La Pensée et le mouvant: Essais et conférences* (1934), in *Oeuvres*, pp. 1249–482. The paperback edition of this translation has a different pagination from the hardback and omits the endnotes. Unless an endnote is involved, references are given to the paperback alone as it is more widely available than the hardback edition.

DS   Henri Bergson, *Duration and Simultaneity, with Reference to Einstein's Theory*, Indianapolis, Bobbs-Merrill, 1965. Translated by Leon Jacobsen, with an introduction by Herbert Dingle, from *Durée et simultanéité: A Propos de la Théorie d'Einstein* (1923), in *Mélanges*, pp. 57–244.

L   *Laughter: An Essay on the Meaning of the Comic*, London, Macmillan, 1911. Translated by Cloudesley Brereton and Fred Rothwell from *Le Rire* (1900), in *Oeuvres*, pp. 381–485.

M   Henri Bergson, *Mélanges*, edited by André Robinet, Paris, Presses Universitaires de France, 1972.

les données immédiates de la conscience

ME   Henri Bergson, *Mind-Energy: Lectures and Essays*, Westport,
      Connecticut, Greenwood Press, 1975. Translated by H. Wildon
      Carr from *L'Energie Spirituelle: Essais et conférences* (1919), in
      Oeuvres, pp. 811–977.

MM   Henri Bergson, *MM*, London, George Allen and Unwin, 1911.
      Translated by Nancy Margaret Paul and W. Scott Palmer from
      Matière et mémoire: Essai sur la relation du corps avec l'esprit (1896),
      in *Oeuvres*, pp. 159–379.

OE   Henri Bergson, *Oeuvres*, edited by André Robinet, Paris, Presses
      Universitaires de France, 1959.

TFW Henri Bergson, *Time and Free Will: An Essay on the Immediate
      Data of Consciousness*, London, George Allen and Unwin, 1910.
      Translated by F. L. Pogson from *Essai sur les données immédiates de
      la conscience* (1889), in *Oeuvres*, pp. 1–157.

TSMR Henri Bergson, *The Two Sources of Morality and Religion*, Notre
      Dame, Indiana, Notre Dame Press, 1977. Translated by R.
      Ashley Audra and Cloudesley Brereton, with the assistance of W.
      Horsfall Carter, from *Les Deux sources de la morale et de la religion*
      (1932), in *Oeuvres*, pp. 979–1247.

Introduction

Every man has two philosophies.[1]

It has been suggested that the preoccupation with language which has characterised philosophy so much this century will be replaced in the next by a 'spiralling return' to the fundamental issue of time.[2] The last number of years have in fact seen a resurgence of interest in the philosophy of time, though it has yet to reach that level of activity which accompanied its first appearance on the modern philosophical scene. I refer here to those early decades of this century when philosophers like J. M. E. McTaggart, Samuel Alexander, and A. N. Whitehead were at the high point of their fortunes. Of these modern philosophers of time it is probably Henri Bergson whom one would have to cite as the first and foremost. Even Bergson's fellow contender for this title, Samuel Alexander, readily admitted that it was probably 'Bergson in our day who has been the first philosopher to take Time seriously',[3] while Jorge Luis Borges believed that anything written on time after Bergson would be anachronistic.[4] While the focus for this study is indeed the question of time, I hope to avoid such anachronism myself by taking Bergson's account – what he calls the philosophy of duration or '*durée*' – as my specific approach.

However, things are never that simple, alas, and this is especially so when it comes to Bergson's interpretation of time. To begin with, he argues that most representations of time abolish what is peculiarly temporal about it. Our supposedly common-sense notions of time stem, he claims, from a philosophical heritage with roots going back to Plato.[5] What that heritage has given us is a constant tendency to ignore what is special about time in favour of confusing its properties with those of various other phenomena – space, language and thought. In other words, time is not an innocent concept: it is neither immediately clear what it is nor immutably given to human understanding. Our ideas about time are themselves transient. And this is precisely what makes Bergson's approach to time so interesting and problematic: the representation of time has a history to it which is not incidental but necessary. Reflecting this evolving nature of the depiction of time, Bergson's own philosophy undergoes a continual process of recreation too. In fact, it is an examination of why Bergson's philosophy, or philosophies, of time are so transient, evolutionary or, in a word, temporal, that lies at the heart of this study.

Not only does this evolution go through many forms in terms of the content of the concept of time, it is equally unstable in terms of the methodology used in reaching it. As our analysis of *MM* in Chapter Two will illustrate, Bergson blends two quite different approaches in his elucidation of temporality, the one emphasising a subjective experience of an enduring continuous *durée*, the other resorting to the objective data of the contemporary sciences, in particular physics and the revolutionary views concerning matter found there at the time Bergson was writing. The interpretative history of Bergsonism testifies to this diversity of method in his work. Traditionally, there have been two ways of taking up Bergson's time-philosophy. The first emphasises its affinities with a naturalistic process philosophy (Whitehead's in particular); the second sees it in the light of the existentialists and phenomenologists who succeeded Bergson in France. Following the first line of interpretation, we find writers like Milič Čapek, David Sipfle, and Gilles Deleuze; taking the opposite track are Jean Hyppolite, Vladimir Jankélévitch, Maurice Merleau-Ponty and Emmanuel Levinas.[6]

This schism has also led to various criticisms of Bergson's work. He has been attacked for what is seen as his residual naturalism by phenomenological thinkers (Martin Heidegger, Jean-Paul Sartre and Gaston Bachelard) just as he has been criticised by philosophical naturalists for his subjectivism. Hence, Bachelard, for instance, reproaches Bergson for ignoring the reality of discontinuity in human time in favour of an unstructured, homogeneous continuity.[7] Nevertheless, Bachelard for his part forgets that discontinuity is perfectly well inscribed within Bergson's naturalism, only at the level of biological evolution rather than conscious human experience. Yet Bergson does not take the direction of a reductive naturalism either: he never reduces reality to one realm of explanation. Most of the errors made in interpreting his work stem from a confusion between the numerous levels at which Bergson's analyses operate. As one commentator has noted, both positions, humanist and naturalist, seem to emphasise their own perspective at the expense of these alternative possibilities:

discontinuity?

variety of possibilities, both humanist & naturalistic

influence of Whitehead (impr & univl) & Exst. (pr & indv.), which was not Bergson

Even as Whitehead gives Bergsonism a final impersonal and universal focus which it did not possess, so does Existentialism give Bergsonism a final personal and individual focus which it did not possess. Bergson's insights survive incorporated within viewpoints other than his own and more sharply drawn than his own.[8]

Just as his own philosophy will assert that there are levels to reality, space and even being, so there are also levels to Bergsonism itself: 'We must always ask which image of Bergson is under consideration'.[9] To think that there is just one image of Bergsonism, be it vitalist or spiritualist, positivist or metaphysical, speculative or critical, testifies as much to one's own reading as it does to his work itself.

levels

The interpretative stance taken in this study of Bergson's work has as its own aim the intention to dispel the view that Bergson ever stuck to one philosophy at all, be it phenomenology, vitalism or, more generally, any form of empiricism. Indeed, as Chapter Five will argue, the import of what empiricism there is in Bergson's thought is also ultimately *ethical*. I say 'ultimately' rather than 'fundamentally' or 'entirely' because it is only in his last major work, *TSMR*, that ethics (termed 'open morality') takes on this mantle: Bergsonism's earlier incarnations remain boldly empirical. While *TSMR* holds one key to understanding Bergson's work as a whole by pointing to the finally ethical orientation of his analyses of time, mind, evolutionary biology and relativity physics, the empirical matters contained therein are no less empirical for all that: neither they nor ethics are reduced to each other. Moreover, the earlier empirical and later ethical concerns of Bergson's thought do not stand outside of each other either: as I will explain, there is good reason for reading Bergson's writings as an implicit ethics of alterity fleshed out in empirical concerns, its moral image becoming explicit only in *TSMR*.

ethical orientra note Bergson's own dvlpmt

The dualism of ethics and empiricism here is not insignificant. In fact, what Bergson's work gives us is a metaphysics by which to understand not only the broader philosophical dualism of fact and value but also all conceptual dualism in general. A supposed weakness of Bergson's work has been its tendency to dichotomise, not simply through its famed dualisms of quality–quantity, mobile–immobile, space–time, past–present and so on, but also in its core 'law of dichotomy' and the underlying rationalism and anti-rationalism, humanism and anti-humanism, physicalism and vitalism (the list goes on), it alternatively countenances. We will see that this affected duplicity is actually the strength of Bergsonian thinking: its metaphilosophical realisation that there is no single foundation or principle on which philosophy can take its stand (even if that principle is 'anti-founda-

strength of his laws of dichotomy

What is a first philosophy?

tionalism' itself), that there are no 'first philosophies' in other words. The merits of any claim to the title of first philosophy, be it from a branch of philosophy like metaphysics or ethics, or a school of philosophy such as empiricism, are usurped in a Bergsonian metaphilosophy which states that, in a creative universe with no static foundations, there will never be a first philosophy for anything or anyone to claim. In other words, if *everything* is changing, then this must be true for philosophy as well.

The expositional dimension of this book consists in unpacking a set of dichotomies within Bergsonism that are increasingly more abstract. Chapters One to Three begin with the first-order dualisms of space and time, mind and body, and finally life and matter, by explaining Bergsonian concepts like '*durée*', 'pure perception', 'attention to life' and '*élan vital*'. The next two chapters take a step up in the order of abstraction as we turn to Bergson's ethical thought, embedding such normative concepts as '*le bon sens*' and 'open morality' within the broader philosophical dualism of ethics and empirics itself. The concluding chapters then thematise this same higher-order bifurcation by allowing Bergson's notions of 'dichotomy' and 'dissociation' to be presented through a methodological and metaphilosophical analysis of time understood, now, not as a simple given to be opposed to some other object like space or matter, but as a support for the perpetual mutations of philosophy itself.

H. Wildon Carr, an early and influential advocate of Bergson's work in Britain, provides a clue to this metaphilosophy in his study of Bergson from 1919. He begins his examination with the assertion that 'The philosophy of Bergson is not a system . . . one of its most important conclusions is that the universe is not a completed system of reality'.[10] Carr makes an interesting connection here between a philosophy – in this case Bergson's non-systematic thought – and the subject of that thought, to wit, an incomplete universe. It is significant in that it implies a link between cosmic incompleteness and the fragmentation of any theory concerning that incompleteness. The alternative, quite reasonable, possibility of a systematic presentation of a non-systematic subject matter is bypassed. Yet, in fact, Carr expresses a profound insight into Bergson's work that is too little appreciated. This connection between content and expression will provide a leitmotif for the latter half of this study, guiding us through our examination of Bergson's thoughts on time, mind, life and ethics that comprise the context of Chapters Five to Eight respectively.

Bergson's writings are replete with classic formulations of a non-systematic philosophy. Our perennial temptation to think that physical laws are eternal, for example, is traced back by him to the mistaken view that the universe must be 'coherent'.[11] Significantly though, incoherence also plays

of Freud

Carr 1919

incomplete universe

univ as coherent/incoherent

always a new effort of research
action on the move baffles all calculatn

a role in the presentational form of Bergson's work, demanding, he argues, the perpetual sacrifice of his firmest convictions and best explanations in order to preserve himself from what he calls 'intellectual automatism'. Hence, when Bergson proclaims '*Je n'ai pas de système*', there is no tone of apology in his voice.[12] Consequently, he openly acknowledged that his works were not coherent amongst themselves.[13] The changes in emphasis as regards the prime 'location' of *durée* – in the continuous present for *TFW*, in the eternal past for *MM* – is just one testament to that fact. Bergson's ambivalence towards the value of instinct and animality – at times closest to life, at other times closer to the lifeless – is another. Indeed, Bergson stated that he never began a new work without also forgetting his previous positions and demanding a new effort of research.[14] Others, however, might not approach such studied incoherence so positively. Isaiah Berlin, for example, accused Bergson of being the thinker mainly responsible for the 'abandonment of rigorous critical standards and the substitution in their place of casual emotional responses' in contemporary thought.[15]

Yet, this casualness or incoherence may have more philosophical import than is usually imagined. Bergson is remembered mostly as a 'philosopher of change', a 'process philosopher', but rarely has this mobility been examined at the metathematic level of philosophical form itself. Readings of Bergson have mostly focused on a certain philosophy of mind and nature, and quite rightly so. Nonetheless, a hint at this higher-order instance of process can also be researched, as can be seen in the following quotation from *TSMR*: 'Action on the move creates its own route, creates to a very great extent the *conditions* under which it is to be fulfilled, and thus baffles all calculation'. The point being made about the conditions of possibility could be taken as merely a question of physical possibility, the removal of an obstacle, for example, rather than a reference to logical possibility. Two facts conspire against this natural interpretation, however. The first is that, as we will explore in Chapter Eight, Bergson saw no qualitative distinction between the physical and the logical. In his most famous work, *CE*, he claims that logic is, in truth, physical in its origins: 'Our logic', he writes, 'is, pre-eminently, the logic of solids'. The 'all or nothing' bivalent logic of what Bergson calls 'materialistic realism' is an abstract from space, the objective space of solid impenetrable bodies where no two objects can simultaneously occupy the same location.[16] Yet, because it is derived from just one type of space, this is not the only type of logic. According to Bergson, there are 'degrees in spatiality', a view that, if seemingly counter-intuitive, is actually no more revolutionary than the contemporary theory of 'fuzzy sets' which is based on an even more paradoxical view of 'different degrees of class-membership'.[17] Fuzzy logic – no less than any other

Berlin like his casual emotl response

action on the move creates its own conditns

logic as physical
degrees of spatiality
altv physical states

of calculus on x, of a change upon change itself / as w no first phil, there is no highest level / of abstraction

individuality of movement, particularly of the sin

logic – could have more to do with alternative physical states than many logicians may be willing to admit.

The second fact is that Bergson thought of abstraction itself as a physical process in its actual operation and not just its origins. In his excellent study of process philosophy, Nicholas Rescher makes a remarkable point when describing Bergson's work which underlines this: 'Everything in the world is caught up in a change of some sort, so that it is accurate rather than paradoxical to say that what is changing is change itself'. He then adds that it would be unfaithful to the spirit of process philosophy to set any ontological categories that would imply concepts and positions that a process philosophy must permanently reject. However, what, we might ask, would this process philosophy be if not a changing-philosophy that must countenance the possibility of permanent transformation, even for itself? Probably to avoid such seeming nonsense, Rescher does add that 'at the most abstract level' all true philosophical positions must be the same, even for process thought.[18] For a Bergsonian, though, this means of escape from paradox is of no help because there is no point which can be called the highest level of abstraction: Bergson believes that abstraction is an ongoing physical process with no highest or lowest levels.

To look at what he understands by the process of abstraction, one must turn to the notion of movement that lies at the heart of his metaphysics. As Chapters One and Six will endeavour to show, in Bergsonian philosophy the *individuality* of movement is its metaphysical status. What makes a movement individual is the rich particularity of the situation in, or rather, with which it unfolds. When represented, however, this movement has each of its various dynamic properties 'extracted' as an abstract concept, leaving a bare, formless and static object behind. Abstraction for Bergson is always extraction.[19] We will come across various cognate terms in our investigation – delimitation, condensation, contraction – each of which corresponds to the physical process of abstraction–extraction operating in a specific field.

of Husserl

Taking on board what Bergson writes about concept-formation as well as logic, one understands why the changing form of Bergson's philosophy is tied to its changing content, and that Bergson's process philosophy cannot be separated from questions of metaphilosophy. From the Bergsonian perspective, metaphilosophy, as its etymology would suggest, simply means change in philosophy. No less than a process meta-physics designates change and transformation in *physis*, so meta-philosophy designates the transformation of *philosophia*. But we must be mindful not to think of this as the documentary traces of such change (that would simply be the history of philosophy), so much as the change itself, what Bergson regards as the

representation seems to be static, bare formless

→ meta-physics!

[handwritten margin notes at top: "thinking in duration / retaining a vital phil must continually be re-invented / Value of truths emerging retrospectively"]

necessary movement of thought. This movement is also named by him 'thinking in duration', which Bergson explains as the inevitability that a philosophical terminology – including his own jargon of '*durée*', 'multiplicity' and so on – will lose its force and have to be replaced with a new language if that philosophy is to remain vital.[20] These novel vocabularies will appear vague, confused and even paradoxical at first – he often cites the example of 'unconsciousness' as it was received in the nineteenth century – but such concepts will eventually, as he puts it, 'become clear' because conceptual clarity is itself a process too.[21] Hence, a certain fidelity to one's philosophy may actually require a systematic inconsistency, perpetual contradiction or, if you prefer, 'casualness'.

[handwritten margin notes: "of UCS", "[Note what F contributed]", "Value of casualness"]

For any examination of a philosopher's work, some simplification and even misrepresentation is unavoidable. Nevertheless, one might justifiably ask how a work that extols a continual creative transformation can be systematically examined without having at once its content artificially petrified and its spirit betrayed? An answer to this problem connects with a closely related disagreement between those who have said that, because it is solely in his final writings that Bergson's metaphilosophy emerges, his work will only be understood when it is read backwards against its own chronology, and those others who say that such a retrospective reading will only ever find a false unity *post rem*.[22] Our own position accords with both these views: any account of another's work must be artificial inasmuch as its vantagepoint is retrospective, but there still remains a certain truth to this artifice all the same and, in fact, we will see that Bergson himself believes that there are truths that can only emerge retrospectively.

[handwritten margin notes: "understndg", "B", "backwards"]

This study's own petrification of Bergson places itself voluntarily on shifting ground, namely on the aforementioned metaphilosophical issue of dualism itself, be it thematic (space or time, mind or matter) or methodological (empiricism or ethics, reductionism or anti-reductionism): such dualities are constantly present in Bergson's work until, in his last published writings, this continual creation of dualities itself becomes the focus of a higher-level metaphilosophical analysis. The order of our own exposition follows the direction of this increasing abstraction as well as the chronological order of Bergson's published work: Chapter One examines the nature of space and time as it is set out in *TFW*; Chapter Two looks at the philosophy of mind in *MM* and the essays collected subsequently in *ME*; Chapter Three, the theory of biological evolution in *CE*; and Chapter Four, the sociobiology and ethical theory of *TSMR*. Each of these first four chapters is devoted to examining one aspect of Bergson's work against the background of current debate within its respective field of investigation. Thereafter, the study takes a more problem-driven orientation, Chapter Five starting with an examination of the role of ethics throughout Bergson's thought by taking a reading of *DS* as its guide. Chapter Six follows the same broad approach, though it tackles ontological questions emerging from Bergson's philosophy of novelty. Chapters Seven and Eight focus in conclusion on Bergson's methodology and metaphilosophy as they are mostly found in the last of his works, the collection of essays published in 1934 and going under the English title of *The Creative Mind*.[23] In pursuit of this reading, our intent is to reintroduce a philosopher with revolutionary views in the metaphysics of space and time, philosophy of mind, philosophy of biology, sociobiology, ethics, ontology and metaphilosophy, and to do so by reading each of his seven major works in the light of contemporary thought.

NOTES

1. *M*, p. 1483.
2. Wood 1989, p. xi.
3. Alexander 1966, vol. 1, p. 44.
4. Cited in Game 1991, p. 196.
5. See *DS*, p. 145 [*M*, p. 200].
6. See Čapek 1971; Sipfle 1969; Deleuze 1988; Hyppolite 1991b; Jankélévitch 1959; Merleau-Ponty 1960; Levinas 1987b.
7. See Bachelard 1963.
8. Hanna 1962, p. 26.
9. Schwartz 1992, p. 303.
10. Carr 1919, p. 14.
11. *CM*, p. 214 [*OE*, p. 1445].
12. *M*, pp. 362, 940.
13. See de la Harpe 1943, p. 360.
14. Ibid. 'I have produced each of my books in forgetting all the others'; see also *M*, p. 798.
15. Cited in Gunter 1986, p. 232; see also Gunter 1995, p. 380.
16. *TSMR*, p. 296 [*OE*, p. 1227], emphasis added; *CE*, p. ix [*OE*, p. 489].
17. *CE*, p. 216 [*OE*, p. 669]; Čapek 1987, p. 145.
18. Rescher 1996, pp. 17, 36.
19. *CM*, pp. 167, 116 [*OE*, pp. 1401, 1354]; *TSMR*, p. 180 [*OE*, p. 1128].
20. *CM*, pp. 34–5 [*OE*, pp. 1275–6].
21. See *M*, pp. 1062–4; *MM*, p. 183 [*OE*, p. 284]; *CM*, pp. 35–6 [*OE*, pp. 1276–7].
22. See Jankélévitch 1959, pp. 2–3, 28; de Lattre 1990, p. 21; Gouhier 1972, p. xix. Norman Kemp-Smith believed that Bergson will only 'come into his own' when he is so read; see Kemp-Smith 1947–8, p. 2.
23. The one work we have excluded from full discussion is *L*, using it instead as a source of corroboratory material when examining other texts. In that it is a popularist piece of work (it appeared originally as three articles in the magazine *Revue de Paris*) as well as being a study in literary theory as much as it is a reflection on the meaning of comedy, its place must be peripheral in an analysis of his strictly academic philosophy.

not dealg w L

1

The Metaphysics of Space, Time and Freedom

[handwritten margin notes:]
donnees immédiates de la conscience
ry of human freedom - durée (real time)
no hint of linear determinato, predictability
simplest psychic elements possess a life of their own,

Time is invention or it is nothing at all.[1] *even repetitn is a new feelg !*
→ not a rearrangemnt of the pre existnce

In 1889 Bergson's first published work appeared, *Essai sur les données immédiates de la conscience*. Its title in English translation, *Time and Free Will* is a better representation of the book's theme, for it attempts to validate the reality of human freedom by an analysis of our immediate experience of time. Central to *TFW* is the distinction – Bergson's first dualism – between this inner experience of 'real time' or *durée* and the space outside and surrounding us. This psychological *durée* is qualitative, heterogeneous and dynamic with no hint of predictability or linear determinism:

> Even the simplest psychic elements possess a personality and a life of their own, however superficial they may be; they are in a constant state of becoming, and the same feeling, by the mere fact of being repeated, is a new feeling.[2] *cf Husserl*

Essential to this philosophy is the realisation that every moment brings with it something 'radically new'.[3] This is opposed to a conception of time as simply a rearrangement of the pre-existing, which is, in Bergson's opinion, its scientific definition.[4] On Bergson's very different understanding, however, time must be creative: if it isn't inventive, it isn't time at all. In real time each new moment is qualitatively different from the last and possesses, as Bergson would put it later, 'an effective action and a reality of its own'.[5]

By contrast, space is quantitative, homogeneous and static. Yet, peculiarly enough, this space is the very medium through which we so often interpret our own actions: we define ourselves in terms of external phenomena. Moreover, it is due to this that we can so easily adopt a determi-

we define ourselves in terms of space, external phenomena

hence we define causoln
w a scientific concepn of time, there is no real change

nistic view of human action in that space is essentially inert and uncreative. Why do we choose to undergo this process of 'spatialisation', to interpret ourselves through the external dimension of our existence where all objects, our own bodies included, appear in a tight chain of determinate causal relations? Part of the blame lies with philosophy, according to Bergson. We have inherited a philosophical notion of time which has a constant tendency to ignore the difference between space and time. Hence, 'When we speak of *time*, we generally think of a homogeneous medium', this homogeneity here consisting in 'the absence of every quality'. This spurious time, however, is but 'the ghost of space' which haunts all our thinking. Thus, when we attempt to oppose space to time or say what is characteristic about time, in each case we most often oppose space only to itself or speak only of what is characteristic about space.[6]

According to Bergson, the scientific definition of time consists of the 'elimination' of real change.[7] Scientific theory and method are predicated on an axiom of mechanism: the world is a machine that can be studied, quantified, predicted and so somewhat controlled. Bergson has no quarrel with that assumption if it is necessary for the pursuit of scientific knowledge: it is the lack of an excuse for our philosophical confusion that both troubles him and stimulates his research. Why do philosophers confuse space with real time and so fail to see that we are not machines but genuinely free individuals? That is the problematic that faces *TFW*.

But we are getting well ahead of ourselves. What has gone before reflects in part a popular and rather superficial interpretation of Bergsonism as a philosophy of time which opposes an extraspatial subjective experience of inner *durée* to a deterministic spatial universe lying outside the mind. This is a hollow reading because, on the one hand, it is based primarily on only one – the first – of Bergson's works, when his later writings will radically alter most of the views contained in it, and, on the other hand, even that picture of *TFW* as intensely and implausibly dualistic is only a partial one. In the rest of this study, we will try to subvert the stereotype of Bergsonism through a close reading of Bergson's whole *corpus*. To achieve this we must return to the ideas above and complicate each one of them: time itself – what does Bergson mean by a qualitative, dynamic process and is that all there is to *durée*? Space – aren't there other ways of looking at space, not merely as a homogeneous and static container, but also as a mobile, rich and heterogeneous phenomenon? Subjectivity – why should the 'immediate data' of consciousness be taken seriously: does Bergson have a naïve view of experience as a pure given with no element of construction? Spatialisation – what motivates this process and what are its precise mechanics? Answering these questions will not only render a more

how do we look at space, subjectivity, immed. consciousness process or passage

complex picture of Bergson's dualism of space and time, but in parts a more plausible one as well: as we will see, deepening the issues also makes them more abstract, so that his defence of human freedom does not remain immune from other difficult issues the exploration of which brought Bergson on to write more than just *TFW*.

SIGNS OF THE TIMES

Time is change – a tautology perhaps. However, Bergson's identification of process or passage with time is certainly not universally accepted amongst philosophers. In particular, there are philosophers of time who are called 'detensers' in virtue of the fact that they deny that the processual tenses of pastness, presentness and futurity are real aspects of time.[8] J. M. E. McTaggart would have named them 'B-theorists' who reduce the temporality of change to the timeless relations between events of anteriority, posteriority or simultaneity.[9] These relations are timeless in the way that the shooting of John F. Kennedy will always be after the assassination of Mahatma Gandhi, simultaneous with (at least) the gunshot of Lee Harvey Oswald and before the assassination of Martin Luther King. These eternal connections stem from taking an objective view of time as a set of relations based on some supposedly non-temporal physical phenomenon such as the geometry of space, increasing entropy or causality. The emergence of novelty is merely how the discovery of these non-temporal states appears to the mind. By contrast, an 'A-theorist' refuses to step beyond the subjective perspective whereby, placed firmly at a moving point in time, events appear to come toward one from the future, enter into one's present and then fall away into the past. To adopt an objective stance outside this procession is precisely to lose the dynamic that makes time that which it is: the emergence of novelty. From the A-theorist point of view, the temporal characteristics of an event are dynamic, passing from being future, to being present, to being past. Hence, from Jacqueline Kennedy's perspective, her husband's death was at one point an unpredictable event in the future, later a vicious actuality and subsequently a regrettable past.

In fact, it is precisely this dynamic nature of events that makes the A-theory so preposterous to B-theorists, for it seems that this process of time would itself require a time *in* which to proceed, leading us on to a vicious regress. If a dimension of time like the present is itself moving, according to what measure of temporality does it move? How fast is it? Must it move in another, second-level temporality or 'super-time'?[10] Yet even if this second-order time existed, it too would need its own repository, and so on *ad infinitum*. Hugh Mellor would be a contemporary example of such a B-theorist. He contends that the process view of time, that it is a

B-theorists
time as objct/
hist/
relps
becomes
its own
space
novelty as
that
moment
(like the
others)

A-theorists
role of
subjectv
(a vicious
actualt/
on-going
now

(cf Husserl) - and how far do we regress, as this event to Jacqueline Kennedy occurs now

processes as fundamental ey

flowing from future to present to past, is an illusion of the mind. Real time for him belongs to a physical substratum (including the physical basis of the mind), a substratum which works according to the laws of cause and effect and which gives rise to a view of time as either 'before', 'simultaneous with' or 'after'. There is no 'flux', 'dynamic' or 'flowing'. There are different states of the world, the temporal direction of which is dictated by the arrow of causality, the cause coming before, the effect coming after. Facts are tenseless, they do not involve the past, present or future and do not concern changeable properties of things themselves: 'Nothing ever was or ever will be caused merely by the passage of time'.[11]

It is because the A-theory places such an emphasis on the passage of time and appearance of novelty that Bergson has naturally been described as a 'thoroughgoing A-theorist'.[12] As we will see in Chapters Six and Eight, however, this neglects aspects of his philosophy which do not harmonise so well with the idea of continual succession, aspects which, in some respects, emphasise the coexistence of different levels of time, but which, to their advantage, answer the problems of regress associated with the A-theory.[13] Bergson allows for a stratified series of temporalities nested together in a relation of ever-larger contraction. In any case, Bergson's own defence of novelty stems less from the subjectivist aspects of his thought than from his metaphysics: the view that processes are the fundamental constituents of reality. If one could summarise the main argument of *TFW* in one phrase, it would be this: movement is different from space. It sounds like another truism but, embedded within a process metaphysics, it results in the far less obvious thesis of the irreducibility of movement. What follows is a sketch of the Bergsonian picture.

Compare also in a strange way to Zeno's paradox

TYPES OF SPACE

The space Bergson has in mind must firstly be distinguished from 'the matter which fills it': it is *Newtonian* absolute space which Bergson opposes to movement.[14] This is space seen as a homogeneous and immobile container wholly unaffected by the material bodies and movements it supposedly contains. Matter in movement, by contrast, is heterogeneous and unstable. But Newtonian space is not the only form of spatiality found in Bergsonism. The idea that Bergson never went beyond the position that all space is homogeneous rests wholly on a reading of *TFW*. There is a historical development in Bergson's understanding of space, with a positive conception of it emerging to counteract the negative presentations that are mostly confined to his first book. By the time Bergson publishes *MM*, what appeared as a real property of space in *TFW*'s depiction has become *[handwritten annotations in top margin: pragmatic interacds w space / establishing our fulcrum of action (or inaction) / ∴ space is not an empty container / of holistic or _____ theories / whole > parts]*

the product of our pragmatic interaction with it: homogeneous space and homogeneous time both

> express, in an abstract form, the double work of solidification and of division which we effect on the moving continuity of the real in order to obtain there a fulcrum for our action, in order to fix within it starting points for our operation, in short, to introduce into it real changes. They are the diagrammatic design of our eventual action upon matter.[15]

The homogeneity of space results from our need to reduce its native alterity to a general set of possible positions, every one the exact same save for their different co-ordinates, an 'empty container' in other words.[16] Real space, on the other hand, is something else: Bergson describes it as 'intermediate between divided extension and pure inextension', giving it the name 'the extensive'.[17] This 'extensive' features properties which beforehand were the preserve of consciousness: qualitative difference and change now inhere within the physical realm.[18]

In stark contrast to the general homogeneity of absolute space, movement is not well-suited to any discourse that treats all movements in common – there is no such thing as 'becoming in general' as he would write later: motion as it is studied in mechanics is nothing other than an abstraction, the 'common denominator' which permits the 'comparison of all real movements with each other'.[19] This point cannot be overemphasised. A movement always proceeds from one unique place to another within a particular context: this is what specifies it as heterogeneous. Indeed, it will be this distinction between the general and the particular, the common and the individual, which will play an enormous role in Bergson's interpretation not only of time, but the mind – body problem, anti–reductionism and his theory of the open society. Movement cannot be analysed into the space whose general, homogeneous and non–directional presence supports its progress. Thus, though movement travels across space, movement itself is not the space it passes over and cannot be completely reduced to it. Indeed, it is the illusion that movement is reducible to space that accounts for the paradoxes of motion posited by Zeno in the fifth century BC. *[handwritten margin note: cf Brentano's intensns also f cowse f's wishes see my note]*

Bergson's understanding of movement is a very broad one that encompasses many other notions of change as well. This can be seen in his exception to the phrase 'the child becomes the man' and its concomitant misrepresentation of the nature of this transformation. To Bergson's process perspective, this phrase would be better rewritten as 'there is becoming from the child to the man'. To say that 'the child becomes the man' is to

[handwritten at bottom: becoming from the child to the man]

motion or change actually implies a change of quality not merely quantity /

extract this particular becoming, as though the man the child becomes pre-existed the becoming, when in fact this becoming actually constituted the being of that man. Becoming is itself no longer a predicate but a subject in its own right: substance is not denied so much as reinterpreted as *durée*, 'a substantial continuity'.[20]

This is plain process metaphysics, but many would say that the validity of Bergson's analysis of change is peculiarly suited to his choice of example. Changes of state in processes of growth or development do seem to be somewhat undetermined, in that their future states obviously remain unconstituted at the outset. But changes of place in processes of movement, it could be said, are not so unrestrained precisely because their future positions do pre-exist their occupation. Their future is the location in space that awaits their arrival. Yet in the example of the child's becoming, it might be said that Bergson falsely conflates growth with movement. Hence, this Bergsonian notion of creative, undetermined change seems restricted to organic, qualitative processes alone. Like that other vitalist, Aristotle, he neglects to think through the specificity of quantitative change.

Bergson's answer to this problem will be found in another central concern of *TFW*: to show that movement is not only different from space but also that (homogeneous) space is a derivative entity. Movement is prior to space. If Bergson is right, then it could be true that changes of place do not proceed toward a pre-constituted future. As he will later observe, we must desist from the thought that it is possible for something to 'change place without changing form' precisely because '*real movement is rather the transference of a state than of a thing*'.[21] In other words, a change in quantity at one level is also a change in quality at another.

This point concerning levels arises in his treatment of Zeno's paradoxes of motion.[22] In Bergson's interpretation of the Achilles paradox, for instance, each of Achilles' steps is an indivisible act 'of a definite kind' all its own.[23] One cannot divorce the actor and action from the movement. If one wants to find out how Achilles overtook the tortoise, one simply asks him because, as Bergson claims, 'he must know better than anyone else how he goes about it'. As reported by Bergson, Achilles' answer would be: 'I take a first step, then a second and so on: finally, after a certain number of steps, I take a last one by which I skip ahead of the tortoise'.[24]

Bergson is not being facetious here. The point being made is that Achilles' steps are 'overtaking-steps', and that is how he overtook the tortoise. If we could use the hyphenated phrase 'Achilles-is-pursuing-the-tortoise', these hyphenations would indicate the description of an

the arrow is only a coordinate

unanalysable movement from which the actor cannot be removed with it remaining the same movement. We do not have the right to 'disarticulate . . . [Achilles' course] according to another law, or to suppose it articulated in another way'.[25] This is not a race between two tortoises, the one slow, the other fast. In other words, we cannot reduce one type of movement – the tortoise's – to its supposed atomic layer and then rebuild Achilles' movement with these atoms. Each of their movements is irreducibly individuated by its character as an action. Yet it is precisely such a reduction that Zeno's analysis fabricates, using homogeneous space as the atomic realm. But a space that is indifferent to the actions it claims to compose cannot be the basis of any adequate explanation. In attempting to reconstruct Achilles' movement with that of the tortoise, one only ignores the particularity of their respective kinds of step in favour of a neutral third variable of little relevance to the matter: homogeneous space. While Achilles and the tortoise may appear to make the same passage, the error of this view will be seen when we think of movement in relation to the actions articulating it rather than the one form of homogeneous and immobile spatiality containing it. a flying arrow caught at rest

Of course, Zeno had more than just one paradox of motion, and talk of actions would seem to be completely inapplicable to the argument of the Flying Arrow, for example. According to Zeno, to move, the arrow must occupy two successive positions, but at any given moment it can only occupy one, therefore it must remain at rest, its apparent mobility an illusion of our senses. Naturally, it is hard to see any actor behind the arrow's movement (no one seriously cites the archer as a candidate), but the fact that Bergson maintains the same solution adopted in relation to the Achilles paradox shows that what is important is not the subjective intention of the actor but the metaphysical individuality of every movement, irrespective of whether or not it is an 'action' in the intentional sense of that term. Bergson's solution is that the arrow is only at a point if it stops there; any other point that we might pick along its course will only represent a possible co-ordinate rather than a real resting place. Like the overtaking steps of Achilles, the course of the arrow is 'a single and unique bound'.[26] essential: what comes between the extremes

What is lacking in Zeno, as well as a certain type of rationality in psychology and biology following the pattern of his paradoxical thinking, is a perception of what comes between the extremes: between the extremes of two points of rest is the intervening movement; similarly, between the extremes of two or more ideas is the interval in which one thought is transformed into the other; and between the extremes of any two species is the movement of speciation. The type of biology, psychology and phy-

one that transformed to another

terminus becomes more sig than movement
space is dead

what is simultaneity, how accurately measured?

sics Bergson's writing resists are all modelled on positing the existence of the extreme terminus over the interval of movement.[27] All are the inheritors of Zeno.[28]

Our preferred clock system

THE ANTINOMIES OF TIME

Aside from tackling these paradoxes, Bergson also unearths some logical perplexities of his own inherent in the notion of time. With the confusion of space for time come others: of the measurable with the non-measurable, of simultaneity with succession and of immobility with movement. The notion of velocity, for example, implies that time is a magnitude. But for Bergson, the so-called 'measuring' of time with the moving hands of a clock cross-sectioned with the activity to be measured is no more than the counting of simultaneities. In homogeneous space there is only one position given of an object at any one time; the past, by which one might be able to picture and compare previous positions with the present one, is not retained. Velocity is therefore only a measurement of immobilities in comparison; it indicates the extremities of movement, not the interval.[29] Intervals of time cannot be measured because they cannot be superimposed upon each other; they succeed each other, and as such, can never enter a relationship of simultaneity.

Simultaneity is, in fact, the hub of the problem. The isomorphism of any two events depends on the type of clock chosen, and with that the level of accuracy attained. The best clock may be deemed the most accurate one, but by what standards of accuracy? If water clocks were in use when Isaac Newton began to devise his system, his ideas would have seemed a crude approximation to the truth. Once mechanical digital clocks arrived his theories would be seen to fit the facts much better, until of course the advent of atomic digital clocks. Thus, as W. H. Newton-Smith rightly says: 'The selection of what I will call a preferred clock system . . . is intimately bound up with the choice of physical theories'.[30] The truth is that there is a good deal of custom necessary in all measurement, not only of time but also of space. Bergson writes, 'There is no doubt but that an element of convention enters into *any* measurement, and it is seldom that two magnitudes, considered equal, are directly superposable one upon the other'.[31] He is perfectly aware of the difficulties that can beset the measurement of space no less than those of time. What is special about the measurement of time, however, is not solely its pragmatic disregard for the integrity of the temporal (as is true also for the measurement of space), but the fact that it is a complete absurdity.

Even were one to adopt a scalar criterion for evaluating clocks where the better clock would measure its object at a finer level, one would still

measurement of time as absurd!

be no nearer the absolute isomorphism defined as simultaneity, as scales themselves are open-ended. Accuracy is relative to one's degree of myopia. As Bergson jests in a later work:

> A thinking microbe would find an enormous interval between two 'neighbouring' clocks. And it would not concede the existence of an absolute, intuitively perceived simultaneity between their readings... Our absolute simultaneity would be its relative simultaneity.[32]

Likewise, Bergson claims that a 'superman with a giant's vision' would see our non-simultaneities as neighbouring simultaneities. Hence, there is a relativity of size, distance and scale for Bergson, and so also of accuracy.[33] There is no absolute 'now' which can contain us all. Indeed, the idea that time in general is impervious to the events supposedly within it stems from an extension of this view of the present as a supercontainer to the past and future as presents departed or yet to come respectively. And from this line of thought it takes little to encourage speculation on the possibility of time travel, as though transporting oneself backwards or forwards 'in' time was just a question (albeit more complex) of either moving about in bidirectional space or rearranging the furniture of space.[34]

So from the moment when *TFW* argues that there can be no apprehension of a pure present, a mainstay of so much of the philosophy that had preceded was suddenly being challenged in the most radical fashion. André Robinet writes of the 'ambiguity of the present' in Bergsonism, while another critic refers to the Bergsonian present as an 'indefinite field' or 'temporal hole'.[35] But Bergson actually amplifies the aporia of time with a puzzle of his own concerning 'the' present. It comes from a later work building on *TFW*'s attack on simultaneity and concerns the distinction between immediate and mediate memory. Bergson finds it illegitimate. There can only be a difference of degree and not of nature between the retention of the short- and long-term past, for it would be no more mysterious were we able to retain a lifetime's past experience than it is to be able to retain twelve seconds of it. Bergson presents the (non-)difference between the two as follows:

> My present, at this moment, is the sentence I am pronouncing. But it is so because I want to limit the field of my attention to my sentence. This attention is something that can be made longer or shorter, like the interval between two points of a compass... an attention which could be extended indefinitely would embrace, along with the preceding sentence, all the anterior phrases of the lecture and the events which preceded the lecture, and as large a portion of what we call

our past as desired. The distinction we make between our present and past is therefore, if not arbitrary, at least relative to the extent of the field which our attention to life can embrace.[36]

Yet by the last sentence that relativises the definition of the present, Bergson has also shown that what is at issue need not necessarily be which portion of the past is being retained, but rather which present is being attended. Bergson does not so much explain the present as problematise it, or, to be more precise, he problematises both those homogeneous objects we call *the* past and *the* present, objects that are supposedly held in common by all subjects and by any one subject over time. The endurance of one hour by a neonate has little in common with how this portion of public time is endured by the human adult other than the shared measurement by a clock. The word 'present' is as relative and multiple as the word 'space'.

Zenoism, we saw, is the error of taking the extreme for the interval, of taking a spatialised present for all of time. But Zenoism is as much a part of the human psyche as it is a set of ancient riddles: this is clear when one looks at Bergson's explanation of the origin of spatialisation whereby the temporal is confused with homogeneous space.

SPATIALISATION

Perhaps we should have said the 'origins' (plural) of spatialisation, for in a fashion we are beginning to recognise as typical, Bergson resolves the issue at a number of levels. Moving from the subjective to the objective, *TFW* firstly discovers the locus of our sensitivity towards homogeneous space in one small part of our experience, namely, the group mind. For Bergson, it is at one with that of our social, public sense:

> The intuition of a homogeneous space is already a step towards social life ... Our tendency to form a clear picture of this externality of things and the homogeneity of their medium is the same as the impulse which leads us to live in common and to speak.[37]

This explains why Bergson thinks that less social animals would also be less sensitive to homogeneity.[38] It seems that the instincts that drive us to form communities that underpin our self-identity ('to live in common') also play a role in forming our obsession with (making) everything the same. The confusion between time and space really concerns the promotion of one type of difference of the simplest sort possible: quantitative difference, or the repetition of the same. Interestingly, when Bergson comes to write his first explicitly sociological study in *TSMR*, a fear of difference will be one

---

[Handwritten annotations:]

relativity of the present to which our attn can embrace — to which present do we attend

of one hour by a child or adult

Zenoism takes the extreme points of the interval, an assumpt of measurm

beginning with a social sci, public group set of Kant (Black) on mathematics

why? to dominate, to exert power

we intend to make everything the same for Lisa Madigan today: vote for

closed soc'y as a fear of difference
yet we gain individually as we respond to our xp for ourselves
homogeneous space as a symbolic image or medium
concepts formed as spatial solids

origin of what he calls the 'closed society' no less than *TFW* describes our spatial sense as a type of 'reaction against that heterogeneity which is the very ground of our experience'.[39]

Beyond the sociological, the reference to language in the quotation above is equally telling. It is clear that *TFW* views homogeneous space as a 'symbolical medium' or 'symbolical image'. A continual theme of this book and the ones subsequent to it is that the confusion of space with time involves our very conceptualisation of the issue; thinking and talking about time distorts it: 'We cannot measure time, we cannot even talk about it, without spatializing it'. Thought about time inevitably becomes lodged in concepts, including duration itself, which petrify it. The reason for Bergson's negativity is due to the very nature of concepts. According to his account, concepts are formed on the model of spatial solids, and it is consequently impossible to think about time without importing into it some of the features of homogeneous space.[40]

This is certainly true as regards subjective *durée*. In the very exercise of its reflective powers, the mind itself has been atomised, firstly into the general features of belief, emotion and sensation, then into the numerous faculties belonging to each feature (attention, anger and so on) and finally into tokens of each faculty – one particular memory or one particular desire, for instance. This encourages us to 'consider in turn the self which feels or thinks and the self which acts'. But for Bergson, the mind, though radically heterogeneous, is still a puzzling continuity for all that: proper reflection (which he will eventually baptise 'intuition') shows that 'From the idea to the effort, from the effort to the act, the progress has been so continuous that we cannot say where the idea and effort ends, and where the act begins'. The continuity mentioned here is not a sameness between isolated tokens of some general type, but between a difference emerging from a complex *whole*: each feeling is a particular, individuated by borrowing an indefinable colour from its surroundings.[41] Such a collective, which nonetheless comprises a group of mutually interpenetrating elements, is given a special name by Bergson: a 'qualitative multiplicity'. However, a full elucidation of this holistic notion must wait our turn to strictly ontological matters later.

continuity of idea & act

we also borrow continuity for our surroundings

Another casualty of this spatialisation is the unity of consciousness itself. Bergson outlines something like a theory of the unconscious formed, like the Freudian version, in tandem with the emergence of society. According to Bergson, modern, social and mechanised existence has cleaved our consciousness in two. The mind exists in two layers, one facing towards and formed after the external, public realm, the other remaining behind in

UCS of F . external
the superficial public self gains ground

we live outside ourselves; we are mostly ghosts
we are acted; we don act ourselves

'profound' seclusion; unfortunately, it is the former 'superficial self' that is gaining ground:

of Jung

> The greater part of the time we live outside ourselves, hardly perceiving anything of ourselves but our own ghost, a colourless shadow...we live for the external world rather than for ourselves; we speak rather than think; we 'are acted' rather than act ourselves.[42]

The division between the superficial and profound is formed where self and world, the qualitative, heterogeneous and indivisible on the one hand, the quantitative, homogeneous and divisible on the other, come into an original contact with one another. Wherever subjectivity touches the external world, it is shaped into the image of the latter. These subjective states, facing inward, transmit this dissecting, publicising action to deeper strata, though they meet with an increasing resistance as they progress. The point where they are finally brought to a halt will indicate what remains of the profound self.

subjectivity touches the external world

Phenomenal
What remains of the profound self

This process does not, however, divorce any part of our personality irreconcilably from the other. Bergson's theory of the unconscious is really a theory of selective inattention. He speaks of different parallel processes in the different strata of the self. The deeper ones go 'not unperceived, but rather unnoticed'.[43] We live even in the deepest of these levels, indeed they are most ours. Later works like MM build on this stratified model, dropping the spatial language of 'surface' and 'depth', 'inner' and 'outer', and replacing it with a picture which differentiates multiple versions of the self according to the various modes of durée, virtual or actual, they embody.[44] This is a multiplicity without the rigid externality characteristic of homogeneous space. The Bergsonian subject is now spread across many planes and myriad versions: in a course given on the concept of personality between 1910 and 1911, he goes so far as to liken it to the pathology of multiple personality and to a series of 'possessions'.[45] Jacques Maritain noted with disfavour that 'it is...impossible, in the Bergsonian thesis, to say or to think I'.[46] But in Bergson's mind, the whole problematic of the ego in psychology boils down to the false hypothesis that the mind is composed of, on the one hand,

> a series of distinct psychological states, each one invariable, which would produce the variations of the ego by their very succession, and on the other hand an ego, no less invariable, which would serve as support for them.[47]

Removing this spatialised image of the mind as a collection of mental states equally removes the need for an ego to underpin these states. As Simon

Clarke has noted in Bergson's regard: 'The "death of the subject"...has roots that go back deep into French philosophy'.[48] But this Bergsonian subject has not been 'decentred': whether the self is essentially and exclusively multiple or singular is not a valid issue for Bergson, for all such imagery stems from the repudiated realm of homogeneous space. It is, on the contrary, what Bergson also calls a 'qualitative multiplicity': 'a unity that is multiple and a multiplicity that is one'. Qualitative multiplicity does not achieve this synthesis of the one and the many (to be examined again in Chapter Six) through a process of abstraction, but by focusing on the particular: it is always the individual's specific multiplicity or unity which is essential.[49]

THE ENDOSMOSIS OF SELF AND WORLD

In what we have seen so far, however, it is doubtless that there is a perceptible circularity at the centre of spatialisation: the *artifice* of homogeneous space is created by a conceptuality modelled on a prior *real* homogeneity. A Bergsonian response to this deficiency can be found in the concept of 'endosmosis'. It describes a process whereby 'each moment [of our *durée*]...can be brought into relation with a state of the external world which is contemporaneous with it, and can be separated from the other moments in consequence of this very process'. By projecting our *durée* into space and thereby giving this 'symbolic medium' the appearance of its own temporality, we inevitably have this projection turned back upon ourselves as we introject the various quantitative and homogeneous attributes of this medium.[50] Objects are flowed into succession *at the same time* as we are atomised into static moments.

But problems remain even with the idea of endosmosis. The question can be asked whether this process initiates in the mind, in space or rather in some hybrid combined action of the two. If it is due to our desire to lead out our existence in public space, how are we able to find the discrete moment within our profound selves to project into space, unless our own *durée* already possesses these distinct moments? Alternatively, if our *durée* is somehow spatialised (given moments) by space before we give space our *durée*, how in its turn is homogeneous space able to find this hold on our mind without already possessing some heterogeneity beforehand? It looks like Bergson has separated the realms of homogeneous space and heterogeneous time too far from each other and that these are the Cartesian problems of dualistic interaction which must follow, though it is endosmosis which plays the impossible role of the pineal gland in Bergson's thought. His escape from this circularity must await the more metaphysical analysis of the same issue found in *CE* that we will look at in Chapter Three.

A second problem, in any case, is that Bergson seems to be in an embarrassed state as regards his own language of time: how can he express a philosophy of genuine *durée* if such a thing is inexpressible in virtue of the spatialisation wrought by language? Once again, however, we must not forget that Bergson wrote other books, ones in which he clearly states that language, thought and conceptualisation come in many varieties, some more and some less suited to describing real time, as Chapter Seven will demonstrate.

BERGSONIAN PHENOMENOLOGY

Behind the notion of spatialised time in *TFW* is the modelling of the human mind upon the material world. At this early stage of Bergson's work there is still a divorce between the two such that disciplines like psychophysics are strongly criticised for their attempt to measure an intensive sensation via the quantitative changes of its external stimulus.[51] Most of the book's first chapter is assigned to detailing how we spatialise our intensive states. Most importantly, it attacks the psychophysical assumption made about intensive states in the work of G. T. Fechner and J. Delboeuf: namely, that they are quantitative at all. In Bergson's view, there are no relations of 'more or less' between our internal states: anger is not a stronger emotion than satisfaction, nor is it more than 'a little anger'; anger, or a little anger, or satisfaction are not on the same scale at all. They are intrinsically different; all they have in common are particular names. It is a certain type of homogenising language that helps to form the impression that they are really variations on the one theme termed 'emotion'.

In fact, it is Bergson's contention that there are no internal scales at all. Scales are quantitative phenomena concerning number and homogenised space; they are both predicated upon a relation wherein one entity can contain another. Indeed, in quantifying our sensations, the relation of container to content is paramount, according to Bergson.[52] Yet, intensities cannot contain each other: a strong emotion cannot contain a weak one and never could. Nonetheless, by defining intensity in accordance with extensity we reduce what in fact are a succession of unique moments into a series of extended states; all moments now are simply 'more or less' in relation to moments that were in the past or will be in the future: nothing is new. Yet, most often we are blind to our own strategy. We are more likely to discuss a subjective emotion without recourse to what is (wrongly) deemed its objective cause, even though we have implicitly modelled the former upon the latter. More disingenuously still, we are also prone to discuss the magnitude of this cause in the light of the apparent quantity of the affect. But this strategy has only a limited use. We are keen to be amateur psychophysicists only when it comes to affects clearly linked with causes: pulling teeth or hair, bending metals, and so on. In these situations we are happiest to quantify the pain or felt resistance in terms of the spatial configuration of the bodies involved, including the muscular disposition of our own body. But there are a variety of intensive states which range from those that are so susceptible to being identified with their so-called cause, states involving physical symptoms normally, to those that are not, such as affective sensations, representative sensations and deep-seated emotions. For each of these categories in particular, Bergson wants to restore the specificity and novelty that has been stripped away by the psychophysicists' quantification. His discussion initially focuses on the milder emotions like desire, joy and pity as well as the more violent ones such as rage, before turning to internal states such as the experience of effort or the various types of sensation, both representative (loudness, pitch, colour, intensity) and non-representative (pleasure and pain).[53]

Take the example of colour. Contrary to the law of colour constancy which states that variations in the illumination of a coloured object will not be perceived as variations in the object's 'real' colour (which remains constant) but only as shades of that real colour, Bergson claims that our immediate impression is of a qualitative change from one colour to another. It is only because of our inveterate desire for a certain type of objectivity that we have developed the habit of attributing these changes to quantitative alterations in background illumination.[54] When the illumination of a white object is decreased, for instance, our immediate sensation is of a new colour, grey. But grey is not an absence of white or a change in the intensity of white; blacks and greys are just as real as white. The same holds for colour saturation. If colour intensity is supposedly on a scale with black as the null point, so too is saturation with white as its end point. For Bergson, however, saturated degrees of the 'one' colour (so-called) are all different colours. While psychophysics can quantify physical causes and sources, it cannot quantify these multifarious sensations directly. Consequently, the experiences of colour can never be fully reduced to any homogeneous physical substratum such as the wavelength of electromagnetic radiation, for instance. What, for example, would be the wavelength of the real experience of black? Physical substrata refer only to an indirect, austere or general aspect of these phenomena, which is not necessarily to say that the electromagnetic theory of light is untrue, but only that it does not provide a complete account of light.[55]

In many of these reductions of our intensive states, the primary medium of quantification is the human body. The analysis of pleasure in *TFW*, for example, shows a conception of the physical which clearly falsifies the

view that Bergson regarded all space as homogeneous. Pleasure is characterised in terms of a pre-conscious bodily intention of the future. Our
body is the first to turn towards a pleasure, our conscious awareness initially lagging behind. When 'our' attraction has caught up with this carnal
impulse, the movement nearer has already begun; yet just as we are at last
enjoying the pleasure for ourselves, so the body becomes distracted again
by another interest of which 'we' later become conscious.[56] Admittedly,
Bergson is portraying this process of reduction to the physical in order to
decry it. It is with *MM*, where the nascent consciousness given to the
body here is expanded into a full-blown bodily intentionality, that such
equivalence is no longer disparaged. Still, Bergson's employment of the
body even in *TFW* remains double-edged. The manner in which he
describes the body in terms of its own inclinations, multiform movements
and developing extensity involves almost as much heterogeneity as his presentation of the intensive states they are used to homogenise.[57] Bergson
also never explains how the two series of extensive bodily quantities and
intensive qualities can be correlated, only that they are: the problem of
endosmosis re-emerges here in another guise.

There is a certain methodological resort to immediate data in all of this,
of course, Bergson asking us to come 'face to face with the sensations
themselves', and even asserting that the self is 'infallible when it affirms its
immediate experiences'.[58] However, in his defence, Bergson is never naïve
as to the self-evident purity of these phenomenological data; gaining access
to the immediate demands effort and is in no way naturally given: as he
himself warns, 'The immediate is far from being that which is easier to
notice'.[59]

FREEDOM

The ultimate significance of spatialisation is summed up by Bergson as follows: 'The very mechanism by which we only meant at first to explain
our conduct will end by also controlling it ... we shall witness permanent
associations being formed; and little by little ... automatism will cover our
freedom'.[60] Having dealt with what *TFW* says about space and time, we
can finally return to the topic of freedom. There is a particular tradition of
philosophising about freedom that does not take radical indeterminacy as a
condition for liberty.[61] Bergson can be placed within it. His own reason is
that the libertarian or indeterminist, or at least one of a particular type,
tends to ground his or her philosophy of freedom on the notion of possibility. Freedom here comprises an array of lines of possible action open to
choice at any one moment: I may have done *x*, but I could have done *y*.

Yet, in Bergson's eyes, a creative act cannot be said to pre-exist its actuality in any way, 'not even in the form of the purely possible'.[62]

In *TFW* it is argued that the supposed lines of possible action grounding the libertarian's freedom of choice are actually created retrospectively by the free act once it has been accomplished. Moreover, it is also argued that the libertarian's prioritisation of the possible is simply an inverted form of mechanism and so plays into the hands of the determinist. Summarising this argument in his lecture 'The Possible and the Real', Bergson describes how libertarians, 'by affirming an ideal pre-existence of the possible to the real ... reduce the new to a mere rearrangement of former elements'. Alas, sooner or later such a strategy can only lead, Bergson continues, 'to regard that rearrangement as calculable and foreseeable!'[63] The possible becomes an alternative, albeit more complex, mechanism by which the past can be understood as having linear effects in the present.

This kinship between possibility and mechanism allows psychological determinism to portray the subject under the control of its own mental states. The truth, however, is that the self is not determined by these states, it creates them.[64] It does not make a choice between really pre-existing alternatives, it creates the image of these alternatives in the retrospective light of its accomplished action. Representations of possibility are based on the assumption of the sameness of subjects and of situations. For Bergson, on the other hand, I was a certain person before choosing that I will never be again: it is incoherent to think that I can travel back in time to amend my choice of action, even in the form of a simple counterfactual hypothesis. To represent choices as fixed is a product of the imagination alone. The only thing that remains constant is the language representing the affair. Only retrospectively do the 'possible alternatives' to what was actually enacted appear to pre-exist as options that I could have chosen but was determined not to. Both the libertarian and the determinist use the schema of 'conception', 'hesitation' and 'choice', which, for Bergson, is merely the verbal crystallisation of a geometrical schema, another atomisation of mind and action.

Every individual is consequently a superlative as well as a comparative. What we have in common with others is precisely that alone, it entails nothing further. It is through thinking that we are essentially and immutably the same as others (including the others we were in the past and will be in the future) that we come to see our differences representing something we are falling short of, things that we *could* have been. They become possibilities for us that some will say we are free to perform and others the contrary. Yet no one worries about not being free to fly; this possibility is marginalised as a physical inability with no relevance for the debate on freedom. But this marginalisation only serves to reinstate other differences as possibilities which are supposedly open to general consumption. Though these acceptable differences admittedly appear more transferable than physical ones, they remain phenomena that are personally owned. It is not a matter of difference *per se*, but of whose difference and which difference. My way of doing x at t can only be my own, at t. Bergson adopts a nominalist position in this respect: Peter is not Paul, so what Peter does can never be a possibility for Paul. It is always my action at a time that was perpetrated, not *an* action that could have been performed as equally by me as by anyone.

Movements belong to individuals and situations. There is no such thing as a general type of movement; there may be a more or less individual movement, but none that can be perfectly general. Such actions that are less individual form the basis for the more homogenised levels at which we most often communicate and otherwise publicly interact with each other. While the differences in question here may be minute, at the level we are concerned with, what is small, particular and nuanced is of the essence.[65] As our introduction outlined, the metaphysical status of a movement is its individual, rich character. When we describe this movement adequately, our portrayal may look like a projection – what Gilbert Ryle might positively call a 'thick description' or what others might negatively call a metaphysical fantasy.[66] In fact, it will be a projection, but only of that individuality that belonged to it indigenously and which was first extracted by precisely our abstract representation of it; as Chapter Eight will show, for Bergson, if abstraction is a type of extraction, then metaphysics must be a form of restoration.

Having said all this, however, *TFW* is not absolutist regarding freedom: 'Freedom, thus understood, is not absolute ... it admits of degrees'. There are degrees of individuality or difference as well as degrees of homogeneity. The reason why freedom admits of degrees is due to spatialisation: at a second-order level, we are perfectly free to lose our freedom through increasing self-automation. Bergson's position on the issue of free will and determinism is best characterised as a peculiar twist on compatibilism. In subverting the opposed theories of determinism and libertarianism, his position bypasses the assumption held in common by both alike: that free will is incompatible with determinism. Libertarians and determinists build their ideas equally on the axiom of their mutual incompatibility. All or nothing. Bergson, on the contrary, believes they are compatible because the characteristic that both constitutes *durée* and differentiates it from determinate homogeneity appears in different degrees at different moments of our conscious existence. There are levels of *durée*, rhythms that more or less approach the minimum-level *durée* of our superficial ego. Consequently, there are varying degrees of freedom amongst our numerous actions. The degree of freedom of an action depends on whether we have got 'back into ourselves' and away from the superficial public realm, away, quite literally, from our 'outer face'. However, paradoxical though this must sound, according to Bergson we are rarely willing to do so: 'Free acts are exceptional'.[67]

In concluding with a notion of freedom based, not on a dichotomy of determinism or indeterminism, but on a plurality of degrees of freedom-mechanism, we still cannot forget the problems of dualism which haunt *TFW*. The origin of spatialisation remains unexplained; concepts like 'endosmosis' involve too many *petitio principii* to bear this explanatory burden. We also saw, however, that the role of the body is one point where the negative reading of Bergson's treatment of space comes unstuck, and it is in *MM*, Bergson's second book, that the body gains its fullest and richest philosophical development just as the themes of dualism and reductive monism come into greater focus.

NOTES

1. *CE*, p. 361 [*OE*, p. 784].
2. *TFW*, p. 200 [*OE*, p. 131].
3. *CM*, p. 35 [*OE*, p. 1276].
4. See *M*, p. 766.
5. *CE*, p. 361 [*OE*, p. 784]; *CE*, p. 17 [*OE*, p. 508].
6. See *TFW*, pp. 90, 98, 99, 232–4 [*OE*, pp. 61, 66, 67, 151–3].
7. See *M*, p. 766.
8. Smith 1994a, p. 1.
9. See McTaggart 1908.
10. See Schlesinger 1994, p. 218.
11. Mellor 1981, pp. 105–9, 119–20, 109.
12. Lacey 1989, p. 56.
13. Clifford Williams has argued that Bergsonian intuition leads to the rejection of both the A-theory and B-theory of time: see Williams 1998.
14. *TFW*, p. 236 [*OE*, p. 154]; see also Newton 1960, p. 322.
15. *MM*, p. 280 [*OE*, p. 345].
16. *MM*, p. 330 [*OE*, p. 376].
17. *MM*, p. 326 [*OE*, p. 374].
18. Even *TFW* can be ambivalent about space, going so far as to say that 'We shall not lay too much stress on the question of the absolute reality of space: perhaps we might as well ask whether space is or is not in space', *TFW*, p. 91 [*OE*, p. 62].
19. *CE*, p. 324 [*OE*, p. 754]; *MM*, p. 268 [*OE*, p. 338].
20. *CE*, pp. 329–30 [*OE*, pp. 759–60]; *CM*, p. 32 [*OE*, p. 1273].
21. *CM*, p. 146 [*OE*, p. 1382]; *MM*, p. 267 [*OE*, p. 337].
22. Some philosophers today might wonder as to the continuing relevance of Zeno's paradoxes in the light of their dissolution by modern mathematics. W. V. O. Quine,

for instance, shrugs off the Achilles paradox (Bergson's favourite example) as simply 'falsidical' in that Zeno's notion that any infinite succession of intervals must add up to eternity shows his lack of appreciation for convergent series: when the succeeding intervals become increasingly shorter, the converging infinite series can give us a limiting finite value, which is 1 (Quine 1976, pp. 3–4). However, more recent writers have shown that Zeno's paradoxes can be rehabilitated as genuinely problematic because they rest on premises different from those of modern mathematics, such as the additivity of an infinity of divisions, for instance: see Sherry 1988, pp. 58–73 and Ray 1991, pp. 11–13.

23. See *TFW*, pp. 112–15 [*OE*, pp. 75–7]. We are also using passages from Bergson's 1911 paper, 'The Perception of Change' in *CM*, pp. 144–9 [*OE*, pp. 1379–81], for the analysis there, though in essence no different from that in *TFW*, brings out the points of interest more clearly. He also turns to the paradoxes at *CE*, pp. 325–30 [*OE*, pp. 755–60] and *MM*, pp. 250–3 [*OE*, pp. 326–9].

24. *CM*, pp. 144–5 [*OE*, p. 1379].

25. *CM*, p. 145 [*OE*, p. 1380].

26. *CE*, p. 325 [*OE*, p. 756]; p. 326 [*OE*, p. 756].

27. See *TFW*, p. 120 [*OE*, p. 80].

28. Some have argued that Bergson failed to realise that Zeno's argument is far from serious but takes the form of a *reductio ad absurdum* against positions which he opposed: see Cariou 1999, p. 111.

29. See *TFW*, pp. 100–17 [*OE*, pp. 67–78]; 117–19 [*OE*, pp. 78–9]; see also pp. 194–7 [*OE*, pp. 127–9].

30. Newton-Smith 1980, p. 160.

31. *CM*, p. 12 [*OE*, p. 1254], my italics.

32. *DS*, p. 56 [*M*, pp. 109–10].

33. See Bergson 1969b; *DS*, p. 122 [*M*, pp. 175–6].

34. See *DS*, pp. 148–9 [*M*, pp. 203–4] where Bergson refers to H. G. Wells' story of the time machine. An old application of common sense, moreover, can quickly dispel the feasibility of returning to the past: wherever the self-proclaimed time traveller may think he or she has just been, it certainly was not the past, because a minimal definition of any one date in history is that it has no elements from any other date, such as 'visiting' time travellers for instance (in other words, part of what it is to be 1982 is *not* to have bits of 1983 cropping up in it!).

35. Robinet 1965, pp. 26–38; Mourélos 1964, pp. 230, 232.

36. *CM*, pp. 151–2 [*OE*, p. 1386].

37. *TFW*, p. 138 [*OE*, p. 91].

38. For other animal minds, 'space is not so homogeneous ... determinations of space, or directions, do not assume ... a purely geometrical form', each would have 'its own shade, its peculiar quality' (*TFW*, p. 96 [*OE*, p. 65]).

39. *TFW*, p. 97 [*OE*, p. 65].

40. *TFW*, pp. 115, 125 [*OE*, pp. 77, 83]; *DS*, p. 150 [*M*, p. 205]; *CM*, p. 35 [*OE*, p. 1275]; *CE*, p. ix [*OE*, p. 489].

41. *TFW*, pp. 172, 211 [*OE*, pp. 114, 138].

42. *TFW*, p. 231 [*OE*, p. 151].

43. See *TFW*, p. 169 [*OE*, p. 112]; see also *M*, p. 810 for a rejection of an unconsciousness that is opaque to and inaccessibly cut off from consciousness.

44. See *MM*, pp. 13, 43–4, 191–3, 288 [*OE*, pp. 176–7, 196, 290–1, 350]; see also Lindsay 1911, pp. 5, 91–2, 156–7, 168–9, which makes a good deal of this development.
45. *M*, p. 858.
46. Maritain 1968, p. 231.
47. *CM*, pp. 148–9 [*OE*, p. 1383].
48. Clarke 1981, p. 16.
49. *CE*, pp. 271–2 [*OE*, pp. 713–14]; *CM*, pp. 164, 165, 176 [*OE*, pp. 1397–8, 1399, 1409].
50. See *TFW*, p. 110 [*OE*, p. 73]. In *DS*, p. 134 [*M*, p. 189], the second half of this process is given the name of endosmosis exclusively, the first half now being clarified as 'exosmosis'.
51. See *TFW*, pp. 1–7 [*OE*, pp. 5–9].
52. See *TFW*, p. 2 [*OE*, p. 6]. A large number is understood as large because it contains smaller numbers; likewise, a large body is understood as large in that the volume it occupies could contain a smaller body with excess. A good part of *TFW*'s second chapter looks at the nature of numerical quantity underpinning the quantification of intensive states as well as the connection of both with space. Our own analysis of Bergson's philosophy of number must await the final chapter of this study, but its primary claim is that mutual exclusivity and impenetrability are facets of homogeneous space and homogeneous number equally (see *TFW*, p. 89 [*OE*, pp. 60–1]). Quantification itself is a process resting upon a type of spatiality.
53. See *TFW*, pp. 7–19, 19–31, 31–60 [*OE*, pp. 9–17, 17–24, 24–42]; see also Moore 1996, pp. 46–50 who analyses Bergson's explanation of the quantification of intensities in terms of 'focal states', that is, a type of restrictive attention.
54. See *TFW*, pp. 50–72 [*OE*, pp. 36–50].
55. Bergson never denies the reality of the electromagnetic theory of light; see, for instance, *CM*, p. 58 [*OE*, p. 1300]; p. 70 [*OE*, p. 1311]; *MM*, p. 272 [*OE*, p. 340]; *DS*, pp. 38–9 [*M*, pp. 92–3].
56. See *TFW*, pp. 38–9 [*OE*, pp. 28–9]. Bergson's point is that it is via these spatial phenomena – the initial inertia, the following movement and the next moment of inertia – that we quantify our inner feeling of pleasure. See also his use of the body in how we quantify our representative sensations (taste, touch, sight) at *TFW*, pp. 39ff [*OE*, pp. 29ff].
57. See *TFW*, pp. 20–8, 35–8 [*OE*, pp. 17–22, 26–8], for what he says on muscular effort, muscular tension and pain.
58. *TFW*, pp. 47, 183 [*OE*, pp. 34, 120].
59. *M*, p. 1148. Milič Čapek points out that in philosophical usage there can be two meanings to the word 'immediate': one corresponding to the immediate *de facto*, the other to the immediate *de jure*; see Čapek 1971, pp. 86–7. Bergson's immediacy is in the *de jure* sense.
60. *TFW*, p. 237 [*OE*, p. 155].
61. See on this Gilson 1978, pp. 67–8.
62. *CM*, p. 19 [*OE*, p. 1260].
63. *CM*, p. 104 [*OE*, p. 1344]. The original argument is at *TFW*, pp. 172–83 [*OE*, pp. 113–20].
64. See *TFW*, pp. 165–72, 219–21 [*OE*, pp. 109–13, 143–5].
65. See Deleuze 1956, p. 86. If this seems to cancel any grounds for morality, this may be because we have set our understanding of both so heavily on models which regard

individuality as a physical isolation automatically requiring either rational contracts or other mechanisms of moral duty to annul its effects. As Chapter Four's study of *TSMR* will illustrate, Bergsonian individuality, on the contrary, naturally brings its own morality with it because it is essentially a tolerance towards difference: a proximity born of the mutual recognition of a real distance.

66. See Ryle 1971.
67. *TFW*, pp. 166, 240, 167 [*OE*, pp. 109, 156, 110].

2

Philosophy of Mind

The truth is that there is one, and only one, method of refuting materialism: it is to show that matter is precisely that which it appears to be.[1]

A constant criticism of Bergson's *durée* has been its lack of structure; that its apparent amorphous fluidity has more in common with the supposed homogeneity of space than Bergson has realised. Such a view, however, as Chapter Six will show, neglects the all-important issue of novelty at the heart of *durée* that makes it a heterogeneous continuity, however paradoxical this phrase may appear. Such a differentiated temporality is full of structure. This ontological refutation salvages *TFW* along with all of Bergson's other writings on time. But *durée* was already internally differentiated along a naturalistic route as early as *MM*.

The consequence of this naturalism for Bergson is that it allows him to introduce *durée* into the physical world while at the same time differentiating the physical variants of *durée* from mental ones. Instead of a simple monism of *durée* everywhere, within and without, leaving nothing to distinguish mind from matter at all, Bergson can now have a mitigated dualism of sorts while still avoiding the parochial privileging of consciousness that distinguishes *TFW*. It will be, as one recent commentator puts it, a 'duality' enforced by pragmatics rather than dogma, a constraint of action administered by life itself.[2] Bergson achieves this, however, without any recourse to idealistic measures such as intentionality or its existential variants like *Dasein* that buy their level of structure at the expense of cutting themselves off from other realities. Just how he pulls this off is one theme for this chapter; the other is an analysis of *MM*'s critique of mind – body reductionism and Bergson's own theory of the mind – body relation.

The book begins with the same attempt at coming face to face with immediacy as was undertaken in *TFW*:

We will assume for the moment that we know nothing of theories of matter and theories of spirit, nothing of the discussions as to the reality or ideality of the external world. Here I am in the presence of images, in the vaguest sense of the word, images perceived when my senses are opened to them, unperceived when they are closed.[3]

The term 'image' is employed universally to designate the objects of every type of perception: 'By "image" we mean a certain existence which is more than that which the idealist calls a *representation*, but less than that which the realist calls a *thing* – an existence placed halfway between the "thing" and the "representation"'. It is this dualism of idealism and realism, said to be brought about by a 'dissociation' between 'existence' and 'appearance', which Bergson is trying to avoid with the notion of 'image'.[4]

Yet this return to a monistic purity is shown to fail almost immediately, for within this world of indiscriminate images there is said to be always one that can be immediately distinguished from the others: the image of my body. An immediately given dualism is reinscribed within the realm of images, in that the body alone is known in two distinct manners: through the perception of its objective form as just one body amongst others and through the affective experience of being incarnated within and possessing this body; the perspectival feeling that 'it is my body'. The body, or my body, is consequently 'a privileged image, perceived in its depths and no longer on the surface . . . it is this particular image which I adopt as the centre of my universe and as the physical basis of my personality'. A further reason for this privilege stems from the fact that the images other than my body appear to influence each other in a determined, automatic and necessary way. Other images influence my body by giving it their movement just as my body returns that influence by giving movement back to them. The difference is that only my body appears to me to choose how it will restore the movement it receives: it constitutes a centre of indeterminacy. This indeterminacy is conditioned in accordance with how these other images present themselves to my body: '*The objects which surround my body reflect its possible action upon them*'.[5] The restoration of the dualism inherent in reality and only temporarily reduced is now complete. On account of the privileged status of the body, every image now seems to be able to exist in 'two distinct systems': one where each image exists '*for itself*', a system Bergson attributes to science, the other where the very same images exist for the one 'central image' of my body, a system he calls '*consciousness*'.[6]

Space no longer constitutes a meaningless void. It is stated that the more a separation decreases, the more the pivotal action of the body becomes real; when it is zero, the image concerned is the body itself. Thus, real action is to possible action what the physical sensation of one's own embodiment is to the perception of other images. The possibility of an action can no longer be thought of as an all-or-nothing affair the occurrence of which depends on whether its object is within range or not. Range and distance are far from being neutral variables; they are precisely the measure of shifting possibility that Bergson is talking about: 'Distance represents, above all, the measure in which surrounding bodies are insured, in some way, against the immediate action of my body'. The choice of 'all or nothing' is an abstract from one type of space only, the objective space of solid impenetrable bodies. It is from this space, where no two objects can simultaneously occupy the same space, that the bivalent logic of what Bergson calls 'materialistic realism' is derived.[7]

From this beginning, Bergson will hold that perception is, in principle, extended and in the things themselves, and, from this, that perception is not the addition of the unextended to the extended but simply a diminishment of the extended. When we come to look at his notion of perception below, we will see how this radical externalism arises, allowing him to state that '*all* sensations partake of extensity'. 'Inside' and 'outside' no longer have absolute value in terms of extensity being opposed to intensity: 'The truth is that space is no more without us than within us', he writes.[8] In place of the old opposition of within and without, we will see instead that there is only a duality of types of action, determined and undetermined. The first origins of dualism are not epistemic, but pragmatic.[9]

LOCALISATION

Just as any image can be given according to either the objective system of science or the subjective system of consciousness, it should be noted that the body too can be taken up from either of these stances. While my body seizes objective images through its subjectivity, it is also an image that can be seized objectively. Its movements and gestures can be stripped of the qualitative heterogeneity that makes them mine to become the general mathematised movements that belong to everyone. Opposed to '*le corps vivant*', there is, as Jeanne Delhomme calls it, '*le corps géomètre*'.[10]

Nonetheless, it is *le corps géomètre*, a general algorithmic understanding of the body wherein physical events are chained together in a linear mechanism, which is Bergson's battleground when arguing his anti-reductionism. *MM* wants to establish a connection between the enduring mind and an enduring world without getting caught up in the one-upmanship of trying to reduce the origins of either one to the other. There are empirical and logical aspects to Bergson's argument: the empirical evidence against reductive materialism is still worth rehearsing in the current climate where such materialism is *de rigueur* within the philosophy of mind, but the logical arguments are independent of whether the target is materialism or idealism: they are concerned with the incoherence of any monistic philosophy as such and operate by raising Bergson's process thought to a metaphilosophical level.

Most of Bergson's empirical argument focuses on consciousness. But by 'consciousness' we should read 'memory', for that is how Bergson characterises mind at this stage in his thought.[11] Bergson's position is that such 'consciousness, even in the most rudimentary animal, covers by right an enormous field, but is compressed in fact in a kind of vice'.[12] His approach, then, is not to argue how consciousness or memory arises so much as to show how it is curtailed.[13] The brain corresponds to or localises only one part of mind, which Bergson describes as the 'actual' phase of a continuous process. This actuality is another term for what *TFW* called homogeneous spatialisation: that part of mind which has been moulded on spatial solids. In this reformed picture of the mental in *MM*, the homogenised dimension of mind accounts for the nature of our perception, while memory represents what remains profoundly heterogeneous. In this respect, perception is to homogeneous space what memory is to *durée*. However, *durée* here does not signify an immateriality so much as a qualitative material movement, in contrast to the brain which remains a part of the static 'geometrical body'.

We must also be careful with the term 'memory': what we call memory *simpliciter* needs itself to be analysed further into homogeneous and heterogeneous aspects. Indeed, Bergson thinks that there are at least three types of state which fall under the rather uninformative catch-all 'memory': there are dispositions or habits which might better be described as bodily memories; then there are as well mental representations or recollections the imagery of which seems so similar to weakened perceptions; and finally, underlying both these two homogeneous kinds termed 'actual' by Bergson, a wholly heterogeneous, 'virtual' memory with not so much a non-physical character as a non-homogeneous one. The greatest extent of memory is this heterogeneous virtuality: the specificity, mutability or sheer difference intrinsic to virtual memory is what renders it irreducible to the actual form of difference found in homogeneous space and, with that, the mechanism of the brain.

But the crucial thing is what connects these forms of actual and virtual difference, to wit, Bergson's process metaphysics: it is always a genesis, a process of actualisation by which homogeneous recollections emerge from heterogeneous virtual memory to colour our actual perceptions. It follows that the terminus of the process – actual memory-images localised in the brain – cannot be equated with the process in its entirety: 'The alleged destruction of memories by an injury to the brain is but a break in the continuous progress by which they actualise themselves'.[14] In fact, diseases of the brain only affect recall – which is a process of actualisation – rather than virtual memory itself: brain damage removes the ability to actualise the memory in full or with the appropriate tonality. Indeed, the evidence from the cases of pathology Bergson studies shows that lost memories can even be restored through an effort of will or an emotional shock, assuming that the tissue damage is not so severe that the mechanisms of actualisation are wholly absent.[15] Of course, there will be clear correlations between mental activity and brain activity as the latest brain-scanning technology reveals; but this evidence only relates to recollection, which for Bergson is spatial.[16] Such recollections will indeed appear as weak perceptions. Moreover, the evidence from brain scans can only indicate a correlation between mind and brain, rather than a relation of production in full, a point Bergson makes repeatedly.

Bergson willingly admits that memory along with the other faculties have some basis in the brain, but each also overflows it in terms of their processual origins: the relation between mind and body is not a constant, nor a simple relation. Bergson's anti-reductionism, then, rests on a complication of memory as regards just how many faculties of memory there are, as well as an inscription of heightened difference within memories themselves that renders them irreducible as a whole. He often says that there is at best only a reduction of *generic* types of mental content. The brain is like a 'frame' or 'organ of pantomime' playing out the public side of our mental life: 'real concrete living thought' always remains unreduced. Hence, mechanistic science lingers in the shallow end of mind, studying an 'artificial imitation' of our deeper psyche obtained by cobbling together stereotypical images and impersonal ideas.[17] That is why Bergson regards the great psychological novelists as empirical psychologists in their own right: they may not use questionnaires or laboratory experiments, but, utilising their own experience and insight, they show us the less stereotyped, more profound and personal aspects of mental life.[18]

One moral of our tale so far is that generalisation aids and abets reductionism. The metaphysical aspect of Bergson's time-philosophy places the emphasis on individuality: tokens of mentality simply fail to reduce to a general algorithmic view of the mind and body. However, this is not to claim that a finer level of description of the body would also fail to find a physical correlate for our more sophisticated mental states. In fact, Bergson as much as concedes this likelihood. Yet, as we will see, such a fine-grained correlation would remain only that, a correlation.

According to the critic A. R. Lacey, however, *MM*'s attack on localisation targets a straw man.[19] The purpose of Bergson's use of data on memory disorder was to show that memory is independent of brain storage, for memories have been seen to return despite their supposed destruction along with particular areas of damaged brain tissue. However, asks Lacey, perhaps the memories were not stored in a locality of the brain, but, as some theories would have it today, in an organisation of the brain? Rebuilding a destroyed cerebral function (rather than the original cerebral matter itself) would then reproduce the vanished memories and maintain the reductionist hypothesis.[20]

Modern trace or engram theories of memory do seem to avoid Bergson's localisation critique – they appear to be functional in the manner Lacey describes: in perceiving an object repeatedly a trace or track is left in the brain coinciding with the operation of the brain in that act of perception (like a hand in the mud might be preserved as a shape but not as a hand).[21] In fact, the Greek term for 'impression' is '*engram*' and the idea of the memory trace goes at least as far back as Aristotle.[22] But another critic, Milič Čapek, rightly claims that Bergson would never have denied the reality of engrams or physiological traces, for his view was that 'every sensory image has its physiological counterpart'.[23] Yet 'counterpart' does not mean 'cause': for Bergson, the brain, the central nervous system or, more broadly, the body are the means by which virtual memory is actualised, but the memories' return is not caused by the brain, nor are the virtual memories themselves stored in the brain. Something may require some other means for it to emerge, but that does not make it thoroughly reducible to those means. Where Bergson's quarrel really resides is in whether that first thing, the memory, pre-existed its actual state *as a memory* (and the mode of difference that entails); if it did not, then it can owe its being as a memory to the second thing (the brain) and be wholly reducible to it; if it did (which is Bergson's view), then only its emergence is reducible, not its entire being.

In Bergson's view, the past is a time and the brain is a place; one should not look for 'where' memories are preserved but 'when', the answer being 'in the past', though even here the metaphor of containment is unhelpful and already a spatialisation of a sort. For Bergson, there is both the actualised memory, which is indeed realised through the brain, and the virtual or 'pure' memory, which overruns all physical correlates. Virtual and actual are best interpreted as phases of a continuous process rather than localities. The brain does not produce or store this memory, in fact, as we will shortly see, its purpose is to retard the attempts of virtual memory to re-emerge into the present: it is a filter only, not a creator.

THE METAPHYSICS OF MIND

We must note as a consequence of this that the observed evidence for localisation could even increase in virtue of the growing homogenisation of mind described in *TFW*. Our thoughts could become as general and automated as the cerebral mechanisms supporting their actualisation. But localisation remains an illusion should it be proclaimed either the eternal truth of a part of the mind or the passing truth of the whole of the mind. In a number of texts Bergson makes it very clear that no *a priori* relationship can be sustained between mind and body, be it in terms of reductive materialism, epiphenomenalism, dualism, idealism, pre-established harmony or whatever else.[24] Bergson sees this dyad as a *sui generis* relation to the extent that, for any given psychological state, there is a playable [*'jouable'*] part of it such as it translates an attitude of the body which is 'in the brain', and another part which has no cerebral equivalent. Just to what degree these respective parts have a hold of the mind is the crucial issue that remains open to change. This transformative property of consciousness is precisely what leads some to believe that what we deemed the caricature of thought in materialist accounts of mind provides an accurate representation of our mental reality. Bergson would admit, in fact, that there are stereotypical thoughts when, as living automata, we exist at a superficial level; but there are also complex, creative thoughts and emotions wherein our whole personality is involved and which can never be repeated. In other words, there are tones or levels to mentality.

The issue of the generality of mind impacts less on a total refutation of materialism so much as its reconfiguration. Specifically, the evidence for localisation – that (part of) the mind reposes in matter, in particular the brain – is not denied but reinterpreted. As a lecture from 1901 states: 'It is a question of determining the exact significance of the facts of localisation'.[25] Bergson's view is that there is a correspondence between matter and mind but no reduction of either one to the other. This might be called a dualism, but we will see that there is a genetic element to this correspondence (which is explained further in *CE*) that makes it more a process of dualisation than a static duality.

As its title would suggest, *MM* attempts to substantiate its claim using data from an area that would appear to favour the opposite view: the pathology of memory. Here it certainly seems as if there is a strict causal relation between areas of the brain and memory states, destruction of the former leading automatically to the annihilation of the latter. The brain, then, produces our memories because the brain contains our memories, or so the story goes. Yet, is it also true that, because the immediate fate of a coat hanging on a hook is partly tied with the fate of that hook (if the latter should fall, the coat would go with it), it follows that the two are either identical or that the former should wholly reduce to the latter? Likewise, in that the movements of a conductor's baton are highly correlated with the music produced by the orchestra, must we repudiate the notion that the music and the baton are separate entities?[26] Clearly not: we know well when to distinguish a relationship of correspondence from one of identity. Now, as science interprets the connection between mind and brain, which is a clear observation, to signify such an identity or reduction, Bergson concludes that 'it does so, consciously or unconsciously, for reasons of a philosophic order'.[27]

Bergson is certainly not naïve about letting the 'facts' tell their story: he believes that there is a constant metaphysics in science, 'already contained in the descriptions and analyses', which renders every fact theory-laden.[28] Even 'brute' perception reflects a certain vital, organic selectivity as well as the exigencies of social life. However, though such 'artefacts' do not pre-exist the act of judgement, this is not to say either that they are pure constructs: there is recalcitrance in them that testify to an untameable objectivity.[29] In the light of both this inescapability of theory and resistance to theory, Bergson's constant complaint is that contemporary philosophy has derogated its duty to interpret the underdetermined fact of mind – body correlation with new metaphysical ideas: in the absence of this, science embellishes them with an old metaphysics, 'a Cartesianism curtailed and narrowed'.[30] Modern materialism is a curtailed or half Cartesianism because it takes only *res extensa* as Descartes has homogenised it while setting aside his other substance, *res cogitans*. This inherited *res extensa* need not involve the vortices of Descartes' physics, but, like his own, it always involves a homogeneous, determinate and linear set of relations, be they modelled on the mechanism of a clock, telegraph, telephone, hologram, Turing machine or whatever other metaphor the latest technology offers.[31] Yet, in blind ignorance of its own metaphysical foundation, materialistic science revolves in an interpretative circle confirming a metaphysical position with evidence already infected with that metaphysics. Materialism becomes a metaphysics for those 'who refuse to be metaphysicians'.[32] Thinking that the primacy of materialism is incompatible with metaphysics commits something of a category error, for materialism, being itself a type of metaphysics, cannot be opposed to metaphysics *per se*.

More broadly, one can distinguish Bergson's metaphysics from materialism's in terms of their movement of thought, for they travel in opposite directions. Modern materialism begins with a general atomic realm and associates these atoms (be they physical, mental or logical) to form ever more complex hierarchies, moving from the many towards the one. Bergson begins with a unity, called virtuality in *MM* but going by other names in his later works, and dissociates it into a multiplicity, moving from the one to the many. The facts of observation can collude with either direction of thought, associative or dissociative, for all they can substantiate is a correlation between phenomena, such as brain and mind, for instance. The formal properties of the brain equate with both the idea that it canalises consciousness (Bergsonism) and that it produces consciousness (materialism). Experimentally, there may well be no crucial test to verify which hypothesis is correct. Indeed, because these are metaphysical perspectives, there may strictly never be any way to falsify either of them, as the long-running attempt to distinguish causation from constant correspondence testifies. If one should be preferred over the other, then it will be on ontological rather than empirical grounds (which we will discuss in Chapter Six).

In that case, one might ask why associative thought is so prevalent when compared with dissociation. Why do we prefer to explain things associatively rather than the other way around? Bergson's answer in *CE* is that this is how the intellect operates, moving always from a plurality at the periphery to a unity at the centre. To adopt the alternative stance requires a massive effort in turning intellect around and against its natural orientation, a reversal Bergson will eventually call 'intuition'. More significantly still, the centripetal movement of intellect has an ontological dimension (that we will also examine in Chapter Six): association goes from the part to the whole to construct the new from the pre-existent on the principle of 'like coming from like'. Intellect cannot comprehend novelty as a genuine emergence but only as a rearrangement of the old: repetition must have priority over difference. Hence the favoured tactic of the materialist is often to justify his or her position on the basis of parsimony: the simplest, least internally differentiated explanation must be the preferred one, which is normally taken to mean one which reduces every reality to its physical substructure. For Bergson, however, this is simply another aspect of our inability to conceptualise *durée* without spatialising it.[33] Furthermore, the appeal to parsimony as well as its cognates, simplicity and economy, neglects the fact that these are all rather complex ideas that come in various forms, as we will see Bergson argue in our final chapter.[34]

THE APORIA OF IDENTITY

This leaves us with one vital issue in Bergson's critique of reductionism, namely, correlation: 'My perception is, then, a function of these molecular movements; it depends on them. But how does it depend on them?' The answer is that they *vary* with them.[35] Yet why is there such covariance, why indeed are there two such 'distinct systems' of consciousness and matter at all? These questions will enter us into the metaphilosophical aspect of Bergson's negative critique. Bergson's own answer, at least in *MM*, is that the reciprocal dependence of these terms is a function of a third, the indetermination of the will. Freedom returns as an essential idea. But while there are reasons why we might find this response unsatisfactory (how neutral can a concept of the will be *vis-à-vis* the mind – body problem?), the value of his metaphilosophical critique of monism remains.

One reductive theory of mind whose fortunes have waxed and waned for the last forty years is called the Identity Theory (IT). As C. V. Borst puts it, this theory of mind and brain, sometimes known as reductive or central state materialism, holds that 'Mental states are quite literally identical with brain states: any given mental state is, roughly, a brain state, brain process or feature of a process in the central nervous system'.[36] He further informs us that the relationship between mind and brain in this theory is a causal one; if the mental is conceived as a special category it is only as a subcategory of the physical in that it is the latter that causes the former.

The main weakness with IT has always been its own assessment of identity as such, and the question of statements of identity in particular. The problem is that when one says that mental events are really brain processes, one seems to be left with no individual reality for a 'mental event' of which it can be said that it reduces to a brain process.[37] Bergson's own criticisms of identity theories foreshadowed this problem clearly. He writes:

> To say that an image of the surrounding world issues from this image of a dance of atoms, or that the image of the one expresses the image of the other...is self-contradictory, since these two images – the external world and the intra-cerebral movement – have been assumed to be of like nature.[38]

Expression and issuance imply a duality, whereas being of 'like nature' invokes a monism. Monisms state that 'everything is *x*', dualisms that some *x* 'influences, causes, symbolises, expresses, issues, or produces' *y*. Despite their best intentions, identity theories usually end up eventually having to state the latter. As Bergson succinctly puts it, '*A relation between two terms is [made] the equivalent of one of them*'.[39]

The problem then for an identity theory stems from its reductive ambitions: it tries but fails to convert a duality into a unity. But what of a non-reductive materialism? Here the problem of accommodating features from both sides of the identity, such as non-localised colour sensations and uncoloured brain-parts, may be offset in favour of simply asserting the identity without trying to correlate its two terms. There are two usual avenues followed to establish this idea. Donald Davidson's theory of 'anomalous monism' is one. At the heart of this approach is what is called the 'supervenience of the mental', a principle whose role in philosophy has been described as the 'last refuge of the modern physicalist'.[40] Simply stated, it holds that there can be no mental change without a physical change. Anomalous monism is a materialist thesis in that it claims that all events are physical, while still being non-reductive in that it does not specify which non-mental event will accompany which mental event. It therefore rejects the thesis that mental phenomena can be given law-like physical explanations.[41] It is a monism in that it takes all events to be physical, but it is anomalous in that the nature of this monism is thought to be indescribable in any nomological manner. Of late, however, there has been less enthusiasm for this approach in that it is 'not a stable position', tending towards dualism in its non-reduction of the mental and towards an outright elimination of the mental in its materialism.[42] In fact, the second variety of non-reductive materialism overtly follows just this latter strategy.

Eliminative Materialism (EM), as it is called, asks us to forget the need for neat reductive matches: feelings and sensations cannot but fail to reduce to the brain simply because they are not real. The only things that exist are material entities such as brain-states. According to EM, if there are no precise correlations between the mental and the physical that will allow the former to be smoothly translated into the latter, it must be because our language of mind is misconceived and false. For Paul Churchland, for example, our perception and understanding of the world evinces a 'thoroughgoing *plasticity*'; our awareness of the world is formed according to the greater or lesser ability we have in exploiting '*the natural information contained in our sensations and sensory states*'. Most of us are quite inefficient at exploiting this information and we have consequently been burdened for too long with the illusion that what we see now under introspection is what is actually there. Churchland asks us to engage in an 'expansion of introspective consciousness', after which we will realise the need to eliminate our old language of the mind.[43] As one commentator puts it: 'Sensations and sensation-talk . . . will simply disappear from a scientifically oriented language, much as demons and demon-talk have already disappeared'.[44] Such linguistic cleansing will remove our naïve vocabulary of beliefs, desires, dreams and so on in favour of the new language of neuroscience: 'A-delta fibres and/or C-fibres' will replace our notions of pain; 'iodopsins', our colour after-images; and 'vestibular maculae', our feelings of acceleration and falling.[45]

The problem for EM, though, is that of the existence of *qualia*.[46] The irreducibility (or ineliminability) of the phenomenological qualities of our experiences of pain or of after-images, for instance, is a truly hard problem. It even has pertinence for the examples Churchland takes as model illustrations of elimination. According to Churchland, heat and burning provide two cases of just the evolution of language advocated by EM.[47] Heat was once deemed to be a fluid, 'caloric', whilst burning was originally thought to involve the release of a substance, 'phlogiston'; in both cases the true explanations turned out to be altogether different: molecular movement and oxygenation respectively. Yet one might still wonder whether the phenomena of heat and burning as experienced (and not simply as previously explained) have been left uneliminated in either case. After all, our experience of burning is incomparable with our understanding of both phlogiston and oxygenation. This is not to say that it is unconnected to either of the two in some way, only that this connection cannot be one of identity. This is basically what Bergson argues in *TFW* and *MM*: our experience of colour or of our own consciousness may correspond in some way with electromagnetic radiation or the activity of our brain and nervous system, but that does not allow us to identify them with these substrata *in toto*. The objective aspects of light are but one perception, and an impoverished one at that: but as Bergson says, 'no work of abstracting, of eliminating, – in short, of impoverishing' perception will bring us closer to reality.[48] As we will see next, Bergson equates representation, both perceptual and intellectual, with a type of elimination: the heightened elimination of abstraction, therefore, is no guarantee of getting closer to reality, despite our mesmeric belief that what is more abstract, more geometrically simple, must also be more real.

THE PRIMACY OF PERCEPTION

'Philosophy made a great step forward on the day when Berkeley proved . . . that the secondary qualities of matter have at least as much reality as the primary qualities'.[49] Turning at last from Bergson's critique of reductive materialism to his own positive theses concerning perception and memory, we begin with the claim that what we call our subjective secondary qualities cannot be discounted as unreal. Secondary qualities originate in the objective realm every bit as much as primary qualities do. What really needs to be explained is how secondary qualities come to be apparently so 'secondary' or 'subjective' in the first place. The answer in *MM* is that their subjective status, what makes them seem so different to primary qualities, is due to the fact that, firstly, they are more complex than primary qualities and, secondly, each individual's perceptual organs inevitably diminish this greater complexity in more various and so apparently subjective ways.

This point makes more sense when seen in the light of Bergson's theory of perception in *MM*.[50] According to his account, perception is not an emergent faculty that adds some sort of subjective accretion to the perceived object. Carried by the brain, it is the product of a process of restriction: it is a subtraction from the world. The form actual perception takes is the result of the brain's canalisation. It may seem that perception adds to the objective, that it conditions or categorises a raw manifold, but in actuality it consists in a removal of what is of no interest to our vital functions. It deletes whatever else is of no practical use to it. These deletions consist of a temporal phenomenon wherein the *durée* inherent in matter is condensed in our perception; a myriad of minuscule differences – the rhythms and movements of the material realm – are congealed in a perceived quality. *CE* puts it concisely: 'The permanence of a sensible quality consists in this repetition of movements... The primal function of perception is precisely to grasp a series of elementary changes under the form of a quality or simple state, by a work of condensation'.[51] The impoverished nature of our actual perception is simultaneously a condensation and an extraction: in being contracted, the complexity of the 'secondary' object, its own specific *durée*, is removed without being eradicated, in other words, it is transformed. The faculty of perception is extractive, the percept is the extract.

In this context, the 'thick descriptions' of *TFW* cannot be described as fanciful embroidery upon an already sufficiently realistic, though spartan world of bare quantities, sense data or information; rather, these descriptions are restorative, reintegrating perfectly real elements previously dissociated by the synoptic powers of perception. In fact, from the Bergsonian perspective, taking a physical phenomenon in its simplest, most abstract form would actually be a 'thin' description. Or rather, it would be less a descriptive affair at all as much as a sign of a depleted perception. Bergson restores to the physical what we erroneously deem to be certain metaphysical (meaning 'suprasensible') attributes, only not in the sense of projecting a mental quality onto a physical quantity, but by allowing each state the individuality that gives it the singularity of being this response to this moment rather than a response to any moment whatever. It is not Bergson who is being 'ornate', 'abstract' or simply 'metaphysical' by adding excess to what is already an adequate reality, but rather the materialist who is being 'pro-physical', so to speak: confining to verbal imagination what is really a part of the world.[52] But where *TFW* utilised a subjective phenomenology to describe what is to be restored, *MM* uses a process metaphysics of multiple *durées* interfering with each other, condensing each other, in order to explain why reality has been so dissociated.

The qualities of sounds, colours, tastes and smells are objective, then, in principle if not in fact, not because they pre-exist their actual sensuous state in some virtual form (for that would assume that they are not the products of omission), but because perception begins with the object *de jure*. Perception is related to the object it represents as a part or condensed extract is related to the whole: it is not only an image *about* reality that may or may not be wholly representative, but a part of reality too. In this respect, there is nothing mysterious about the world 'beyond' the mind:

> Between this perception of matter and matter itself there is but a dif-
> ference of degree and not of kind...the relation of the part to the
> whole...My consciousness of matter is no longer either subjecti-
> ve...or relative...It is not subjective, for it is in things rather than
> in me. It is not relative, because the relation between 'phenomenon'
> and the 'thing' is not that of appearance to reality, but merely that of
> the part to the whole.[53]

AGAINST REPRESENTATION

It would be a profound mistake, however, to think that we might effect a reintegration of the baroque mind and formless matter simply by rejoining the concept to the thing. Thinking is not an innocent activity. Intellect is for Bergson an extension of the digestive power of perception. So what becomes of representation in this new Bergsonian scheme of things? Bergson sees perception as an action rather than a duplication of reality; likewise, he sees the brain as an action rather than a theatre for observing this duplicate reality:

> There is the implicit...hypothesis of a *cerebral soul*, I mean the
> hypothesis that the world as idea is concentrated in the cortical sub-
> stance. As our presentation-world seems to accompany us when our
> body moves, we reason that there must be, inside that body, the
> equivalent of the world-presentation. The cerebral movements are
> thought to be this equivalent.[54]

The commonest theories of perception in contemporary philosophy of mind, causal theories, are so favoured because they purport to explain how and why perception should be generally faithful to 'external' reality.[55] If we are truly related in any sense to what we perceive as it is in itself, it is only because perception is connected to the object of perception via a chain of causal mechanisms. The content of perception, however, is deemed an access to a world of information and the mind the processor of this information on account of this veracious replication. Yet, there is another philosophical tradition (including most notably Maurice Merleau-Ponty, Emmanuel Levinas and Gilles Deleuze) which does not see perception as a true or false duplicate of reality, but as a reality in itself. Bergson heralded this view with the contention that perception is an action within a world of actions.

Rejecting the informational and speculative picture of consciousness and situating it back in the world as Bergson does leads to the predication of extension, not to the causes of perception, but to the perceptions' contents themselves. As noted earlier, Bergson has already given up the myth of an entirely immaterial mind: 'The truth is that space is no more without us than within us'. Those, on the other hand, who continue to maintain that mental content is immaterial must face the inevitable objection. How are mind and matter ever to be related if the former is allowed to emerge mysteriously from the latter as an unextended representation of it? Materialism, according to Bergson, holds precisely this view: matter does have the ability to produce something entirely different from itself, namely the perception of matter. Materialism views this perception as '*wholly speculative interest; it is pure knowledge*'.[56] Of course, it may see perceptual knowing as confused and only generally true compared with the perfectly faithful standard of scientific knowledge (the scope of the former being determined by evolutionary constraints perhaps), but perception is still deemed informational at heart. Therewith, an odd and unacknowledged dualism is constituted of 'formless matter' and 'matterless thought', as Bergson labels it.[57] On the one side is the hardware, the information processing mechanism; on the other, the software, the information itself. Though efforts have been made to remove this duality by reducing this very notion of information to that of negentropy as understood by communications engineering, extending this specialised understanding of information and communication to explain conscious informants and communicators seems to many like a verbal sleight of hand.[58] Likewise, the whole idea that the brain's neurones can play the role of hardware switches that are either 'on' or 'off' to facilitate the conveyance of this digital information has come in for some strong criticism.[59]

Bergson argues that what provides representation with its passive and purely informational *appearance* is of a sensory order: it stems from a pre-reflective identification of our powers of perception *in toto* with one sense alone: that of touch. The tactile sense gives us the solidity of the object: its resistance, intransigence and threatening impenetrability. Referring all our other senses to touch creates, by analogy, a solipsism of images. The idea of the body or a part of the body (such as the brain) being able to recreate an image of an external reality follows from seeing it as one of these discrete and entirely self-sufficient entities. The imperialism of touch precludes the body from being taken up through those other senses that throw it outward and into the world. According to Bergson, we must learn to think with our other senses and actively distend the body.[60] Doing this would leave us in greater doubt as to whether perception actually does either double, mimic, reproduce or recreate the world in any immaterial or informational manner.

What is also implausible about a causal theory of perception is that such a physicalism should separate out a part of the world, the sentient body, and have the remaining world orient itself towards that body as the cause of its perceptions. According to Bergson, it is a tenet of physicalism that 'behind ideas is a cause which is not idea'. Yet, surely these divisions and orientations between body and world are our ideas imposed on the physical.[61] Talk in terms of 'external' and 'internal', 'input' and 'data-reception' clearly implies a point of view that sees only a part of the whole, it really assumes an opacity of vision that can only belong to a situated perspective:

> But is it not at once clear that to consider the brain separately, and separately also the movement of its atoms, involves now an actual self-contradiction . . . [if materialism] defines the object not by its entry into our presentation, but by its solidarity with the whole of a reality supposed to be unknowable?[62]

To say that there is a brain with objects external to it and which 'modify it in such a way as to raise up ideas of themselves' is to pass surreptitiously to the idealist's language and posit *'as isolable by right what is isolated in idea'*.[63] Thus, Bergson finds materialism incapable of keeping consistently to a non-idealist language when it discusses representation.

The brain, as we learnt, acts as an instrument of mediation: it analyses in regard to movement received and selects in regard to movement executed; in both cases it is 'an instrument of action, and not of representation'.[64] Our perceptual mechanisms neither mirror nor create reality, they select from it. Not that an alternative Kantian model, for instance, which sees the world conforming to the mind would have no place for deletions and delimitations either.[65] But by seeing the body enact a narrowing or restriction, Bergson has no ontological difference in mind between the agency of this action (or its product) and the world on which it acts; perception is not of any stuff of which the rest of material reality is not already made:

'*There is in matter something more than, but not something different from, that which is actually given*'.[66]

If one consequently asks where representation takes place if not in the brain, Bergson's answer will be that, *de jure*, it takes place at the object! This will sound ridiculous only if one is determined to believe that perceptions must be contained in the brain. But if one claims that they are unextended or informational, how can they be 'contained' at all? If, on the other hand, they are extended and are thereby truly *of* the world and not just *about* it, then they must be in or rather 'at' the object in some manner. Bergson's whole argument is that it is just as likely that perception should occur at the object where we perceive it as it is for it to occur at our eye or our brain. In fact, because the perception is of the object, it is more likely *de jure* to occur at the object than anywhere else.

There is a famous sophism in the philosophy of mind, known as the 'homunculus fallacy', which is often found in materialist thought. It consists firstly in thinking that either a part of an organism like the brain, or an artificial system like a computer, can plan, communicate or contain information as though that did not imply the need for a fully sentient planner, communicator or informant. Philosophers fall victim to this fallacy by then inadvertently placing such a tiny living homunculus (in some guise or other) within their favoured system to carry out the very functions that their materialistic analysis was supposed either to eliminate or reduce to non-sentient physical mechanisms. Bergson's apparently absurd view that perception occurs at the object is no more than a radical extension of the critique of this fallacy: 'A sensation cannot be in the nerve unless the nerve feels. Now it is evident that the nerve does not feel . . . [and] if it is not in the nerve, neither is it in the brain'.[67] Imagining the stimulation of the nervous system by a ray of light at a source P, Bergson notes:

> The truth is that the point P, the rays which it emits, the retina and the nervous elements affected, form a single whole; that the luminous point P is a part of this whole; and that it is really in P, and not elsewhere, that the image of P is formed and perceived.[68]

The pure image of the thing is formed and perceived then, not in the nervous system but at the thing itself: 'The visual perception of an object the brain, nerves, retina *and the object itself* form a connected whole, a continuous process in which the image on the retina is only an episode'.[69]

Conceiving perception as a diminution of the extended world obviously goes against the view that sees its action upon and existence within the world as an addition to rather than a subtraction from it. But that the activity of perception is itself reductive is essential to Bergson's solution to the mind–body problem. It makes more sense to understand perception as a loss of matter rather than as a magical superaddition to it of something non-material (the representation of it). So long as a dualism of perceptual information and material world is maintained with one as the passive spectator upon the other, the relationship between the two will never be explained. Perception is an action, a deletion of what is of no interest to our body in the world, not a mysterious appendage of something entirely different from that world. As Frédéric Worms' commentary on Bergson points out: 'It is not the world which is a content of consciousness, but consciousness which is a property of the world'.[70] And this world, remember, is one composed of processes, not static objects.

BERGSON'S THEORY OF RECOLLECTION

What renders perception subjective is the contraction of 'external' reality in a diminished image. But this deletion is a temporal phenomenon, a contraction of worldly rhythms of *durée* that is administered by perception coloured by memory:

> If every concrete perception, however short we suppose it, is already a synthesis, made by memory, of an infinity of 'pure perceptions' which succeed each other, must we not think that the heterogeneity of sensible qualities is due to their being contracted in our memory and the relative homogeneity of objective changes to the slackness of their tension?[71]

It is when a theoretically pure perception is alloyed with memory that subjective consciousness emerges. After all, while a pure perception may be at the one object in principle, the many different actual perceptions we each have of it must be variegated alongside the introduction of personal memories. Simultaneously, what creates the apparent dualism of mind and body will be the emergence of a certain type of memory termed 'actual'. On all accounts, then, memory is central to Bergson's positive thesis. We have looked already at his use of data from the pathology of memory in his critique of reductionism; now we can turn to how he reshapes the significance of memory for his own ideas.

According to several presentations of Bergson's theory, it involves two forms of memory, the one named 'habit-memory', the other 'representational-memory'. The first is a set of physical motor-mechanisms wholly bent on action; the second are iconic recollections representing the past. *MM* illustrates this distinction by asking us to contrast the ability to learn a poem by rote with the ability to remember the specific occasion of that lesson. Learning by rote creates a cerebral motor-mechanism, a habit of the body that can be repeated at will when called upon. The body is not an inert machine but a concentration of action, an encapsulation of the past. A representational-memory, on the other hand, is of a specific event in a life, it has a date and as such can never recur identically.[72]

Not only this distinction, which foreshadows the contemporary theory of 'declarative' and 'procedural' memory, but also the emphasis Bergson puts on the body, were radical innovations for his time.[73] Despite the lack of credit given to him initially, Bergson is at last being acknowledged in various quarters as the thinker 'who first saw … the genuine significance and peculiarity of the body', he also being the earliest modern philosopher fully to realise 'the body's pivotal position … as a continual "center of action"'.[74] This carnal memory, however, is not one by proxy of the beliefs and intentions of an incorporeal *cogito*. It is a true body-subject with its own intentionality, Bergson writing explicitly of an 'intelligence of the body' and a 'logic of the body' as well as 'bodily memory'.[75]

Amongst his criticisms of atomistic psychology is a rejection of those theories of recognition making recourse to supposedly objective processes of association and recollection.[76] Seeing that each image is objectively similar in one way or another to every other one, such associations must beg the question by implicitly assuming a partial recognition which can evoke precisely the desired line of association rather than any other. By contrast, Bergson places the subject's body, anchored to a particular place and time, at the centre of recognition. There is a type of recognition consisting of bodily action without any representation. To recognise an object is firstly to know how to use it. The habit of utilising an object organises various bodily movements together such that any one of these movements 'virtually contains the whole'. Re-encountering one automatically results in bringing back the memory of the others. Thus, for example, one's familiarity with a town would be composed more of a 'well-regulated motor accompaniment' acquired during repeated walks through it rather than any set of representations in one's head.[77] As this interpreter describes it: 'One's body *knows* this city; one's body *recognizes* this city … One's body does not picture or imagine or think: it acts out, plays out, and this is its memory'.[78]

This bodily cognition acts as the basis for our more seemingly disincarnated recollections, intellections and understandings. He calls the preceding form of recognition 'inattentive'; there is equally an 'attentive' recognition linked to the operation of representational memory. This also begins with bodily movements but, whereas the former takes us away from the object perceived to a set of ready-made habits, attentive recognition brings us back to it in detail. Bergson shows how this type of attention is initiated

with an 'inhibition of movement'. An 'arresting of action' leads to a rever-
berative process as an attempt is made to reconstruct the broken movement
with representational memory-images. This is a looping, cyclical effort at
restoration: 'The operation may go on indefinitely – memory strengthen-
ing and enriching perception, which, in its turn becoming wider, draws
into itself a growing number of complimentary recollections'.[79] These
memories 'echo' both the initial interrupted movement as well as the subsequent memory-enhanced perceptions trying to reconstruct the object.
Hence, attention does not analyse a given object so much as repeatedly
attempt a series of syntheses in order to recreate the object:

> Reflective perception is a *circuit*, in which all the elements, including
> the perceived object itself, hold each other in a state of mutual ten-
> sion...so that no disturbance starting from the object can stop on its
> way and remain in the depths of the mind: it must always find its
> way back to the object from where it proceeds.[80]

Attentive recognition, then, is a set of circuits or reverberations within
perception caused by the disturbance of some novel event. Conscious
awareness is amplified by shock, resistance or disorder interrupting our
habitual actions, following which perception is more and more enhanced
with memory-images in an attempt to reintegrate the object or dissipate
the shock of the disturbance. In short, 'The sense of familiarity is largely
due to the diminution of the inward shock which constitutes surprise'.[81]

Bergson illustrates this theory in a discussion of the attentive perception
of language. Over time, he argues, auditory impressions organise nascent
bodily movements that can scan the salient outlines of any token of speech.
In the recognition of one such token, we firstly co-ordinate these motor-
diagrams to the impressions made on the ear by analysing the latter into a
skeletal framework. But these diagrams indicate only the conspicuous outlines of the speech, the attentive part of recognition follows, as

> *the hearer places himself at once in the midst of the corresponding ideas*, and
> then develops them into acoustic memories which go out to overlie
> the crude sounds perceived, while fitting themselves into the motor
> diagram.[82]

To understand another's words is to reconstruct, from the ideas, the continuity of the sound that the body has firstly decomposed.[83] Both types of
memory are utilised, and in each case it is a type of action which is
involved – of decomposition or reconstruction – it is never a passive information processing. The motor-mechanisms Bergson alludes to would be
hopelessly wide of the mark for current psychologists and neuroscientists –

an occupational hazard for philosophers who embed their ideas in empirical data rather than ascend above them – but the principle behind his argument – the *basis* of cognition in motility – remains timely. Only recently has this approach, though now reworked in a different and somewhat reductive context, entered the philosophical mainstream with the development of parallel processing in artificial intelligence and non-cognitivist theories of mind such as Gerald Edelman's Neural Darwinism.[84]

BERGSON'S THEORY OF MEMORY

What is specific to habit-memory is that it rests wholly on motor-movement; whereas the second form of memory only begins with a movement, habit-memory is pure motility.[85] This has led some to regard representational memory as the definitive form of memory in Bergson's account such that habit-memory barely deserves the name of memory at all. But there is more to his picture of memory than this duality. In fact, we noted at the start of this chapter that Bergson's is a tripartite theory with a concept of 'pure memory' alongside those of habit- and representational-memory. Moreover, there are two phases to the presentation of his theory in general. On the one hand, he gives us an explanation of recollection that espouses a dualism between representational-recollection and habit-recollection (Chapter Two of *MM*); on the other, he gives us a three-part theory of memory involving these two types of recollection and one form of unrecollected pure memory (Chapter Three). This last memory, he tells us, is pure because of its unrecollected or virtual state, whereas any form of recollected or actual memory is one simplification or another of this virtuality.[86] As Gilles Deleuze rightly says, in contrast to the virtual, every type of actual image 'implies, according to Bergson, a corruption of pure memory, a descent from memory into an image which distorts it'.[87] So we now have a new opposition, this time between two forms of recollection that we can generically term 'image-memory' and one form of true memory called 'pure memory'. So, while Bergson states at one point that representational-memory '*imagines*' the past whilst habit-memory merely '*repeats* it', his final position becomes clear later; true memory is neither habit nor imagination: '*Imaginer* n'est pas *se souvenir*'.[88]

The significance of this new opposition is all-important for it allows us to excavate the meaning of pure memory or virtuality in *MM*. Bergson is determined not to be added to the number of philosophers who see only a difference of degree or intensity between perceived images and pure memory: 'Memory actualized in an image differs, then, profoundly from pure memory'. He repeats this principle in other texts going so far as to state that 'The recollection of an image is not an image'. The crucial point to be retained in understanding Bergson's distinction between recollection and pure memory is this: whereas a recollection actualises the past, pure memory *is* this past.[89] This is without doubt a thoroughly realistic view of antiquity. Pure memory is not a mental duplicate referring to the historical past, rather, the past really persists into the present and this survival actually manifests itself as our recollections![90] Not that this realism is gratuitous: in Bergson's view, one can only substantiate an ontological difference between memory and perception, that is, show that memory is more than a weak, faint or copied perception, by establishing its direct relationship with the past as a real existent. Bergson here prefigures phenomenologists like Sartre who also combated the empiricist view which interprets memory as simply weak perception. But, unlike the phenomenologists, Bergson does not utilise anthropocentric differences (existential structures usually based on the affective realm) to ground the distinction between the two; he shows no such recourse to idealist tendencies. Bergson takes the bull by the horns and, just as he showed that a pure perception must begin at the object alone rather than 'in' the brain or the nervous system, so too a pure memory must begin with the past itself rather than any present phenomenon, be it a perception or an emotion.

Our past psychical life (of pure memory) is always there; it survives as a whole, pressing forward to regain entry into the present as an actual recollection. The present inhibits this pressure of our past by literally being that which is present. When there is a disturbance in our present activity, when, in other words, our recognition fails, the ensuing embellishment of our perception with recollections is less a result of *our* need than an opportunity for pure memory to fulfil *its* need: '[Pure] memory merely awaits the occurrence of a rift between the actual impression and its corresponding movement to slip in its images'.[91] A movement's fullness, then, drives away the image, while its lack or interruption contributes to its approach from the past. In neither case, though, can pure memory ever be recollected without bodily movement: it requires some form of movement to actualise itself. Hence, lesions of the brain affect our possible movement and nothing else; they destroy the ability of pure memory to actualise as a memory-image, but not pure memory itself. Psychic blindness, for instance, has more to do with the disturbance of motor-habits than with the loss of memory.[92] Which memory-image is actualised is a selection prepared by the movements of my body in the world rather than by any general laws of association. In Bergson's view, this selection most probably begins in accordance with vital interests – what we need to survive in a situation. While our past tries to manifest all of itself in the present, only the most useful images succeed.

Not surprisingly, a host of criticisms has arisen from this identification of the past with memory. Bergson has either failed, it is said, to differentiate the '*being of nature*' of the past from the '*intentional being*' of this same past, or he has confounded 'an act of knowing with that which is known'.[93] We might add ourselves that Bergson's realism here must lead one to wonder how the present, being in part the actualised image of the past, can be anything more than the realisation of some stored-away memory. If the next actual present is already contained in some form of virtually present memory, are we not back again with the problem of seeing the present as a rearrangement of the pre-existent?

FROM THE AMBIGUITY OF THE PRESENT TO THE END OF MEMORY

We should note, however, that Bergson in any case reformulated both his theory of memory and his realism towards the past in later works, especially the essays and lectures collected in *CM*. It was there that he forwarded the puzzle concerning the vague distinction between mediate and immediate memory. In the same location, he argues that 'the preservation of the past in the present is nothing else than the indivisibility of change'. In place of 'the indivisibility of change' he also uses the phrase 'undivided present'.[94] But we might ask in relation to both, how we should infer the preservation of the past from the indivisibility of the present. In *MM*, Bergson states that there is a 'continuity which we have thus broken between the perception, the memory, and the idea'.[95] What becomes vague (and we will look closely at the technical use Bergson makes of vagueness in Chapter Eight) is the distinction of memory and perception, and with that, of past and present. If Bergson can argue for the preservation of the past in virtue of its being 'automatically' preserved within the indivisible structure of an extended present, we might question in turn whether this 'indivisible' structure tells us as much about the ambiguous and polyvalent nature of the present (or presents) as it does of the mysterious immanence of the past.[96] Indeed, it has been proposed that Bergson's argument as regards the continuity of mediate and immediate memory actually undercuts his earlier dualism of memory and perception, and marks as a result the abandonment of his hypothesis of the integral conservation of the past.[97] We might add in agreement that the differences highlighted by Bergson in respect to our varying 'attention to life' do not delineate different types of memory so much as different types of perception, and, with that, different forms of 'the' present. The mystery of the past's retention, even as we understand the term 'retention' in the most orthodox fashion of 'remembering', only arises if we think of ourselves as contained in the same present wherein each of us individually develops. Yet, this notion is precisely what *TFW* tries to subvert in its attack on simultaneity. If we alternatively posit a multiplicity of presents, each with a correlatively different past and future, the need to enlist the services of a conserved past, virtual memory or any other ethereal entity has been removed. 'The' present is merely the most impoverished, abstracted and impersonal *durée* that overarches all others: the lowest, most dilated common denominator.

Confirmation for a multiplicity of enduring presents comes from the fourth chapter of *MM*. Where *TFW* simply opposes the *durée* of consciousness to space, in this fourth chapter Bergson introduces a serial, tiered model of *durée* which is more ontological than psychological. This comes through primarily in *MM*'s depiction of virtuality and its own stratified configuration. There is not one virtual *durée* opposed to an unenduring material world; rather, there are 'planes' of virtuality, 'infinite in number', representing a myriad different degrees of *durée*.[98] *Durée* is scalar, allowing for a mutual impregnation of past and present in varying degrees. It has different rhythms, large and small, nested within each other, just as the *durée* of a day bounds the *durée* of a lecture or a walk in the park:

> In reality there is no one rhythm of duration; it is possible to imagine many different rhythms which, slower or faster, measure the degree of tension or relaxation of different kinds of consciousness and thereby fix their respective places in the scale of being.[99]

We saw in Bergson's puzzle concerning attention that our perception is quite elastic, mixing a pure perception with any amount of memory. *MM* fleshes this out with two paradigms of perception which represent polar opposites: that of someone living wholly in the present, a person of impulse reacting inflexibly and immediately to any stimulus; and that of someone living completely in the past, the 'dreamer' with 'no sense of the real', to borrow Pierre Janet's phrase.[100] The effort of living, according to Bergson, is keeping these poles at bay through the continual exchange between past and present, between an ideal pure perception that would be identical with matter – *durée* at its most dilated rhythm – and an ideal pure memory wholly removed from matter and completely formal. But these ideal purities are just that, theoretical poles: reality consists in different dilations of *durée* intervening between them rather than centred on one or the other extremity.

'Attention to life' is one name Bergson gives to this effort, but it is really 'a-tension' which is in question, a holding together of opposites. This is not a voluntary attention, which would be momentary and individual, but a range of mental plasticity that is species-specific, imposed by nature.[101] Only brain damage or extreme fatigue can disturb this natural range. Sleep and mental disorder detach memory from the sensory – motor functions by which it normally enters present reality.[102] In one of the companion essays to *MM*, 'Memory of the Present and False Recognition', Bergson describes psychopathology as less a disorder in relation to the subject in isolation (insanity may actually enrich one's life with new ways of feeling and thinking), so much as the subject's relationship with the world. The enhancement of one set of faculties upsets the equilibrium in our continuous adaptation to the environment. Maintaining this equilibrium requires the effort that Bergson calls this attention to life. Though this attention is very fatiguing, it is one which, simply by being 'more complex' and 'delicate' in the precision of its adjustment to reality, is thereby 'more positive'.[103] 'Balance' here is not a passive equilibrium, but a continual active adjustment, always on the brink of losing its balance, always on a knife-edge.[104]

DURÉE IN THE WORLD

We must be wary not to think of this tiered virtuality as only psychological: the proliferation and generalisation of *durée* in *MM*'s fourth chapter takes it beyond human psychology towards an ontology such that using the term 'matter and memory' as an exclusive disjunction is no longer helpful.[105] It is 'matter *and* memory': both belong to *durée* in terms of their substance: 'We can conceive an infinite number of degrees between matter and fully developed spirit... Each of these successive degrees, which measures a growing intensity of life, corresponds to a higher tension of duration'. In support of this process metaphysics of substance, Bergson subsequently rehearses some of the then newly emerging theories of physics wherein force was being increasingly materialised and the atom increasingly idealised:

> 'They show us pervading concrete extensity, *modifications*, *perturbations*, changes of *tension* or of *energy* and nothing else. It is by this, above all, that they tend to unite with the purely psychological analysis of motion that we considered to begin with'.[106]

Yet, while both matter and mind endure at their own range of speeds, they also, as actions, differ in their orientations: indeed, such orientation is essential to their identity. 'Matter' is really a 'materialisation', a divergent tendency towards increasingly ex-tended *durée*. Mind too is a process, this time of tension, of an ever-increasing condensation of different rhythms into its *durée*. Hence, it is the work, not so much of personal memory but of time itself which contracts secondary qualities in a manner which renders them apparently subjective; our personal memory – indeed our very subjectivity – is simply one other symptom of this, a phase-part characterising the particular rhythm of our *durée*.

What this allows for, ultimately, is a temporal solution to the mind – body problem, what Bergson has been searching for all along: '*questions relating to subject and object, to their distinction and their union, should be put in terms of time rather than of space*'.[107] Body and mind are irredeemably isolated only when understood spatially by taking matter to be extended and perception unextended, rather than seeing that they differ only by degree. The reality is that their difference is stated best in terms of the admixture of different rhythms of past, present and future, that is, not in terms of space but in terms of time or *durée*, which admits of degrees. Within *durée*, there is not one reality but a plurality. What remains to be discussed, in conclusion, is what generates this tension and ex-tension, two directions that spawn a plurality of *durées* from a continuity of time.

CONCLUSION

With virtuality so thoroughly placed on a continuum with actual forms like perception and matter, we are now at last faced with the issue of what generates the dualisation of mind and matter along this scale of different *durées*. Why indeed are there such strong correlations and covariances between mind and matter? Why, finally, are there two series at all rather than just one realm of matter or mind? Bergson's answer in *MM* is no less disappointing than was the recourse to endosmosis in *TFW* in a similar context. It is also surprisingly related to that last work: the answer is freedom: 'Thus, between brute matter and the mind most capable of reflection there are all possible intensities of memory or, what comes to the same thing, all the degrees of freedom'.[108] Time's internal differentiation between the most dilated *durée* of matter and the most contracted *durée* of mind is effected, in the last resort, by an injection of freedom, be it termed an indetermination of the will or our power of action. That this explanation is one-sided, either because it favours mind over matter or because it mentalises matter with will, shows how inadequate it is for the task of going beyond this duality. At a minimum we need a non-psychological explanation of will, power or action. *Durée* itself provided a plausible medium to straddle the poles of mind and matter, but we still need to understand why *durée* itself is multiple and serial, offering membership to both mind and matter rather than being the exclusive property of mind as it tends to be in *TFW*.

TFW understood Achilles' movements as actions that could not be reduced to the immobile homogeneous space subtending them. *MM* placed a peculiar twist on that tale, for it added that it is specifically our action that generates this reductive medium of homogeneous space! Homogeneous space and time represent the diagrammatic design of our eventual action upon matter.[109] Process seems to undo itself naturally in places. It will be Bergson's third major work, *CE*, which attempts to resolve this paradox by locating action within the larger context of life and by showing how and why life too is its own worst enemy. In fact, explaining the internal schism within life will also help to answer our question concerning the genesis of the mind – body duality: in *CE* there is an avowed and necessary dichotomy at the heart of life which generates dualities like mind and matter, instinct and intellect, and even freedom and determinism. If life invokes a monism, it is a dynamic one that feeds on its own continual dissolution and dissociation. Bergson will begin the third chapter of *CE* with an attempt to explain the genesis of intellect and materiality by proposing that the two 'are derived from a wider and higher form of existence' and that it must have been the one process that 'cut out matter and the intellect, at the same time, from a stuff that contained both'.[110] Our next chapter will try to throw new light on the dynamic production of mind and matter as well as on the meaning of this original 'stuff'.

NOTES

1. *MM*, p. 80 [*OE*, p. 219].
2. Worms 1997a, p. 41.
3. *MM*, p. 1 [*OE*, p. 169].
4. *MM*, pp. xi–xiii [*OE*, pp. 161–2]; see also p. 260 [*OE*, p. 333].
5. *MM*, pp. 1, 64, 4–5, 6–7 (translation altered) [*OE*, pp. 169, 209, 171, 172].
6. *MM*, pp. 14, 12 [*OE*, pp. 177, 176]. He also calls images for themselves 'matter' and images for the body the 'perception of matter' at *MM*, p. 8 [*OE*, p. 173].
7. *MM*, pp. 57–8, 6 [*OE*, pp. 205, 172]. Two-valued logic, as Hans Reichenbach pointed out, is a product of the 'corporeal substance' we find in the zone of middle dimensions into which we are born (Reichenbach 1959, pp. 189–90). But this 'zone' is not for Bergson the simple given that Reichenbach takes it to be.
8. *MM*, p. 288 [*OE*, p. 350].
9. See Worms 1997a, p. 21.
10. Delhomme 1954, p. 54; see also Alexander 1957, p. 37.
11. See *ME*, p. 68 [*OE*, p. 857].
12. *CE*, p. 189 [*OE*, p. 647].
13. See *MM*, p. 34 [*OE*, p. 190].
14. *MM*, p. 160 [*OE*, p. 270].
15. *CM*, p. 154 [*OE*, p. 1389].
16. The anti-Bergsonian criticisms of Jean-Pierre Changeux and Jean-Noël Missa (see Missa 1993, pp. 137–63) which make recourse to this neuroscientific evidence fall

foul of this misreading: Bergson would agree wholeheartedly that recollection is spatial. But recollection is not all there is to cognition: as a process it has various other phases.

17. See *TSMR*, p. 263 [*OE*, p. 1199]; *ME*, p. 58 [*OE*, p. 850].

18. See *M*, p. 707. In fact, the descriptions of a psychological novelist are often superior and 'more scientific' than those of many psychologists whose observation is tainted with woolly generalities and metaphysical hypotheses.

19. See Lacey 1989, p. 119.

20. Ibid. pp. 120–21.

21. See Rose 1987, p. 456.

22. Lyons 1987, p. 141.

23. See Čapek 1971, p. 165.

24. *M*, p. 481; *TSMR*, p. 263 [*OE*, p. 1199].

25. *M*, p. 483.

26. *ME*, pp. 45–6, 92 [*OE*, pp. 842, 871].

27. *MM*, p. xvi [*OE*, p. 164].

28. *CE*, p. 205 [*OE*, p. 660].

29. In his theory of secondary qualities and 'pure perception', we will find that Bergson understands perception as a dynamic movement between the ideal poles of pure objectivity and pure subjectivity, such that it is never wholly constructed nor wholly 'given'.

30. *ME*, p. 50 [*OE*, p. 845].

31. And this is to leave aside the whole question of what a physicalist, whose material substratum boils down to whatever contemporary physics says it is, means by the term 'matter'. Just where modern physics will take our concept of matter is unbounded because its own ontology is so abstract; see Wagner 1994, p. 88, 90; see also Davies and Gribbin 1991, on where the ontology of physics may go next.

32. Alfred Binet, cited in Grogin 1988, p. 3.

33. Dissociative thought, on the other hand, goes from the whole to create genuinely emergent parts.

34. Teichman 1988, p. 16 wonders whether obedience to Ockham's razor always leads to the best explanation: 'Is the best explanation the one which helps us to understand things and predict events? Or is it one which conforms to scientific theory? . . . in astronomy, say, the best explanation will clearly turn out to be a scientific-mathematical one, when it comes to the behaviour of individual human beings ordinary commonsense folk psychology is usually better than any other explanatory model'. The value of parsimony for evolutionary theory has also been a matter for debate; see Sober 1993, pp. 179–80.

35. *MM*, p. 8, [*OE*, p. 174].

36. Borst 1970, p. 13.

37. One reply is that the identification is an empirical one. It is not saying that *x* is *y*, but rather that *x* has been identified as *y*. Analogously, a stranger at the door may turn out later to have been the doctor at the door. But that does not mean that all statements concerning that stranger are identical to ones concerning the doctor; each has its own logic. Yet it will eventually be found that what those stranger-statements were referring to was really the doctor, just as, for instance, science discovered that lightning-statements were really referring to an electrical discharge; see Smart 1970, pp. 55–6, 62. The apparent individual reality of both the entity to be reduced and

the entity it will be reduced to actually pertains to the different types of logic we use in making statements about the two. It is nothing essential to them. Yet problems with identity persist: see for just one example Stevenson 1970, pp. 87–92.

38. *ME*, p. 238 [*OE*, p. 964].
39. *ME*, p. 246 [*OE*, p. 969]. This dilemma of IT is actually asserted initially in the context of Bergson's attack on idealism here; but the point stands against any monism including reductive materialism. Materialism in particular, he writes (*ME*, p. 237 [*OE*, p. 963]), involves an illegitimate movement between two 'notation-systems', the one idealist, the other materialist. If we were to try to follow the reasoning of either, we would find that 'we pass instantly from realism [materialism] to idealism and from idealism to realism, showing ourselves in the one at the very moment when we are going to be caught in the act of self-contradiction in the other'.
40. Crane and Mellor 1990, p. 203.
41. See Davidson 1980, p. 214.
42. See Kim 1994.
43. Churchland 1979, p. 7; Churchland 1988, pp. 76–9; Churchland 1979, p. 116.
44. Borst 1970, p. 20.
45. Churchland 1979, p. 119.
46. There is also the lesser issue of the absense of conditions for EM's very own expressibility; see Casey 1992, and, as a response to the sort of argument Casey poses, Churchland 1990, pp. 221–2.
47. See Churchland 1988, pp. 43–4.
48. *ME*, p. 253 [*OE*, p. 973].
49. *MM*, p. xiii [*OE*, p. 162].
50. See *MM*, pp. 26–31 [*OE*, pp. 185–8].
51. *CE*, p. 317 [*OE*, p. 749].
52. In fact, the charge of artistic licence being at work in Bergson's method actually connects with his theory of aesthetics outlined in *L*: in the genuine artistic imagination there is no question of any 'projection' on to reality occurring at all; it is not an idiosyncratic faculty creating *ex nihilo*, it simply reveals what we have hidden from ourselves in our perceptual power of condensation which is at the same time an abstraction from the individual to the general; see *L*, pp. 150ff [*OE*, pp. 458ff].
53. *MM*, pp. 78, 306 [*OE*, pp. 218, 361].
54. *ME*, p. 251 [*OE*, p. 972]. Thinking of the brain as a 'Cartesian Theatre' for viewing the contents of mind has been attacked again more recently by Daniel Dennett in Dennett 1991.
55. See Tallis 1991, pp. 79–82.
56. *MM*, p. 288 [*OE*, p. 350]; *MM*, p. 17 [*OE*, p. 179].
57. *MM*, p. 9 [*OE*, p. 174].
58. See Tallis 1991, pp. 88–101.
59. See Globus 1995, pp. 136–47.
60. See *ME*, pp. 234–50 [*OE*, pp. 962–71]; *M*, pp. 411, 643–4.
61. *ME*, p. 243 [*OE*, p. 967].
62. *ME*, p. 244 [*OE*, p. 968], second part of quotation not in interrogative form originally.
63. *ME*, p. 245 [*OE*, p. 968].
64. *MM*, p. 83 [*OE*, p. 221].

65. See Goodman 1978, pp. 7–17, in Kantian voice on the five ways the mind can be seen to construct its world.
66. *MM*, p. 78 [*OE*, p. 218].
67. *MM*, p. 62 [*OE*, p. 208]. One materialist response to the fallacy is to invoke a hierarchy. As Daniel Dennett proposes, one begins by consciously placing homunculi with their own beliefs and desires at the highest level of the physical system (subsystems such as 'rememberers', 'evaluators', 'overseers' and so on), be it a brain or a computer (see Dennett 1979, p. 80). But these homunculi themselves are continually analysed into smaller and 'less clever' homunculi until a level is reached when all anthropomorphising has ceased and we are dealing purely with 'adders and subtractors' (p. 81). The successful activity of one homunculus is thereby explained, not through recourse to another homunculus within it, but through positing a team consisting of smaller and individually less talented homunculi (see Lycan 1990, p. 80). Our initial set of full-blown homunculi are thereby 'discharged' of their duties (Dennett 1979 p. 81), and can be replaced by a cumulative structure comprised solely of levels which are entirely mechanistic. See also the attempt in Minski 1988 to explain mind, which he views as a project 'to show how minds are built from mindless stuff' by recourse to increasingly more elemental and stupid subsocieties of agents with simple tasks, which in composition generate sophisticated powers (p. 17). However, the problem with this type of answer to the fallacy is one of emergence. It is one thing to see how an activity normally performed by a single agent of certain intelligence could be effected by lesser beings with their talents pooled together; it is quite another thing to believe it possible that beings with no intelligence whatsoever could muster anything beyond this level, irrespective of how many of them are collected together. Though Bergson would wholeheartedly endorse the reality of emergence in nature, we can be less sure of his approval when it involves making such a massive category error as is seen here. 'More clever' can be resolved into 'less clever', but a total absence of intelligence cannot be inflated into anything else (even 'adders and subtractors' represent a degree above mindlessness): this clearly shows that it is always easier for the 'reverse engineer' to explain things by working backwards rather than forwards.
68. *MM*, pp. 37–8 [*OE*, p. 192].
69. *MM*, p. 285 [*OE*, p. 349].
70. Worms 1997b, p. 103.
71. *MM*, p. 238 [*OE*, p. 319].
72. See *MM*, pp. 89–98 [*OE*, pp. 225–31].
73. See Squire 1986, p. 1614. According to Edward Casey, Bergson's introduction of habit-memory 'was potentially revolutionary for Western theorizing about memory' (Casey 1984, p. 280).
74. Zaner 1971, p. 243; Casey 1987, p. 179.
75. *MM*, pp. 137, 139 [*OE*, pp. 256, 257]; *MM*, p. 197 [*OE*, p. 293].
76. These criticisms are still very pertinent today where the neurosciences, though having complicated matters substantially, remain reliant on the scheme, 'recognition equals perception plus associated memory'; see Missa 1993, pp. 70–1.
77. *MM*, pp. 213 105–18, 112, 111 [*OE*, pp. 303, 235–44, 240, 239].
78. Tallon 1973, p. 487.
79. *MM*, p. 123 [*OE*, p. 247].
80. *MM*, p. 127 [*OE*, p. 249].

81. *MM*, p. 112n [*OE*, p. 240]. Bergson is here endorsing the view of Alfred Fouillée.
82. *MM*, p. 145 [*OE*, p. 261].
83. See *MM*, pp. 120–31 [*OE*, pp. 245–52].
84. See Edelman 1992, pp. 81–2.
85. See *MM*, p. 93 [*OE*, p. 228].
86. See *MM*, p. 171–2 [*OE*, pp. 276–7] and *CM*, p. 153 [*OE*, p. 1388].
87. Deleuze 1973, pp. 57–8.
88. *MM*, p. 173 [*OE*, p. 278].
89. *MM*, p. 181 [*OE*, p. 283]; *ME*, p. 165 [*OE*, p. 917]; *MM*, pp. 170–3, 180–1 [*OE*, pp. 276–8, 283].
90. *MM*, p. 319 [*OE*, p. 369]. Note that some might not regard 'realism' towards the past as this view that the past somehow still exists (in itself or in memory), but instead that the past did once exist (was present), as opposed to an anti-realist who would say that it never even existed even as a previous present but is always constructed so retrospectively in the present (which is all that exists).
91. *MM*, p. 113 [*OE*, p. 241].
92. See *MM*, p. 115 [*OE*, p. 242].
93. Maritain 1968, p. 220; Russell 1914, p. 21.
94. *CM*, p. 155 [*OE*, p. 1389]; *CM*, p. 152 [*OE*, p. 1387].
95. *MM*, p. 155 [*OE*, p. 267].
96. *CM*, p. 153 [*OE*, p. 1387]; *CE*, p. 5 [*OE*, p. 498].
97. See Wolff 1959, pp. 335, 337 and Wolff 1957, pp. 55–71.
98. *MM*, p. 222 [*OE*, p. 309].
99. *MM*, p. 275 [*OE*, p. 342]. Some writers argue against the possibility of degrees of consciousness, for consciousness can only be either present or absent. What might appear as a low degree of consciousness is rather a perfectly standard consciousness of either a vague object or with vague content; see Tallis 1991, pp. 255–6n13. Bergson, however, would have rejected such a stark divide between the form and content of consciousness.
100. *MM*, pp. 296, 313, 331 [*OE*, pp. 355, 365, 377]; Bergson cites Janet at *MM*, pp. 229–30 [*OE*, pp. 313–14].
101. *MM*, pp. 226, 113–14 [*OE*, pp. 311, 240–1].
102. In dreams, the attention is not fixed by the sensory–motor equilibrium of the body; see *ME*, pp. 104–33 [*OE*, pp. 878–97].
103. See *ME*, pp. 151–2 [*OE*, p. 909]; *ME*, p. 153 [*OE*, p. 910]; *ME*, p. 155 [*OE*, p. 911].
104. See Cohen and Stewart 1994, p. 245 on the many meanings of the word 'balance'.
105. Unlike Freud, 'Bergson does not use the word "unconscious" to denote a psychological reality outside consciousness, but to denote a nonpsychological reality – being as it is in itself' (Deleuze 1988, p. 56).
106. *MM*, pp. 296, 266 [*OE*, pp. 355, 337].
107. *MM*, p. 77 [*OE*, p. 218].
108. *MM*, p. 297 [*OE*, p. 355].
109. See *MM*, p. 280 [*OE*, p. 345].
110. *CE*, pp. 197, 210 [*OE*, pp. 653, 664].

3

Philosophy of Biology

Your book risks remaining in darkness for a hundred years.[1]

It has been said that *CE* marks a shift in Bergson's thought from a philosophy of human consciousness towards a 'super-phenomenology for life itself'.[2] One might dispute this point – a pluralist ontology of process might seem a more appropriate label than simply an extension of the method of immediate data – but it is certainly true that this book is definitive in Bergson's own philosophical development, not only because of the early and ultimately destructive fame it brought to his work, but also because it does represent the most general extension of his philosophy of time.[3] This last fact must be made clear from the outset: *CE* posits a theory of time first, and only second a philosophy of life. Even *TFW* suggested that 'The past is a reality perhaps for living bodies', and it is this temporal property of biological phenomena which draws Bergson towards this area in his third major work.[4]

Why it should be evolutionary biology in particular that Bergson tackles is self-evident: in any ordinary sense of the term, evolution means 'change'.[5] That is all there essentially is to Bergson's theory of life: a theory of time generalised. Bergson frequently describes biology in a temporal fashion, the living body being a *'register in which time is being inscribed'*.[6] Within evolutionary theory, of course, there have been constant struggles between those who would direct this phenomenon of change towards some or other end and those who would defiantly resist such a move. Yet, while we will discover that teleology is in fact present in even the most apparently mechanistic approaches to life, the most notable exemplars of finalism in biology have always been animism, orthogenesis and vitalism. Bergson has been wrongly placed in the last of these categories of teleologism. It should already be clear that in his time-philosophy the emphasis has always been on the unforeseeable and indeterminate creation of novelty, and this will be no less true in his application of that theory to evolution. Nevertheless, we still find eminent evolutionists characterising Bergson as a 'teleological' philosopher, who believes that 'evolutionary change necessarily proceeds along determined paths'.[7]

This misrepresentation of his work is so prevalent than one is tempted simply to say that Bergson is not a vitalist at all were it not that what is really at issue here is the meaning of the word 'vital'. Bergson does use the term '*élan vital*', but the emphasis is on the first part of the phrase rather than the second, the vitality in question is a type of time, a type of organisation, rather than any mysterious notion of an *anima sensitiva*, vital fluid or *archeus*. It is noteworthy in this respect that the entry in *The Encyclopedia of Philosophy* under 'vitalism' does not discuss Bergson's work, finding that more suitable for treatment in the context of his general metaphysics of time.[8] In his own survey of the contemporary literature in evolutionary theory, Bergson does of course discuss vitalism, but only to reject it on account of its finalism. What he does admire is its heuristic virtues: it acts as a label for our ignorance, showing the insufficiency of mechanism in explaining life, while that mechanism simply 'invites us to ignore that ignorance'. This critical aspect of vitalism does have real value, but Bergson has no truck with any positive content that 'superposes on mechanism' some additional agency, such as the entelechy of Hans Driesch.[9]

Bergson's own work in *CE*, like that of his previous books, has its own critical dimension as well as a positive thesis to forward, and our presentation now will follow that structure again. Our *via negativa* here looks at evolutionary theory's main protagonists in terms amenable to Bergson's critique: the debate over neo-Darwinian adaptationism; gradualism versus punctuated equilibria; internalism and externalism; the unit of selection problem; and lastly the new sciences of complexity. Naturally, the oppositions here are constructed in a manner which will allow Bergson's ideas to gain their foothold in the debate – there are various other issues we have had to omit – but these concerns belong to the mainstream of theory nonetheless, and lead on to what Bergson has to add which remains original and of value. This originality stems from his introduction of a philosophy of creative time into the science of life; a perspective that has only quite recently been rediscovered by biology itself after a long period mired in reductive mechanism. Some of the territory covered will be familiar; reductionism in psychology is very similar to and often works hand in hand with reductionism in biology: just as mind is regarded as a product of the molecular and electrical processes of the brain, life for some evolutionists is a product of the molecular processes of genes.[10] Tackling these issues will also add a new stratum to our own investigation into Bergsonian dualism, this time throwing new light on the dynamic, genetic element of dualisation.

DISSOCIATION

'Life', Bergson writes, proceeds '*by dissociation and division*'. A living entity is not what has been composed from cells so much as what 'has made the cells by means of [a] dissociation'.[11] Again, this term 'dissociation' is given priority over association. What began as a concept in psychopathology prevalent in the nineteenth century gains increasingly more significance in Bergsonian thought.[12] But what is at question here is not what type of thing life is – a lot of little things coming together or one big thing breaking up – rather it is a question of what mode of process life constitutes. Bergson often uses the term 'organisation' instead of life, which is quite appropriate as 'organisation' connotes the residual effect of past actions accumulated within the present. Organisation is a type of movement rich with history. Bergson describes it as a continuous change of form linking the embryo with the adult organism, while ageing is explained as the further development of the embryo.[13] The cell itself, in being formed by dissociation, is not the deposit of some ethereal vitality from above, but one phase of a process whose temporality, rhythms or phases are essential to its nature.[14]

Life as such, on the other hand, when understood as a mode of organisation, is a capacity prior to, or the condition of possibility of, any organic form. The antecedent unity implicit in the concept of dissociation will itself need further exposition when we look back to its ultimate origin; but certainly at the stage when cells and individual organisms are being formed, the generative unity in question is only relative. Any unity can itself be regarded as the product of an earlier dissociation, an ongoing creation formed through the cascading dissolution of earlier, provisional and relative unities. There is only the 'inexorable law', Bergson says, which dooms every living entity to eternal division and subdivision until it covers 'the widest possible extent in space'. This continual 'bifurcation' is not incidental to life but lies at the heart of evolution.[15]

Consequently, Bergson would take issue with the image of the tree of life prevalent in many contemporary versions of evolutionary theory. As the strong version of this thesis goes, there is a single tree of life with all species branching off from what was originally one common ancestor.[16] This idea remains too Aristotelian and hierarchical for Bergson, for it pictures life as a successive linearity rather than as a network of coincident dissociations in every direction. Bergson's alternative image is of an explosion outward (with each exploded fragment itself generating a new explosion) rather than of growth upwards. Likewise, organisms should not be regarded as natural kinds but as collections or nexuses of different tendencies, for no species, genus or kingdom uniquely possesses any one characteristic. All vary primarily in their tendency to emphasise these common characters: as he advises, we should seek '*dynamic* definitions' in biological taxonomy.[17]

It follows that there is no '*life in general*' marching inexorably towards some goal, but simply sporadic currents of life with real creation ongoing at all points along them. Evolution does not operate gradually by slowly accumulating minute changes mechanically until a new species is created. For Bergson, life is a continuum of heterogeneity, with each species representing a sudden emergence of novelty and invention: 'Discontinuous evolution ... proceeds by bounds, obtaining at each stopping-place a combination, perfect of its kind'.[18] This is not to claim that the constant creativity of evolution is harmonious or progressive (whatever that 'progress' might entail): disparity, disharmony and failure, Bergson writes, 'seems to be the rule, success exceptional and always imperfect'. Life is replete with 'deviations, arrests, set-backs' at the level of both bodily formation and the ecological integration of species. What unity and coherence there is, is again the product not of a movement towards unity, but the disintegration of one 'implied in this movement itself'.[19]

Admittedly, Bergson does present evidence for evolutionary convergence, taking as his example the independent evolution of light sensitivity in molluscs (an 'eye' of sorts) and vertebrates.[20] But he is not arguing for a teleology here so much as confirmation of some (strictly non-theological) anterior source of organisation as against the accumulation of traits by pure chance being proposed by mechanistic theories at the time he was writing. What this source will consist of, ultimately, will be a tension between two opposed forces or tendencies, an originating impulse that is already internally divided and perpetually divisive, a symmetry which was always already broken. This divisiveness is precisely what propels evolution forward and informs any point on its progress. Hence, it must always be regarded as a type of complex movement rather than a mysterious power. Any specific point on its path, any organism in other words, represents a forced accommodation between these opposed tendencies. Discovering what these tendencies are will take us into metaphysical and metaphilosophical territories, for the two are self-referential: on one side the tendency towards having an end and so ceasing to create, on the other the tendency towards never-ending creativity. 'Aims' and 'convergences' are admissible in Bergson's theory of life, but they must be understood at a second-order remove and dualistically: one aim is simply not to evolve at all but re-volve in a circle with a fixed nature; the other aim is aimless movement itself, continual invention. This internal contradiction fuels the motor of life's engine.

We can conclude for now by putting some flesh on the bones of this rather abstract scheme of dissociation. In the extended quotation that follows, Bergson clearly shows what his so-called vitalism actually comprises: life simply consists of two modes of movement, that is, nothing more substantial than time itself:

> Two things only are necessary: (1) a gradual accumulation of energy; (2) an elastic canalization of this energy in variable and indeterminable directions, at the end of which are free acts. This twofold result has been obtained in a particular way on our planet. But it might have been obtained by entirely different means. It was not necessary that life should fix its choice mainly upon the carbon of carbonic acid – ... We go further: it is not even necessary that life should be concentrated and determined in organisms properly so called, that is, in definite bodies presenting to the flow of energy ready-made though elastic canals. It can be conceived (although it can hardly be imagined) that energy might be saved up, and then expended on varying lines running across a matter not yet solidified. Every essential of life would still be there, since there would still be slow accumulation of energy and sudden release.[21]

Accumulation and sudden release. Which material is involved is irrelevant. Which type of energy is less relevant too in comparison with the mode of organised movement it instantiates.[22] When one realises that the latest understanding of living organisms sees them as 'far-from-equilibrium dissipative structures' that must 'take up and dissipate energy in order to maintain their structural integrity', the probity and timeliness of Bergson's nearly century-old depiction seems startling.[23] Let us now examine why so many think differently and continue to reject this theory of life.

PUTTING THE PART BEFORE THE HORSE

In the final pages of *CE*, Bergson rebukes the mechanistic model of biological and social evolution propounded by Herbert Spencer, whose writings a generation earlier had made him the most popular evolutionist of his day. In particular, Bergson takes exception to what he calls Spencer's 'false evolutionism':[24]

> The cardinal error of Spencer is to take experience already allotted as given, whereas the true problem is to know how the allotment was worked...A true evolutionism would propose to discover by what *modus vivendi*, gradually obtained, the intellect has adopted its plan of structure, and matter its mode of subdivision.[25]

Spencer does not follow a true genesis or evolution but is simply '*reconstructing evolution with fragments of the evolved*'. Such a reverse engineering deals only with 'reality in its present form'. What Bergson sees here is the diametric opposite of his own theory of a creative evolution: a materialistic, mechanistic, reductive and deterministic picture resting on the two sins of retrospection and conformism: we can only adopt this view if we 'place ourselves in one of the points where evolution comes to a head...and it is this part that we declare representative of the whole'.[26] But this simply removes what is temporal from evolution. The present is idolised, evolution having supposedly reached its best possible outcome in its current state. Likewise, the past is made into a fixed inevitability that could only have taken one direction: towards us. Finally, the future is abolished as there can be no genuine creation of novelty but only and ever the predetermined implementation of the one outcome made possible by the present. What we have behind these two rival approaches to evolution are consequently two rival philosophies of time.

Use of the concept of progress is a sensitive issue amongst evolutionists. Is there a tendency to global progress or is there only local improvement? And what do we mean by 'progress' anyway: diversity, physical fitness, longevity, individual fecundity, resilience or complexity? Complexity is in fact a popular option, but then the question transforms into what sort of complexity – greater compositional (internal) complexity, greater relational (external) complexity, or some (perhaps necessary) combination of these going hand in hand. Whatever the specific version employed, some type of complexity is usually taken for granted as the general direction evolution has moved in from the pre-biotic soup onwards. Yet, on the other hand, no one wants to be accused of finalism and, certainly, no one wishes to attach a normative value to the term 'progress'.

Stephen Jay Gould and Richard Lewontin's critique of the neo-Darwinian adaptationist paradigm is worth mentioning here.[27] Just as Bergson accused Spencer of lionising the present, Gould and Lewontin similarly portray the adaptationist as a modern Dr Pangloss (from Voltaire's *Candide*), picturing the organism as a collection of phenotypic traits – like the hump of a camel or the spots of a leopard – each one of which has evolved as the best possible response ('fittest adaptation') to the selective pressure of the external environment. The reply from adaptationists has often been to concede that there are various obvious constraints on perfection, but that that only excludes the thesis of strong adaptationism – the view that all traits are perfect and none maladaptive.[28] A weak adaptationism, the reply continues, still stands as a defensible alternative. But Gould and Lewontin never targeted strong adaptationism in fact, just as Dr Pangloss never advocated perfectionism. Pangloss does not deny evil, only that evil is gratuitous: our world represents the best possible outcome given the constraints of necessary human weakness and physical misfortune: unlike God, it is not perfect. Likewise, even the (weak) adaptationist thinks that each and every phenotypic trait somewhere along the line, in the past or the present, through this environment or another one, is an adaptation to selective pressures which, while not perfect and perhaps even maladaptive on its own, constitutes the best compromise possible for the whole organism given any alternative. It is a form of mechanistic biological fatalism.

The contentious issue, for non-adaptationists today as it was for Bergson in his time, is whether such a mechanistic view can exhaustively explain the phenomena of evolution. Bergson argues eloquently that the environment which 'causes' the formation of similar biological forms is not like a ready-made container awaiting whatever liquid might fill it. Living organisms actively contribute to and partly create their environment: there is mutual interaction. Adaptation is more like a solution to a problem than a passive moulding into shape from external pressure: 'Such adapting is not *repeating*, but *replying*, – an entirely different thing'.[29] Clearly, there is a difference between seeing adaptation as active problem solving instead of passive imprinting: as two current theorists put it, 'Organisms grow in environments, they are not moulded by them'.[30]

The lately developed theory of coevolution allows different species to act as part of each other's environment. The evolutionary success of one species can be affected by that of another: new fitnesses evolve in a species as a reaction to new traits in another so that each evolves, not in triumph over the other, but so that each survives within an ecology that includes its coevolving cohabitants. Such coevolution is plausible once one notes the complexity of the evolutionary landscape. This complex picture of evolution radically alters the dualistic image of competing organisms passive before an alien environment; competition is still there, but what is newly admitted is an evolutionary process which is partly internal to a set of species seen as a dynamic system in its own right. There is then a self-organising, active dimension to life. We will soon see that taking evolution beyond the dichotomy of either being wholly prone to external pressures (orthodox adaptationism) or internal forces (Lamarckism) is also a facet of Bergson's theory.

Another major feature of certain brands of adaptationism is the propensity towards reductionist thinking. In Richard Dawkins' notion of the 'selfish gene', we have what has been called 'The ultimate reductionist scenario yet concocted in evolutionary biology'.[31] Across a number of books, Dawkins argues that adaptations are not for the benefit of the organism but for the active germ-line replicator. The organism is merely the vehicle for that replicator. Genes mould the world to facilitate their replication, be it through the phenotypic traits of the vehicular organism or the extended phenotypic traits of that organism's behaviour, manufactured artefacts, relations with other organisms and so on.[32] The significance of individual organisms is eliminated, as they become, in Dawkins' infamous words, 'gigantic lumbering robots' programmed to preserve the selfish molecules we call our genes.[33] Dawkins' point is that the organism does not hold a privileged place, and that what is essential in evolution – replication with intermittent errors of information across generations – is a role fulfilled sufficiently by the genome alone.

Strange as it may seem, Bergson might not necessarily disagree: indeed, he sums up his position at one point by agreeing that 'evolution takes place from germ to germ rather than from individual to individual'.[34] That heredity (phylogenesis) should now be understood in terms of molecular biology and the RNA–DNA replication machine is not his concern. His view would rather be that Dawkins has not gone far enough in the direction his argument follows. Seeing the inadequacy of one level of biology, the organismic, Dawkins simply miniaturises the phenomenon by now allowing genes to carry the active role in evolutionary process. But the fundamental picture remains the same. The difficulties attendant to this miniaturisation are well rehearsed in the literature and only include the role of mitochondria, the mathematical and physical dynamics of organic form, and the context-dependency of genetic causal activity.[35] What they testify to is a deferment of the issue rather than its resolution, for the closer biology comes to understanding life in terms of its physico–chemical covariants alone (Bergson would not say 'causes'), the closer it comes to letting what is vital about it slip through its hands.[36] Just as one can place perception neither in the nerve nor in the brain but only at the perceived object itself, so Bergson's quarrel with Dawkins would be that one must identify the process of life only with life itself as a type of organisation and not with any one of its stages, be it the gene or the organism. Evolution does not need any vehicle or container. No privileged locus is required because it is not a space of that type at all; it is a mode of order, a movement. In a sense, Bergson rehabilitates the organism along with every other level of biology: they all have as much or as little reality as preferred, for they are all phase-parts of a process.

Taking one part of evolution, the gene say, and bestowing all the features of vitality upon it actually reinstates all the old dualisms rather than eradicating them. DNA now becomes the informational replicator or software, the organism becomes the vehicular hardware. *CE* takes pains to show where materialist evolutionary theory tries to seclude a covert finalism within itself – in the organism's *effort* to survive for example: if it were consistently materialist, it would have no need to talk of survival or struggle at all. Bergson himself is clearly against the internal finalism of Lamarck – in place of acquired characteristics, he espouses directionless deviation. Yet, mechanism does not evade finalism either. This can be found in any functionalist analysis for instance: in place of the spiritual telos found in vitalism, a functional telos is substituted to explain the evolution of phenotypic traits; instead of an external programme, an internal one comprised of the organism's physiological functions.[37] In a similar vein, we find theorists like Jacques Monod, the supposed scourge of vitalist biology, nonetheless writing of a 'telenomy' in nature and so readmitting a crypto-finalism to explain the emergence of complex organisms.[38] Bergson would not have been surprised:

> Mechanism, here, reproaches finalism with its anthropomorphic character, and rightly. But it fails to see that itself [*sic*] proceeds according to this method – somewhat mutilated! True, it has got rid of the end pursued or the ideal model. But it also holds that nature has worked like a human being by bringing parts together.[39]

To segregate one piece of matter from the rest and discuss its self-identical persistence against a background of non-replicating, non-evolving matter is already to inject some ideation into the scene. Hence, to think of DNA as information plays upon the same slide of meaning we saw active in the homunculus fallacy in psychology.[40]

ANTI-GRADUALISM

We have seen Bergson's critique of a retrospective fallacy at work in mechanistic evolutionary theory, its propensity being to reconstruct evolution with '*fragments of the evolved*'. The whole organism is atomised into traits and remanufactured in imagination with the assumption that nature works in the same way as human technology, that is, by associating parts into wholes (rather than dissociating whole processes into phase-parts). Richard Dawkins admits that geneticists have to work in this manner, going backwards from the differing phenotypic traits of two adult animals which are known to differ in one gene, so that they can then posit the influence of that gene on those traits. But aren't they confusing homogeneous space with time, a fragment of the evolved with evolution? In Dawkins' view, however, the evolution of the animal *can* be spatialised in the most stark manner, with the metaphor of 'genetic space' allowing us to see each species' development localised within a multidimensional field of all possible genetic configurations. There is no novelty here: every possible future is mapped out in a storeroom of possibilities.[41]

The advantage this spatialised viewpoint gains us, says Dawkins, is that it permits evolution to be thought of as a 'gradual, cumulative process'. Successive changes are small relative to the organism's immediate ancestor but cumulatively massive over the time-periods involved in evolution. Were the changes not individually incremental but complete transformations, each one on its own would most probably be maladaptive simply on account of the fact that they produce an adult less like its successful parent.[42] In defence of gradualism, Dawkins shows admirably why these myriad contributory changes are retained rather than eradicated before the final cumulative evolution of the trait in question is completed, the point being that each and every retained step towards that evolution constitutes a trait in itself conferring a fitness advantage that thereby 'pays its way', so to speak. In the debate over the value of assumed incremental changes, he has more than answered anti-gradualist criticisms, including Bergson's.

The real problem with such gradualism, however, has always been that the simple accumulation of variations may explain the modification of the species but not the emergence of a new species.[43] And here Dawkins' defence of gradualism fares less well. Stephen Jay Gould and Niles Eldridge's theory of 'Punctuated Equilibria' is one response to this challenge of explaining speciation. The theory gains its title because it melds two processes with opposite temporal properties: the stasis of natural selection and the creative change of speciation. This picture of 'stasis punctuated by episodic events of allopatric speciation' has also helped to reinstate the integrity of species. Species and species formation are real agents in evolution rather than simply vehicles for another fundamental process.[44]

Punctuated Equilibria theory has been invoked as a position with resonance for Bergsonism.[45] After all, Bergsonian evolution is not incremental or gradual either, but a 'discontinuous evolution which proceeds by bounds'. Certainly, there is some substance to this point once we have divested Bergsonism of its vitalist stereotype (which would surely scare off Gould and Eldridge from such an association) and realise that it is at heart a theory of time.[46] In his own argument against gradualism, Bergson cites Hugo de Vries' 'theory of mutations', the idea that

> a new species comes into being all at once by the simultaneous appearance of several new characters...Species pass through periods of stability and transformation. When the period of 'mutability' occurs, unexpected forms spring forth in a great number of different directions.[47]

Of course, de Vries' evidence for mutations was eventually discredited, as also was the kindred theory of saltationism forwarded by Richard Goldschmidt in the 1940s when no credible mechanism for its operation could be found either.[48] But Bergson, in any case, ultimately rejects de Vries' theory for its reliance on the operation of chance: the sudden emergence of multiple co-ordinated changes in a species is unlikely to have arisen by pure accident. The real issue, as always, is not to find a privileged locus to act as *the* carrier for evolution, but to show that each and every locus is no less real than any other as a resting place, but equally no less unreal than any other as the bearer of an evolutionary movement which must never be confused with an immobility.

This point can be illustrated if we look again at the weakness of gradualism in terms of logic rather than its empirical explanation. Species are normally defined as interbreeding individuals capable of producing fertile offspring. But there is a genuine vagueness attaching to the cut-off point in real populations between groups that will and will not interbreed.[49] Behind this lies a puzzle which has bothered evolutionists from Darwin to the present day: how can an ape have a child that is an ape that has a child that is an ape...that has a child that is a man that has a child that is a man? On account of this paradox, we could claim that all evolution is spurious. As it is impossible for any one non-*Homo sapiens* to beget a *Homo sapiens*, it follows that there is no evolution between species at all. But this is akin to the query behind Zeno's Achilles paradox: how can Achilles overtake the tortoise if each of his steps must be behind the steps of the tortoise in advance? The question behind how speciation works is very similar. Gradualism thinks evolution homogeneously just as Zeno thinks movement homogeneously: how can one evolve beyond what one is, for to be what one is not is not to be at all? But if evolution is regarded as a heterogeneous continuity, 'one' is to one's ancestors just as Achilles' 'overtaking' steps are to his earlier 'catching up' steps: a new irreducible creation of novelty. There is real creation for Bergson at all points along the continuum, indeed, this is what makes it a continuity, because each point is *similarly* new in some way.[50]

INTERNALISM AND EXTERNALISM

We have seen the tensions amongst contemporary theorists as regards what exactly natural selection selects: does it operate for the benefit (or duplication) of the organism or its genes? Before the advent of genetic reductionism the earlier debate involved claims for selection amongst groups of organisms versus claims that selection acted on individual organisms alone. The advocates for group selection lost that argument to the individualists. But our interest now is with Bergson's subversion of the whole notion of a unit of selection in evolutionary theory through his attempt to steer between outright externalism and internalism. In fact, whether one is branded an externalist or an internalist depends on which unit of selection one favours and so where one locates the forces of selection: if the unit is the gene, then its environment comprises both its phenotype and extended phenotype as they extend outward to the benefit or detriment of the gene's chances of being duplicated. If it is the group, then the environment consists of an entirely different configuration where what would seem external from the gene's perspective will be internal from the group point of view.

Bergson attempts to follow an intermediate route between externalism and internalism by integrating these partial views into a larger, though thereby less definite, perspective. But he does so, not because he favours some new alternative unit of selection, but because the individuality of all such units is questionable. Both internalism and externalism wrongly place the emphasis on the part – irrespective of whether that part is the gene, organism or group – rather than the whole, which is life. Certainly, the organism is not individual enough for Bergson. Its individuality is both relative and unstable, being decentred spatially, with 'elements composing the individual . . . [having themselves] a certain individuality', as well as temporally, with each organism being connected with its 'remotest ancestor' and 'all that descends from the ancestor in divergent directions'. But this is not then to confer the prize on either the group above or the gene below: the issue of individuality – what is inside and what is outside – is not just undecidable in all directions, up and down, it is actually indeterminate for reasons which are intrinsic to life itself.

In a self-referential manner we will explore more later, one part of the motive force of life resides in the tendency to create isolated individuals; as Bergson puts it: life 'manifests a search for individuality, as if it strove to constitute systems naturally isolated, naturally closed'. Life in part concerns the *creation* of an inside and an outside and so cannot be explained in terms which take a particular inside and outside for granted. That this search is in vain, that life must incessantly move in an open direction without ever reaching closure, is the other part of the aforementioned motive force driving it. This is the one type of finality Bergson allows within the vital realm, one that involves the whole notion of life as such rather than any specific unit.[51]

THE NEW BIOLOGY

For the most part, the relationship between life and matter will be our main concern from this point onward, as it is in the later chapters of *CE*. That this relationship must lie at the heart of any understanding of biology is obvious: but behind that again must be one's understanding of matter *per se*. The problem, according to Bergson, is that the two cannot be understood in isolation from each other, so that getting our picture of either of them right entails getting it right for both together.

As against the charge of vitalism, Bergson clearly believes that organised, living matter is made of entirely the same stuff as inert matter. He is thoroughly aware that there is no principle that might stop physics and chemistry from synthesising living matter from non-living matter.[52] What differentiates the two are modes of organisation, types of order or, in other words, movement. What is certainly not the same as living matter, however, are those 'artificial systems' cut out of inert matter by science:

> That life is a kind of mechanism I cordially agree. But is it the mechanism of parts artificially isolated within the whole of the universe, or is it the mechanism of the real whole? The real whole might well be, we conceive, an indivisible continuity. The systems we cut out within it would, properly speaking, not then be *parts* at all; they would be *partial views* of the whole.[53]

The only material systems which are bereft of all genuine temporal qualities – and so allow for perfect repetition, bidirectionality and quantification – are artificially closed or isolated systems, that is, ones which either do not exchange any matter with their environment (but do exchange energy) or exchange neither matter nor energy.[54] Bergson defines inert matter itself as the tendency to constitute closed systems, but the closure is never perfect and is only completed artificially by scientific theory: 'There is no reason, therefore, why a *durée*, and so a form of existence like our own, should not be attributed to the systems that science isolates, provided such systems are reintegrated into the Whole'. What is needed then is not some extramaterial principle but a new theory of matter: a dynamic materialism as far apart from classical materialism, Bergson hopes, as modern mathematics is from classical mathematics.[55]

The new interconnected sciences of chaos (which looks at the complex behaviour of simple phenomena) and complexity (which looks at the complex or simple behaviour of complex phenomena) appear at last to be providing Bergson with his long-awaited new vision of matter and life. With regard to both we must point out that neither assumes the existence of pure chaos or disorder: it is a deterministic chaos in question, 'where precise laws lead to apparently random behaviour which is in fact minutely organised'.[56] This tallies with Bergson's critique of disorder in *CE* where he argues that there is no such thing as pure disorder, this notion being an illusion generated through a confusion between two different types of order: material (or geometric) and vital.[57] In the modern parlance, one might call the first 'deterministic chaos' and the second 'complexity'.

Between these two types of order, then, the sciences of chaos and complexity make the general point that life is comprised of 'complex non-linear dynamic systems with rich networks of interacting elements' which are attracted to 'settle dynamically at the edge of chaos'.[58] In other words, life is a dynamic phenomenon *par excellence*, a metastable transitory phase between frozen order and (deterministic) chaos. The echo of Bergson's theory of life to be heard in these new ideas is uncanny. Nearly one hundred years ago he had characterised life as '*a reality which is making itself in a reality which is unmaking itself*'.[59] In his theory, these two realities, that of vital order and that of geometric order (deterministic chaos), border each other as two movements, and life, the vital order, lies always on the brink or edge of falling into the opposite form of order.

As to the features of this vital order, Bergson contrasts the evolution of artificially isolated systems with that of living systems: whereas the former evolve algorithmically, living systems evolve chaotically, that is, they are not influenced at a time T by the previous moment T_{-1}, but by whole of their history.[60] Instead of a linear progression, we have a non-linear creativity or radical novelty.[61] A present moment expresses the action of any amongst an infinity of possible influences from the past, a contraction, so to speak, of the past into the present. But there are no general laws for any one of these contractions: they are chaotic. These ideas from Bergson's nascent biophilosophy, though necessarily vague and episodic, show the new relevance of his thought in the light of work done by Stuart Kauffmann, Brian Goodwin and others.

THE GENETICS OF MATTER AND MIND

Were we to continue to talk of two types of order and two types of movement, the impression would naturally arise that Bergson has simply redrawn the dualism of *TFW* on a cosmic scale. His anti-reductionist critiques in both *MM* and *CE* recourse to the quite proper metaphysical distinction between covariance and causation, but to conclude from this that Bergson proposes some form of non-reductive parallelism along the lines of Leibniz or Spinoza would be wrong. Parallelism or dualism is only one moment in evolution, though it is a crucial one. The third chapter of *CE* shows why it is only a phase and what fundamental process brings it forth.

The origin of this explanation lies in a puzzle concerning what could be described as Bergson's evolutionary epistemology, an area I touched on earlier and will deal with extensively in Chapter Eight. On the opening page of *CE* Bergson tells us that one aim of his work will be to show 'That our concepts have been formed on the model of solids; that our logic is, pre-eminently, the logic of solids; that, consequently, our intellect triumphs in geometry'.[62] Concepts are shaped by the imprint of homogeneous space. Yet, in the same text he also states the following:

> If everything is in time, everything changes inwardly, and the same concrete reality never recurs. Repetition is therefore possible only in the abstract: what is repeated is some aspect that our senses, and especially our intellect, have singled out from reality, just because our action, upon which all the effort of our intellect is directed, can move only among repetitions.[63]

But repetition is no less a feature of homogeneous space than is the impenetrability of solids. We also learnt from *MM* that homogeneous space and time are the products of our actions on the 'extensive'. So, we are told first that our concepts are modelled on homogeneous space, and then that it is our concepts which contort a really enduring extensity into that homogeneous space. We are left, therefore, with a dilemma as to whether homogeneous space is prior to and active upon our mind or whether it is our conceptual intellect which distorts concrete extensity into homogeneous space, for as things stand the two actions seem to revolve in a circle. Indeed, this circularity is one more symptom of the weakness in Bergson's theory of the endosmotic relationship between space and mind that we first encountered in *TFW*. A. R. Lacey notes of it as follows:

> What is not very clear is how they [concepts] could be modelled on objects if we require them to pick out objects as such in the first place – for objects after all depend for their reality *as* objects on being picked out by us for pragmatic purposes... There seems to be a certain chicken-and-egg puzzle here.[64]

And yet an answer to this puzzle is also to be found in *CE*, for there we learn of Bergson's belief that *'the more consciousness is intellectualized, the more is matter spatialized'*. According to this account, the only coherent hypothesis to explain the intellect's apparently adequate adaptation to the physical world – its covariances or correspondences – is to suppose that it has *'been brought about quite naturally, because it is the same inversion of the same movement which creates at once the intellectuality of mind and the materiality of things'*.[65] The same movement by which mind is homogenised into an intellect of 'distinct concepts' also forms concrete space into a homogeneous collection of 'objects excluding one another'.[66] Georges Canguilhem has described this as 'the formation of form ... correlative to the materialisation of matter'.[67] It could also be described as an inverted hylomorphism: our intellectual representation of the object stemming from becoming increasingly non-identical with it. But the crucial difference is that the duality of *hyle* and *morphe* is derivative and engendered. Dissociation is prior to association.

We are now in a position to find a way out of the problematically circular process by which our concepts can apparently be homogenised by space before they have homogenised matter into that space. The homogenisation of the two consists in the one movement: 'The space of our geometry and the spatiality of things are mutually engendered by the reciprocal action and reaction of two terms which are essentially the same'. So this movement can be taken up from different vantage points. What occurs to concrete extensity to produce homogeneous space is now but one side or pole of an activity that can just as well be viewed from what happens to mind to produce intellect. It would be just as inaccurate to describe the process entirely in terms of this alternative pole of intellectualisation: Bergson insists that the genesis of the one cannot be considered 'without making the genesis of the other'.[68] Alongside Bergson's evolutionary epistemology, therefore, we find an evolutionary physics.

Just what this process begins with and operates on is described as 'a wider and higher form of existence' in one location, an 'initial force' elsewhere, and will require a fuller examination soon.[69] The mysterious order of the cosmos at which we wonder only arises due to an interruption and decomposition, though precisely of what we do not yet know. But what this decomposition creates is real all the same. The physical mechanisms of the brain, for instance, do not merely symbolise the operations of the mind (a view sometimes found in *MM*), they are real, actualised accommodations between a capacity for intellect and another for homogenised matter contained in an initial force:

> This order, on which our action leans and in which our intellect
> recognizes itself, seems to us marvellous. Not only do the same gen-

eral causes always produce the same general effects, but beneath the visible causes and effects our science discovers an infinity of infinitesimal changes which work more and more exactly into one another, the further we push the analysis: so much so that, at the end of this analysis, matter becomes, it seems to us, geometry itself. Certainly, the intellect is right in admiring here the growing order in the growing complexity; both the one and the other must have a positive reality for it, since it looks upon itself as positive. But things change their aspect when we consider the whole of reality as an undivided advance foreword to successive creations. It seems to us, then, that the complexity of the material elements and the mathematical order that binds them together must arise automatically when within the whole a partial interruption or inversion is produced. Moreover, as the intellect itself is cut out of mind by a process of the same kind, it is attuned to this order and complexity, and admires them because it recognizes itself in them.[70]

INSTINCT AND INTELLECT

To corroborate these rather contentious points my final chapter will have to look more closely at Bergson's ideas on abstraction and concept formation. For now, we can begin by examining what *CE* has to say about mind in the context of evolutionary biology. Alongside his duality of matter and intellect Bergson places another, this time wholly set within epistemology: that between instinct and intellect. Bergson makes it clear that there is a real distinction here, instinctive intelligence being an 'as if' intelligence that should not be analysed in terms of trial and error or acquired habits.[71] Naturally, for some contemporary thinkers Bergson's opposition is too simple: to throw all instinctive activity together as a mindless automatism bereft of intelligence is misguided and testimony to a lack of ethological knowledge. Instincts can at least be distinguished into open and closed varieties, the former allowing a range of behaviour, the latter a fixed response to stimuli.[72] It is noteworthy how aware Charles Darwin was of this problem: 'It is a significant fact, that the more the habits of any particular animal are studied by the naturalist, the more he attributes to reason and the less to unlearnt instincts'.[73]

In his defence, we should add that Bergson is here describing intellect and instinct in their theoretically pure forms, what they consist of in principle. In actuality, of course, 'neither is found in a pure state', as he says himself. Hence, Bergson allows that instinct, 'although it does not form concepts properly so called, already moves in a conceptual atmosphere'.

That is why, he argues, it is so easy to confuse what lies at the heart of instinct with a form of intellectual labour, be it deemed fossilised or occurrent. Moreover, while instinct in principle is not to be thought of as a variety of intelligence and must be kept separate from it, neither is it a pure mechanism for Bergson. It is certainly conscious, but something '*felt* rather than *thought*'. Bergson uses one specific example to illustrate instinct as a 'sympathy' (in the etymological sense of the word) between two organisms. He describes how a predator, the Ammophila wasp, seems to have a magical knowledge of the physiognomy of its traditional prey, the caterpillar, such that it can apply its sting to just the degree required to paralyse it without causing death (and so creating a living food resource for the longer term). But this instinct will only appear to be a miraculous intelligence if it is seen in terms of two related things rather than as simply one developing relationship.[74] One might say that it is really one continuous activity with two protagonistic dimensions.

This is the way in which we can build a link between a genuine understanding of evolution and a genuine understanding of instinct: through a process metaphysics. The best means to explain the enigma of instinct (how do past behaviours persist without intelligent learning?) is not through some mysterious emergence from genetic coding or some other physiological substance but, as we saw before when explaining memory, simply by a comprehension of the indivisibility of change. An instinct is one among many indivisible movements carried across a *durée* of past, present and future. That is why Bergson repeatedly asserts how difficult it is to distinguish the work of biological morphogenesis from its continuation in the activity of instinct. Whereas intellect is 'at ease only in the discontinuous, in the immobile, in the dead', and has a '*natural inability to comprehend life*', '*instinct, on the contrary, is moulded on the very form of life*'.[75] Like the ghost of memory, the ghost of instinct only haunts those who fail to see the continuity of the evolutionary movement both within 'biology' strictly speaking, and from biology to epistemology. Organic bodies belong to a continuum of behaviour, indeed, as processes, they are that behaviour.[76]

The qualitative difference between instinct and intelligence actually rests less in their respective powers, according to Bergson, than in their objects; the objects of instinct are the organic relationships inherent within life itself while those of intelligence are more flexible, abstract relations. Or rather, intellect has no specific object as such but is a form applicable to any object. The formalism of intellect can contain or frame an infinity of objects and finds a natural home in relations such as of like with like, content to container, and cause to effect.[77] One commentator has described the Bergsonian picture of intellectuality as the mobility of mobility, that is, the dissociation of one type of movement – action – into another type of movement – a type of meta-mobility.[78] Hence, in *CE* two types of sign are described: the '*instinctive sign*', which 'is adherent', and the '*intelligent sign*', which 'is mobile' and 'free'.[79] Yet the intelligent sign's freedom is purely abstract, a free-floating form without content, a frame for thought rather than a genuine thought (which Bergson will instead call an intuition). For Bergson, therefore, intellect does not merely dissociate form from content, it also *is* form dissociated from content. It is as much a faculty for such dissociation as it is the product of dissociation itself, both producing and produced at the same time in an autocatalysing movement.

THE AMBIGUOUS ORIGIN OF MATTER

Yet if intellect is an extract or derivative as we saw earlier, so is instinct. It too has dissociated from a 'common origin' along with intellect. Once again, we have two progeny that point back towards something primitive relative to them, only now it is instinct which is coproduced with intellect rather than intellect with matter. The issue of the emergence of instinct and intellect from this third element connects with and returns us to the issue of the emergence of matter and intellect from the aforementioned 'wider and higher form of existence', as can be clearly seen in the following: 'We have good reason, then, for believing that the evolving force bore within it originally, but confused together or rather the one implied in the other, instinct and intelligence'.[80]

We will return to the relationship between instinct and intellect when we come to discuss intuition in Chapter Seven. A broader issue now, however, is the further ambiguity in Bergson's work as to whether or not matter is a coeternal but separate entity from *life*, or whether these two as well are implied forms incubated within something else. Bergson can appear, at times, as an idealist allowing only consciousness any reality, with matter then becoming an epiphenomenon. A confusing use of terminology does not help things either. Matter is sometimes opposed to life, sometimes to 'spirit' or 'consciousness' and sometimes to the *élan vital* (the latter four being made equivalent). Alternatively, life is also regarded as a primitive, holding matter and spirit as potential forms within itself. These issues clearly need to be negotiated with care, because where the confusion really arises is between the two moments of Bergson's genetic dualism, between the moment of unity and the moment of duality.

Matter appears as a negative epiphenomenon when it is regarded as an 'arrest' of the 'action that generates form', or in other words, of life.[81] But other related texts clearly show that, while matter is indeed regarded as 'the inverse of consciousness', it remains wrong to thing of either of them as derivative relative to each other. Rather they are 'coexistent and inter-dependent' or 'complementary aspects of creation'. This interdependence of the two can be examined from the standpoint of paradox. Life, being dissociative in the actual biological forms it takes, must divide if it is to create in any concrete, material reality. Materiality is regarded by Bergson not so much as a principle of individuation *per se* as of spatialisation and so what splits the *élan* into a stream of ramifying channels. And yet it is also said that what is creative about life *are* its acts of division; there never is a pure creativity without material division. In opposing the creativity of life, matter also ensures that creativity.

The way out of this paradox is through the introduction of different *types* of life into our reading: life as it is actualised in organic form, and life in its virtual potentiality, as a type of organisation. *TSMR* later indicates this distinction with the nomenclature of 'nature' and 'life' respectively. Phenomena connected with 'the generative effort of life' are at the same time 'breaking with nature'. These two forms of vitality indicate two phases in a continuous evolution, from virtual to actual, from life to nat-ure. Consequently, dissociation is produced by two phenomena: the resis-tance of matter to life *qua* virtual, as well as 'an unstable balance of tendencies' or 'duality' of tendency which this virtual life bears within itself and which is actualised as organic nature and inorganic matter.[82]

However, if we can by pass our paradox by admitting different forms of life, actual and virtual, we cannot by pass the corollary that follows from this: if there are two forms of life, there must also be two forms of matter: the one actual form constituting the obstacles which resist life in its actual-ity, and the other a virtual type that takes the form of a 'tendency' within the virtual form of life. In other words, the actual forms of both life and matter are dissociated from each other and cause further dissociations, but the virtual forms are held together in a tension that is confusingly also called life or *élan vital*. But this last could have equally been baptised an '*élan matériel*', and in fact *CE* frequently describes matter too as a move-ment.[83] One could thus paint a mirror image of the Bergsonian stereotype – a Bergsonian materialism depicting life as merely matter turned against itself. But both pictures are partial points of view, for every inversion of a movement is nonetheless a movement all its own. Nothing can be described as the opposite of movement *per se*, for as Bergson would later admit, 'There never is real immobility, if we understand by that an absence of movement'. Movement is reality itself, and what we call immobility is a certain state analogous to that produced when two trains move at the same speed and in the same direction on parallel tracks.[84]

Hence, neither matter nor life is prior to each other in time or ontological status – they are mutually dependent because they imply each other at a virtual level. When 'life' dissociates in its collision with matter, there is here a meeting between life in its virtual form (where matter and organic life are merely potential) with previously actualised forms of life. We might say that matter is external to organic life while being internal, in its virtual form, to life as a principle of organisation. Yet, we must remember that these virtualities are theoretical: as internal, the existence of a pure undissociated life with matter as its interior disparity is only an ideal. There is no pure creativity or inertia just as there are no pure virtualities or actualities in Bergsonian thought. These are not immobile states but phases of a movement. In actual form, matter is always external to life, but one might say that its condition of possibility is contained within life understood as a mode of organisation. It is by a feedback loop that the external form of matter acts on its own internal form (in the inherent tension of life) so as to actualise both more matter and organic life: a cosmic form of autocatalysis, one might say.[85] That both matter and intellect take this autocatalytic form of production is no coincidence, for their genesis has a common origin in *CE*'s description.

The careful commentators bear this out in their own reading of this difficult area of Bergson's thought, H. Wildon Carr describing Bergson's picture of mind and matter as 'divergent tendencies' which point to 'an original and necessary dichotomy'.[86] But it is William E. May who has definitively analysed this subject:

> It is better to say that Bergson includes *both* matter and spirit within the *élan vital* . . . It does not precontain matter as a 'seminal seed', for this would be to fall into the mechanistic view that 'all is given'. That is, it does not precontain matter *in its material existence*. Yet it does, in a very real sense, precontain matter in a virtual, unrealized state. This is brought out by Bergson when he teaches that matter comes into being as something actual or realized by passing from an 'intensive' to an 'extensive' state . . . In other words, the *élan* precontains both consciousness and matter as interpenetrating virtualities, and it gives rise to both in the course of its actualization, in the course of giving rise to what is *other* than itself.[87]

CONCLUSION

In tackling the question of the origin of matter, we seem also to have stumbled upon the motive force behind the genetic element of Bergson's dualism, a substitute for the role inadequately played by freedom in *MM* and endosmosis in *TFW*. Dissociation is driven by the 'unstable balance of tendencies which life bears within itself'. Contrary forces are in play. But what are these forces? Here arises a new difficulty. If they are in any way again one-sided, lapsing into the vocabulary of consciousness or that of mechanism, then our apparently genuine explanation of dualism dissolves before our eyes into a unilateral idealism or materialism. We have heard that virtual states of matter and life are at work, but what is special about their virtual forms that allows them to interpenetrate or commingle in a manner not open to their actual incarnations? What is needed is something more than a new word like 'virtual' or 'intensive'. The answer comes when we look a little deeper into the different types of organisation represented by life and matter. What we find are two opposing hierarchies, one privileging continuity over heterogeneity, the other an exact inversion of this. Here is a basic question for ontology. We have seen already that time itself for Bergson is regarded as a heterogeneous continuity and we have remarked on the paradoxical nature of this concept. It seems as though life and matter articulate this paradox in their ongoing mutual antipathy and forced accommodation. Matter as repetition, life as creation. Bergson even writes that the two appear to us 'as radically different forms of existence, even as antagonistic forms, which have to find a *modus vivendi*'.[88]

This ontological paradox will be our concern in Chapter Six, but in preparation for that we will have to look at the social form these antagonistic modes of existence take in Bergson's work, for we will see that the issues discussed here are not immune to such social matters. Bergson evidently believes that social life appears as a major feature of evolution, and that evolving societal forms must deal with two 'contradictory requirements, which have to be reconciled' and which he names 'individualization and integration'. These two poles indicate an existential side of our ontological puzzle: in place of heterogeneity, we have individualisation or freedom, instead of continuity we have integration or equality. Like organic life, social life seems to express the same exploration of a fundamental dilemma. In addition and perhaps more startlingly, Bergson believes that it is a socio-ethical trait that overcomes this dilemma, one which can provide us with an insight into 'life's secret', to wit, self-sacrifice or love.[89] Self-sacrifice reconciles egocentric liberty and altruistic equality, the individual and the communal.

Before the reader sneers in derision, we should note two things. Firstly, in following this line of thought Bergson does not moralise the natural facts of evolution by transforming it into a progress towards some value like increased complexity, linguistic capacity or rationality. Rather, Bergson makes morality or ethics the direct object of his analysis. If evolution could be said to tend towards an end, it is to the non-end of continual creativity which, translated into ethical language, becomes the 'open morality' of his next major work *TSMR*. The second point is that modern evolutionary thought itself is also plagued by an ethical dilemma, as is seen in the modern controversy over 'selfish' genes. Where the quandary enters is with the apparent reality of altruism.[90] The dilemma of altruism for evolutionary theory is that it seems impossible that it should be able to arise in nature given the thesis of the selfish gene. But it clearly does. And again, *TSMR* also takes this topic as its focus, though in a slightly different context which we will expore in Chapter Four.

NOTES

1. Letter to Bergson from William James in 1907; see *M*, p. 725.
2. Moore 1996, p. 9.
3. The introduction to *CE* (p. xv n [*OE*, p. 494n) claims that what it takes from *TFW* are the notions of 'continuity and creation' – metaphysical ideas concerning time rather than appearances.
4. *TFW*, p. 153 [*OE*, p. 102].
5. Sober 1993, p. 1.
6. *CE*, p. 17 [*OE*, p. 1239]; see also *M*, p. 1149: '*La vie déroule une* histoire'.
7. Thom 1975, p. 159; Dobzhansky et al. 1977, p. 503. If philosophers really did read scientific work as poorly as some scientists read their philosophy, then some of the criticisms made of the misappropriation of science by philosophers might begin to ring true.
8. See Beckner 1972, p. 255.
9. *CE*, pp. 45, 44n [*OE*, pp. 531, 530n].
10. See Goodwin 1994, p. 219.
11. *CE*, p. 94 [*OE*, p. 571]; see also *CE* pp. 106, 272 [*OE*, pp. 581, 714]; *CE*, p. 274 [*OE*, p. 715].
12. See Rycroft 1987, pp. 197–8. The American Psychiatric Association 1994 (p. 477) tells us that multiple personality disorder is now known as 'dissociative identity disorder'. A dissociative symptom is defined as 'A disruption in the usually integrated functions of consciousness, memory, identity, or perception of the environment' (p. 490).
13. *CE*, pp. 19–20 [*OE*, pp. 509–10].
14. It has been suggested that, perhaps, the cell should best be regarded as an event rather than a thing; see Gunter 1983, pp. xli, xliv.
15. *L*, p. 65 [*OE*, p. 102]; *CE*, p. 57 [*OE*, p. 541], translation altered.
16. See Sober 1993, p. 7.
17. See *CE*, pp. 112–13 [*OE*, p. 586].
18. See *CE*, pp. 27–8 [*OE*, p. 516]; *TSMR*, p. 127 [*OE*, p. 1082].
19. *CE*, pp. 136, 109–10, 102 [*OE*, pp. 129, 104, 96].
20. See *CE*, pp. 64–72 [*OE*, pp. 546–53].
21. *CE*, pp. 269–70 [*OE*, pp. 711–12].
22. See Boundas 1996, p. 91: '*élan vital* is not an occult power, but rather the name of the force(s) at work each time that a virtuality is being actualized, a simplicity differenciated, a totality divided up'.

23. Goodwin 1994, p. 26; Brooks and Wiley 1988, p. 33. They are called 'dissipative structures' in that the system dissipates the entropy (increased randomness in matter-energy) it produces into the environment (Coveney and Highfield 1991, pp. 167–8). In that organisms exchange matter and energy with their environment, they are open systems; but in that they dissipate some of their own production of entropy into the environment, they are 'partly closed' (Brooks and Wiley 1988, p. 9). Again, we will see that Bergson thinks of life as a flawed attempt to constitute closed systems through dissociation.

24. *CE*, p. xiv [*OE*, p. 493].

25. *CE*, p. 389 [*OE*, pp. 805–6].

26. *CE*, pp. 385, 52 [*OE*, pp. 802, 537].

27. See Gould and Lewontin 1994.

28. See Dawkins 1982, pp. 46, 51.

29. *CE*, p. 61 [*OE*, p. 544].

30. Brooks and Wiley 1988, p. 29.

31. Eldridge 1995, p. 169.

32. See Dawkins 1982.

33. Dawkins 1989, p. 19.

34. *CE*, p. 179 [*OE*, p. 639]. This is Weissmann's thesis of the eternal germ-plasm which Dawkins admits is a forerunner to the concept of the selfish gene; see Dawkins 1989, p. 11.

35. See Sober 1993, p. 4; Cohen and Stewart 1994, pp. 293–4; Sterelny 1995, p. 157.

36. See *CE*, p. 238 [*OE*, p. 687].

37. *CE*, pp. 62, 80ff, 42–3 [*OE*, pp. 544–5, 560ff, 528–9].

38. Wolsky and Wolsky 1992, p. 159 concur; see Monod 1972, pp. 23, 32.

39. *CE*, p. 94 [*OE*, p. 571]. It has been argued that evolutionary explanation can be teleological *and* naturalistic, involving 'matter and nothing else' (Sober 1993, p. 86). The 'why' of evolution – why do birds have wings? – merges with the 'how' of physiology by explaining the dynamics of flight and its part in the bird's organic integrity and survival. Where a functional ascription is legitimate is where it is etiological, explaining the causal background to how the trait got there (Wright 1994, pp. 33–9). But this seems to ascribe a very large role to causation and an assumption that how we describe the origination of a part equates with a purpose. Admittedly, Bergson allows that we can speak retrospectively as if nature follows ends. But this weak finalism is merely retrospective: though nature appears from this vantage point as though it has specific values, such directions are never seen as an anticipation of the future.

40. See Ingold 1995, p. 28: adaptationism 'instals the genotype at the heart of the organism, as a kind of intelligence'.

41. See Dawkins 1986, pp. 54–5, 66–7.

42. Ibid., pp. 67, 73.

43. See Goodwin 1994, p. 166.

44. Eldridge 1995, p. 94; Gould and Eldridge 1972, p. 98. Gould and Eldridge employ the work of Ernst Mayr and Theodosius Dobzhansky whose biological species concept defines a species as a group of actually interbreeding populations that are reproductively isolated from other populations.

45. See Wolsky and Wolsky 1992, p. 160.

46. 'Time' is also the last and keyword in Gould and Eldridge's famous 1972 essay; see Gould and Eldridge 1972, p. 115.
47. *CE*, pp. 66–7 [*OE*, pp. 548–9].
48. Though new evidence for the existence of regulatory genes has made some people think again about the possiblity of macromutations; see Eldridge 1995, pp. 99–100.
49. See Cohen and Stewart 1994, p. 369.
50. See *CE*, p. 30 [*OE*, p. 518].
51. *CE*, pp. 45, 15 [*OE*, pp. 531, 506–7].
52. See *ME*, p. 26 [*OE*, p. 830]. Experiments with 'pre-biotic synthesis' have shown that amino acids (the building blocks of proteins which are essential to life) are formed under wide-ranging conditions utilising water, nitrogen, ammonia, hydrogen cynanide and methane, provided that there is a source of energy supplied such as an electric discharge. Likewise, the biosynthesis of the living cell is wholly explicable in terms of current physics and chemistry; see Eigen 1992, pp. 31, 48.
53. *CE*, p. 32 [*OE*, p. 520].
54. *CE*, pp. 10–11 [*OE*, pp. 502–3]; see also Coveney and Highfield 1991, pp. 152–3.
55. *CE*, pp. 12, 33–4 [*OE*, pp. 503, 521–2].
56. Coveney and Highfield 1991, p. 183.
57. See *CE*, pp. 244–9 [*OE*, pp. 691–6].
58. Goodwin 1994, p. 169.
59. *CE*, p. 261 [*OE*, p. 705].
60. This past is described as 'very long'; see *CE*, pp. 21–2 [*OE*, p. 511].
61. *CE*, pp. 24, 30 [*OE*, pp. 513, 518].
62. *CE*, p. ix [*OE*, p. 489].
63. *CE*, p. 48 [*OE*, p. 533].
64. Lacey 1989, p. 158.
65. *CE*, pp. 199, 217 [*OE*, pp. 656, 670]. The other hypotheses Bergson discusses are empiricism, idealism and pre-established harmony.
66. *CE*, p. 199 [*OE*, p. 656]; see also *MM*, p. 239 [*OE*, p. 319].
67. Canguilhem 1943, p. 206.
68. *CE*, pp. 213–14 [*OE*, p. 667]; *CE*, p. 210 [*OE*, p. 664].
69. *CE*, p. 197 [*OE*, p. 653]; *M*, p. 989.
70. *CE*, p. 229 [*OE*, p. 679].
71. See *CE*, pp. 176, 178, 185 [*OE*, pp. 636–7, 638–9, 644].
72. See Midgley 1980, pp. 51–7.
73. Cited in Rachels 1991, p. 133.
74. *CE*, pp. 142, 197, 181, 183 [*OE*, pp. 610, 654, 641, 642–3].
75. *CE*, pp. 146, 174 [*OE*, pp. 613, 635].
76. See Liedloff 1986 for an examination of this continuity between mind and organic being as well as within life itself in terms of its significance for child-rearing.
77. See *CE*, pp. 155–7 [*OE*, pp. 619–21].
78. See Miquel 1994, p. 209: 'La connaissance se dissocie de l'action'.
79. *CE*, p. 167 [*OE*, p. 629].
80. *CE*, p. 142 [*OE*, pp. 609–10]; *ME*, p. 25 [*OE*, p. 829].
81. *CE*, p. 252 [*OE*, p. 698].
82. *ME*, p. 23 [*OE*, p. 828]; *TSMR*, pp. 255, 256, 52–4 [*OE*, pp. 1192, 1193, 1018–20]; *CE*, pp. 103, 268 [*OE*, pp. 578, 711].
83. See, for instance, *CE*, p. 263 [*OE*, p. 707].

84. See *CM*, pp. 143–4 [*OE*, p. 1378].
85. This would place Bergson's cosmological views somewhere in the area of a steady-state theory; see on this Gunter 1971.
86. Carr 1975, p. vii.
87. May 1970, p. 634.
88. *CE*, p. 103 [*OE*, p. 578]; *ME*, p. 17 [*OE*, p. 824].
89. *ME*, pp. 33–4 [*OE*, pp. 834–5]; *CE*, p. 135 [*OE*, p. 604].
90. See Rachels 1991, p. 77. Altruism has worried evolutionists ever since Darwin, and the leading sociobiologist E. O. Wilson has described it as 'the central theoretical problem' for his discipline.

4

Sociobiology

It is primarily as against all others that we love those with whom we live.[1]

In turning to this relatively short study of *TSMR*, we should note that we are jumping a quarter of a century in Bergson's *oeuvre* from the date when *CE* appeared in 1907. Hence we will be looking at ideas which are the product of a good deal of reflection beyond that found in the earlier works on time, mind and biology that make up the first entries in Bergsonian philosophy. That said, while we will discover new twists to Bergson's line of thought, there remains a continuity with his older ideas such that *TSMR* can also throw a retrospective light on them.

TSMR has been described as an attempt to temper the primacy given to the 'group mind' in modern sociology by drawing greater attention to the role of the individual.[2] As such, what *TSMR* takes as two symptoms of this group mind, closed society and static religion, 'were the last entries', it has been said, 'in a column of partial negatives, beginning with mathematics and science generally'.[3] In Chapter Five, we will go further and argue that Bergson's struggle against the symptoms of closed society and the group mind was present in all his analyses, be they empirical, metaphysical or socio-ethical. That is why this interlude is centred here, on the last major book written by Bergson, before we turn to issues in ontology, methodology and metaphilosophy with relevance for all his work in general.

The first noteworthy distinction about *TSMR* is that it is primarily a work in sociobiology rather than metaphysics; indeed, as regards its analysis of religion, it is *the* sociobiological study, according to Charles Hartshorne.[4] Bergson's main claim is that the nature of social relations is not fixed, but an ongoing creation.[5] This is not to argue that it is a by-product of intrin-

sically individual human endeavour – at all times in this book Bergson tries
to balance the claims of methodological and theoretical individualism with
those of collectivism – but rather that society and cultural are evolutionary
rather than self-explanatory.[6] We must seek their origins or 'sources' in the
biological exigencies of life, as a creator both of the species and of individuals: 'All we have to do is to consider man again in his place among living things, and psychology as a part of biology'. Having done so, we will
have replaced sociability back within the 'general evolution of life'.[7]

Two caveats must be added to this rather bare manifesto: first, that Bergson's is certainly not a reductive sociobiology; there is no hint here that he
wishes to deflate culture to 'merely' animal, biological or genetic forces. In
tandem with his redemptive and anti–reductionist views in biology, his is,
if anything, an inflationary discourse; biological influence merits much
more worth than we give it: 'Let us then give to the word biology the
very wide meaning it should have, and will perhaps have one day'. Secondly, this will be a truly evolutionary sociobiology. Bergson's complaint
against similar analyses of that time and earlier (one thinks again of Herbert
Spencer) was that they 'take society for granted', and end up using biology
to aggrandise and consolidate a particular status quo: they are conformist
rather than evolutionist.[8] It is irrelevant whether the analysis is liberal or
conservative in political orientation: the error of false sociobiology is its
search for legitimising natural essences, when in truth the 'sources' of
society only provide us with natural tendencies, one of which will actually
be the tendency to renounce all notions of natural essence in favour of the
continual creation of new social forms – what Bergson will dub 'open
morality'. Hence, Bergson sidesteps the frozen essentialism of reductive
naturalists as well as the liquid relativism of culturalists: society is indeed
moulded by nature, but by a creative nature which in part tries to break
its own moulds!

NON-RATIONALIST ETHICS

Irrespective of what form sociobiology takes, its main struggle will be with
those who reject its premise altogether and seek to explain society and
morality wholly in terms of the instruments of human intelligence. There
are two attacks Bergson makes on this intellectualist view. One of them
rests on his earlier work which shows that intelligence itself is the offspring
of biology and so must 'correspond to vital needs'; this evolutionary epistemology (to be examined fully later) shows that rationality cannot be the
direct agency behind culture and ethics but acts at best by proxy for vital
forces. Of course, Bergson is careful not to reduce reason to a parody of
itself when rejecting its efficacy; it would be too simplistic to say that pas-

sion rules wholesale over rationality. He accepts that moral decisions must be channelled through reason in any particular situation. It is also true that the more 'economical' a society becomes (in the literal sense of that term), the more the dictates of its operative morality are logically integrated, giving succour to the intellectualists' conviction as to their ultimate origin.[9] The sources Bergson is invoking do not bear down transparently on our every decision, indeed, it would be impossible to act if we did have to refer to them explicitly. The two sources are both varieties of proto-morality, as the term 'source' implies. They represent the conditions of possibility, so to speak, for making moral judgements at all and for having a moral sensibility. But neither fits an intellectualised model of ethics for, as we will see, they are infra-rational and supra-rational. *TSMR* does not set out an alternative system of ethics or '*morale*'.[10]

By an 'intellectualised model of ethics' Bergson does not mean a specifically rationalist ethics such as Kantianism, so much as any ethical model which systematically derives a set of codes from some initial premise or premises on the assumption that coherence is a facet of morality: 'General interest, personal interest, self-love, sympathy, pity, logical consistency, etc., there is no principle of action from which it is not possible to deduce more or less the morality that is generally accepted'. In each case, morality is deemed deducible from and reducible to an evidential base, whatever it may be. But, just as we found in the reductive analyses of mind or life, the essential is thereby omitted. In other words, what is moral in morality, that is, what is 'moving' (in every sense), remains unexplained by intellectualism. This point relates to Bergson's other line of attack: the old idea that the virtue of coherence or consistency lacks any real impetus to practical action: 'Reason can only put forward reasons, which we are apparently always at liberty to counter with other reasons'. Moreover, just as we found that psychological and biological reductionism required some form of covert homunculus or teleology to sustain its analyses, so too the explicitly rationalist moralities in particular (Kantianism, for instance) can operate only by tacitly assuming a moral homunculus at some level within the rational scheme, even when it is morality which is supposed to have been explained in terms of reason.[11]

We should take care, however, not to think that Bergson's meta-ethics is emotivist. At least in respect to sympathy (which we know already to be one characteristic of instinct in *CE*), Bergson clearly argues against its adequacy as a starting point for ethics.[12] But something more complex again distances Bergson from any possible identification with emotivist theory: his conception of emotion itself. One comprehends only one side of the affective realm by thinking of emotion in terms of sensations, hormonal processes or, less physiologically, simple blind impulses. Alongside such desiccated, spatialised feelings, Bergson will argue for the primacy of 'creative emotion' in ethics, emotions that are opposed to neither reason nor representation but incubate a certain form of intentionality. At this level too, Bergson tries to reconcile (or reverse) the dichotomy of emotivism and rationalism in ethics by means of an inflationary or redemptive picture of emotion itself:

> Alongside of the emotion which is a result of the representation and which is added to it, there is the emotion which precedes the image, which virtually contains it, and is to a certain extent its cause ... an emotion capable of crystallising into representations and even into an ethical doctrine.[13]

There are, of course, 'natural', easily recognised emotions, ones which are inspired by thought, social convention and even nature itself; but a genuinely new, creative emotion is not caused by a representation or inspiration; it is 'pregnant' with its own representations: it is supra-rational. Bergson does not draw a clear line between the conative and the cognitive: emotions already embody a grade of intentionality, belonging, as they do, not to a supposedly raw and meaningless physical realm but rather to a material world already imbued with an ineliminable degree of representation. That our emotional repertoire is not tied down by physiological constraint or socio-linguistic convention seems difficult to contemplate, but Bergson is making a metaphysical point here too: morality is linked to a certain type of emotion precisely on account of the creative nature of emotion itself: 'Creation signifies, above all, emotion'.[14]

We concluded the previous chapter by referring to the vital insight that Bergson believes the nature of love provides us: it reconciles egoism and altruism, freedom and integration, creation and repetition. In *TSMR*, it is again asserted that 'creative energy is to be defined as love'.[15] But increasingly, this emphasis on emotion takes a distance from any psychologistic view and heads towards something more: love or, as he also names it, 'fraternity', is not

> intensification of an innate sympathy ... It is not the extension of an instinct, it does not originate in an idea. It is neither of the sense nor of the mind. It is of both, implicitly, and is effectively much more. For such a love lies at the very root of feeling and reason, as of all other things ... It is still more metaphysical than moral in its essence.[16]

What Bergson alludes to here – the metaphysics of this or any morality – will become the central issue for our study before long.

THE MOVEMENT OF CLOSURE

The metaphysics of Bergson's theory of life must always be kept in mind when discussing his sociobiological examination of ethics and religion. That said, the first manifestation of this is the dualism evident in this work from the very beginning. There are *two* sources of morality and religion, and both are biological. They can both be biological because there are two major facets to Bergson's theory of evolution, what we described as a virtual type of organisation on the one hand and the expression of that order in actual organic forms on the other: evolution itself and fragments of the evolved. Two facets of time, in other words, time flowing and time flown.

In *TSMR*, these biological influences appear in morality as two types of motivation: moral obligation and moral aspiration, each corresponding to the evolved and the evolving respectively. The first acts as a type of pressure, a centripetal movement of closure, fostering a closed model of society (or association) and a static form of religion. The second is an outward, dissociative and centrifugal movement, bearing within it the seeds of open sociability and dynamic spirituality. As neither source of the two is 'strictly and exclusively moral' it would be foolish, Bergson writes, to try to explain either in terms of moral or religious theory.[17] Our sociobiology must be genuinely social *and* biological.

Bergson compares the first type of movement, that of moral obligation, to the integrative pressure that maintains the unity of cells within an organism, only in society it is habit that plays the role of the binding force. We must note that there is no causal agency implied going from the biological substratum to the sociological superstratum here: rather, both realms evince a type of movement which is not modelled on one or the other but on a third principle we might call 'transcendental'. The force maintaining the unity of animal societies bound by instinct is another parallel given, though again instinct *per se* is not meant to be the 'cause' of our sense of obligation but simply another manifestation of this type of movement.[18]

We ought to remark here that such collectivist thinking as this has often been accused of a romantic organicism along with the dangerous political implications purportedly attendant on this. It is the totalitarian fantasy *par excellence* to see the body politic literally as an organism, one understood as 'a single, homogeneous body proper recognising no exteriority or otherness vis-à-vis itself other than in relation to itself'.[19] Defenders of collectivism might reply that any appearance of organicism in their thought is merely metaphorical and thereby inoffensive: the communities in question have nothing to do with biology and have everything to do with convention, tradition, an *esprit général* and so on.

Yet while much of this collectivism does indeed have a cultural basis – intermittently connected with a theory of linguistic holism as well – the charge of a more literal organicism need be neither so unpalatable nor unwelcome as most collectivists assume it is. The impasse between a cultural view of morality, a rationalist one, and a sociobiological one is undone by Bergson's plea that biology be understood 'broadly'. In Bergson's sociobiology, organicism leads to political views exactly opposite to those often repudiated. He does not argue for a closed image of the social on the basis of a rigid biological essentialism: rather, because his so-called vitalism is embedded in a process metaphysics, the organic and the social are both left ideally open. Bergson does not believe that organic systems are wholes, rather they are dynamic dissociating phenomena which are only relative unities. Political organicism need only be feared if one's picture of the organic, the biological or the vital is of a particular variety.

As regards these social obligations, Bergson argues that no particular one has any superior value over the next in terms of its being closer to a biological origin; the only social form which is significant to Bergson is the very general one that there are obligations as such, the 'totality of obligation' that plays the role of an infra-rational social adhesive. However, we never feel the action of this totality except when we depart from it: rarely is it that obligations or duties do not harmonise with our own habitual tendencies. It is only when we make a transgression that we become conscious of them, for consciousness is the very 'hesitation' (in the language of *TFW*) or 'disruption of movement' (as *MM* would say) evinced when we struggle between social and personal motives. Deviating from accepted moral convention causes an internal resistance within ourselves which, 'if we resist this resistance', leads to a 'state of tension or contraction'. From this abnormal, limit case stems the mistaken notion that obligation is an independent self-explanatory principle of ethics. Generalising from the particular brings about the erroneous idea of the self-sufficiency of duty, set (at least potentially) within a rationalistic ethics. But, at heart, this view confuses a perceived pressure to restore an obligation with the origin of the obligation. Intelligence only supplies the hesitation, the resistance to a resistance, not the obligation itself.[20]

FROM THE CLOSED TO THE OPEN

Arising from this obligation is a type of conscience that we properly call 'social' in that it indicates the desire for socialisation and the preservation of our social identity. One trait of social obligation is that it immediately installs a 'closed society, however large'. It is in its nature to form social groupings like the family, the nation, the race and so on, each of which acts as an intermediary reinforcement of habitual social mores. Society in general occupies the broadest and most abstract of these concentric circles surrounding the self. Within each circle, all are regarded in an equal light and all are allowed the same rights and freedoms. What is essential about such bounded domains, however, is that they are more or less closed to the outside. A social formation may be very broad and even continue to grow broader by incorporating previously ostracised groups; no matter, they remain closed in the type of movement they instantiate: 'Their essential characteristic is nonetheless to include at any moment a certain number of individuals, and exclude others'. Every in-group requires an out-group or 'enemy' (as Bergson puts it) such that our bonds of social equality and tolerance are purchased through an act of exclusion 'against all other men'.[21] It would not be going too far to say that closed morality barely deserves the name of morality at all if we mean by that some wholly unself-interested altruism. And yet, from Aristotle to John Rawls, most theories of ethics maintain their systems of justice on the basis of some type of opposition: be it the non-political animal or the non-reciprocating animal, to take just two examples, something must be excluded from the moral realm by definition.[22]

Without noticing it, the contemporary French political philosopher, Etienne Balibar, has recently reinvented Bergson's exact idea thus:

> Equality in fact cannot be limited. Once some x's ('men') are not equal, the predicate of equality can no longer be applied to anyone, for all those to whom it is supposed to be applicable are in fact 'superior', 'dominant', 'privileged', etc. Enjoyment of the equality of rights cannot spread step by step, beginning with two individuals and gradually extending to all: it must immediately concern the universality of individuals...This explains...the antinomy of equality and society for, even when it is not defined in 'cultural', 'national', or 'historical' terms, a *society* is necessarily *a* society, defined by some particularity, by some exclusion, if only by a *name*. In order to speak of 'all citizens', it is necessary that somebody not be a citizen of said polity.[23]

Whatever feelings we have for the group, writes Bergson, 'imply a choice, therefore an exclusion; they may act as incentives to strife, they do not exclude hatred'. This is closed morality: a set of rules and balances, pressures and obligations bearing down on the individual, homogenising him or her by removing his or her evolutionary alterity. In terms of religion, the closed society tends towards a static form of faith, a codified, institutionalised spirituality that expresses above all the interests of the group rather a supposedly universal divinity. Static religion is not the same as closed morality, however, for the former can often demand acts of superstitious barbarism deemed immoral by the latter: yet it remains that the two serve the same form of social order and are often found together.[24]

It is impossible for abstractions such as 'universal love' to raise this social egoism to a genuine altruism, for the goal is as daunting as any of the infinite tasks in Zeno's paradoxes.[25] A movement of closure cannot be transformed into a movement of openness; they are no less different than are the catching-up steps of Achilles different from his overtaking steps.

But alongside social obligation, social conscience and the closed societies they sustain, there is another type of conscience which responds, not to the need to be kept within the closed fold of society, but to the desire for openness, specifically the desire to be open towards openness: a welcome owed to those who are themselves 'opening'. Behind the command to 'love all' lies this other morality – biological too, but in another sense than 'merely' naturalistic. Bergson talks now of a 'complete morality' or 'absolute morality' and, in a passage that will become increasingly significant, describes the 'extreme limit' of its movement as follows:[26]

> The other attitude is that of the open soul. What, in that case, is allowed in? Suppose we say that it embraces all humanity: we should not be going too far, we should hardly be going far enough, since its love may extend to animals, to plants, to all nature. And yet no one of these things which would thus fill it would suffice to define the attitude taken by the soul, for it could, strictly speaking, do without all of them. Its form is not dependent on its content. We have just filled it; we could as easily empty it again. 'Charity' would persist in him who possesses 'charity', though there be no other living creature on earth.[27]

Pure openness sympathises 'with the whole of nature', but it is also a contact with a principle of nature which expresses itself in quite a different attachment to life than that found in a sympathy for the other members of one's group. It is described as an objectless emotion that loves who or what it does only 'by passing through' rather than aiming for them.[28]

Now, it must be added that both these moralities, closed and open, are only 'extreme limits', and are never found in any actual society in their pure form separate from each other. The forces of openness and closure are present in varying degrees in every society and are intermixed in actual morality. Such actual morality encompasses what Bergson describes as a 'system of *orders* dictated by *impersonal* social requirements', as well as a 'series of *appeals* made to the conscience of each of us by *persons* who represent the best there is in humanity'.[29] Nonetheless, the two remain distinct while being united in their difference, for they represent 'two complementary manifestations of life'.[30] There never has been nor could be either a truly open society or a fully closed one. These are ideal limits.[31]

We have seen Bergson argue that there can be no genuine moral reformation of the circle of society through expansion; there is only the possibility of a reduction rather than an elimination of universal inequality. Of course, none of these theses tallies well with those moral discourses which place the emphasis on political emancipation through conceptual reformation. Bergson is less confident in the value of increasing the boundaries of enfranchisement through winning larger and larger associations so much as dissolving the discourse of 'boundaries' altogether. It is not by a process of expansion that we pass from the closed state to the open, and Bergson brands as 'intellectualist' the idea that it is so possible. Open morality is not about calculating the distribution of justice, it is a 'disposition of the soul'.[32]

Such relative, distributive justice is, in fact, a perfect mix of closed obligation and genuine open aspiration: it is a question of distribution, reciprocity, equivalence – a mathematical balancing act of quantity with quantity, quality with quality. This relative justice similarly creates a form of equality that remains set against the outsider.[33] In part, the notion of reciprocal freedoms and shared rights still serves the need for social order. The transition from the idea of this form of justice to that of absolute justice is supposedly gradual, but Bergson regards it as an incommensurable 'leap forward', the gradualist thesis being a product of retrospection. Absolute justice has another source altogether: it refuses to let even one individual suffer for the good of the group. While it was the prophets of Israel who gave justice this categorical nature, Bergson also argues that it was Christianity that made it genuinely universal, the Judaic form remaining insular. But still the principle of universality continues to be a theory barely actualised in reality. Indeed, Bergson laments the fact that so many philosophers have failed in practice to implement a principled ethical universality in preference for a parochial justice.

To summarise, what we might term 'moral associationism' must always bring its own boundaries with it: an increase in the association, the enfranchisement of a particular 'minority' or group, can only sustain itself on the basis of redefining the boundary all the more forcefully against whatever or whoever remains beyond its limits. It would be nice to think, as Darwin did for instance, that our moral sentiments expand incrementally to include all mankind, regardless of race or social status, and that they would even finally extend to the 'lower animals'.[34] And yet all the evidence indicates otherwise. Just as members of one group, *Homo sapiens*, have distributed amongst themselves every right and privilege through the course of an enlarging enfranchisement, they have done so by invoking an identity that necessarily ostracises a vast out-group ('non-human animals' so called) to the extent of either defining them in some jurisdictions as non-sentient beings or practically treating them as such in most others.

Evidence of the exclusionist nature of liberation morality can be seen in the fact that any newly enfranchised group – the aged, the obese, persons of different colour, and so on – were only persecuted in the first place on account of a mere relative difference being turned into an absolute distinction. A type of spatialised perception made one group fall outside the closed moral sphere which, now, in more luxurious times, can afford to reintroduce it. And Bergson is quite sure that economics is an important motivation for the apparent tolerance of closed morality. He describes consumerism as an instant economy of excess, not a gradual increase in decadence. There never is 'sufficient wealth' for a class beyond which any further affluence is distributed equitably. The idea that greater wealth within a liberal economy facilitates greater liberalism in ethics is simply wrong. Wealth and technological advance within one group leads to heightened consumption within the group (be it of food, other commodities or various freedoms and rights) rather than a more equitable distribution amongst the less fortunate beyond the group. Hence, 'millions of men never get enough to eat', while others squabble over which of their luxuries should be necessities and which should even be proclaimed a basic right (for them).[35] In utter disdain, Bergson describes such a world where 'everything...is arranged for our maximum convenience' as simply being 'cold as death'.[36]

A CREATIVE SOCIOBIOLOGY

At any one moment, the form a society takes represents an accommodation between these two types of morality, open and closed, simply because human culture is an artefact of nature in both its evolving and evolved orders. Society is pulled in two opposed directions: inward, by the tendency to consolidate what identity it has, to revolve in a circle, to repeat, and outward, by the tendency to destroy its own identity, to evolve new heterogeneous forms of social arrangement, to create. The manifest result of these different forces is of a circle, but one that is gradually expanding.

By expanding, it testifies to the aspiration towards openness, but by remaining at any one moment a circle, it affirms the fact that it is still closed.

This sociobiological model bears comparison with Peter Singer's own concept of 'the expanding circle'. His too is an exercise in sociobiology that posits society as an extending form driven by two different forces. He borrows the leitmotif for his idea from W. E. H. Lecky's *The History of European Morals*:

> At one time the benevolent affections embrace merely the family, soon the circle expanding includes first a class, then a nation, then a coalition of nations, then all humanity, and finally, its influence is felt in the dealings of man with the animal world.[37]

It is the differences between this and Bergson's theory which are illuminating. Singer argues that once the obligations of kinship are fulfilled within the boundaries of our own group, our sense of moral obligation expands to the next largest community with which we identify.[38] Clearly, Singer does not hold with the idea of an economy of excess as Bergson does. On this front, then, the issue dividing them is the question of why there should be a 'next largest' community with which one identifies. Why not simply circulate within one's own group, bestowing ever more luxury, advancement and legal right upon its members? How do we come to identify with the outsider at all?

The forces manipulating Singer's model are twofold but, oddly for a work in sociobiology, only one of them is directly biological. What maintains group identity is genetically determined. Altruism beyond the individual's immediate egoism is clearly necessary to maintain some form of community, but as natural selection takes place at the level of genes, altruism must be genetically determined and, if adaptive, selected for at the genetic level.[39] The problem, however, is how any altruism actually appeared in the first individual to spread throughout the community. Within the paradigm of the 'selfish gene', such non-self-interested behaviour would seem highly maladaptive and sure to be weeded out quickly. Singer's answer comes in a limited form of group selection whereby members of some isolated groups of the same species (most probably all interrelated) engage in altruistic behaviour, such as mutual grooming for instance, which the other groups refrain from doing. Whereas altruism cannot survive in competition amongst individuals, it actually flourishes in competition amongst groups where the example of an acquired habit of mutual grooming would confer a definite advantage. Hawk-natures perform best within groups, but dove-natures perform best between groups.[40] Altruism gets going in a particular group with a notion of inclusive fitness – the members of the group are all related, remember – and, once up and running, such co-operative natures do then compete well with wholly self-interested groups of individuals. Thus, altruism survives.[41]

But this biological factor only ever maintains group identity, it could never facilitate altruism beyond the group towards the universal. So far, the likeness with Bergson's ideas is conspicuous; in his theory of closed morality, altruism is also regarded as deferred egoism.[42] One difference between the two theories, however, is that Singer utilises a reductionist account of genetic determinism to support the biological force of closure.[43] The other difference concerns the forces of expansion towards a universal ethic. For Singer, only reason can embody this role. Reason breaks beyond the boundary of customary morality; it alone is genuinely universalist because it alone can be genuinely disinterested. Only through reason, then, is it possible to leap from parochialism toward universalism. In itself, this reason is wholly open but, mixed with the genetically determined forces of group-identity, it can work only to extend the circle of morality rather than break it.

Again, the similarity with Bergson's open morality is marked, but Singer's intellectualism is the major point of variation. In Bergson's theory, biological life plays two roles, neither of which implies a genetic reduction, and one of which confers the possibility for genuine universalism. Biology need not be superseded by reason precisely on account of openness being a biologically driven emotion rather than a product of disinterested intellect. Admittedly, Singer does concede to David Hume's view (and so to Bergson's as well) that reason alone 'cannot give rise to action', but he adds that love of reason and consistency can be motivating in itself.[44] To be sure, love of reason can be extremely motivating, but, in as much as it spurs us to action, it is because it is a *love* first and a love of *reason* second. As *TSMR* states: 'For we may be obliged to adopt certain means in order to attain such and such ends, but if we choose to renounce the end, how can the means be forced upon us?'[45] The end may be reason, but it is worth nothing unless we desire it. Desire, in the broadest sense of the word, is the key, and far from taking the puritanical view that desire is only and ever egotistic, Bergson believes that it can be universalist and creative. As we saw, it is possible to create new emotions, and it is such creativity that gives us an insight into the nature of life.

THE OPEN AND THE VAGUE

Bergson holds that moral evolution captures the essence of biological evolution, a 'dynamic morality... is related to life in general'.[46] Both move towards openness or creativity itself. But what is interesting is that this movement is self-perpetuating, for 'openness' as such is a necessarily vague formula and requires continual creativity to fill in its content in each concrete situation. We mentioned already that the form open morality takes 'is not dependent on its content'. Its 'aim' is only to pass through its object. In other words, the evolution *to* openness is not teleology strictly speaking but, in a self-referential manner, an evolution that places itself at issue: an evolution that can either continue or fail to evolve further.

Fleshing out the vague formula of openness actually entails an accommodation with its opposite biological and moral tendency towards closure. In concrete terms, Bergson explains how any new particular liberty for one individual or group of individuals must encroach on the liberty of others. Liberty conflicts with equality no less than heterogeneity conflicts with continuity. But how the two conflict cannot be determined *a priori*, for others in the community may adapt their behaviour in recognition of this new liberty, that is, there is a feedback mechanism which subverts any possible algorithmic formula being written for social evolution.[47]

In political terms, democracy is the name given to this vague social evolution. The idea of democracy rests in the attempt to reconcile liberty and equality. But this can only be achieved each time, not by reason, but through fraternity or love. The vagueness of the democratic formula provides latitude for the moral creativity that will work empirically to produce 'forms of liberty and equality which are impossible of realization, perhaps of conception, to-day'. When this formula is given content, however, Bergson warns us that the direction of openness 'risks turning into an incurvation in the direction of private interest'. Such an incurvation creates a new circle of identity that will persist until its own inherent contradictions require a creative leap forward in ethical thought and political organisation.[48] This is why Bergson proposes that the 'secret of life', what reconciles but never eradicates the inherent tension between equality–continuity and liberty–heterogeneity, and also what propels life forward, is love. Simon Critchley's recent study of the current work of Jacques Derrida, Emmanuel Levinas and Claude Lefort has adventitiously shown how Bergson's ideas have retained their immediacy despite their formulation seventy years ago:

> Democracy is an indeterminate political form founded on the contradictions of individual freedom versus . . . [amongst other things] complete uniformity . . . *Democracy does not exist*; that is to say, starting from today, and every day, there is a responsibility to invent democracy, to

extend the democratic franchise to all areas of public and private life.[49]

So new liberties are real inventions that cannot be predicted. Though it is generally true that liberty and equality are always in tension, how they are reconciled each time cannot be anticipated but only invented by what Bergson names 'moral creators'.[50]

ETHICAL CREATION

We have seen that open morality finds its inspiration in a personal appeal rather than through the impersonal pressure which regulates the morality of a closed society. Some form of direct or indirect interpersonal relationship is required. Where closed morality lies in obedience before the law, open morality lies in an 'appeal', 'attraction', or 'call'. But the call does not come from just anyone: it requires a privileged personality. What is best in our society is bequeathed to us by individuals Bergson calls heroes, and each hero − living or dead − 'exerts on us a virtual attraction'. Bergson certainly is not asserting a hard and fast dimorphism between leaders and their followers here − every individual possesses within him or herself 'a leader with the instinct to command and a subject ready to obey' − it is simply that our closed societies are configured to ensure a herd-mentality in the majority.[51]

The heroism Bergson describes is of a religious variety, though one that is dynamic and wholly active rather than institutional and reified.[52] Bergson also calls these heroes 'mystics', though again, the notion of some ascetic contemplative is far from what he has in mind. These mystics are creators, transgressing the boundaries of life, mind and society in their inspirational morality. As an earlier essay puts it, their moral existence is nearest to life itself: such 'inventive and simple heroism' is 'the great success of life', being at once its 'culminating point' and most primitive 'source'.[53] In crossing all frontiers, mysticism goes 'beyond the limits of intelligence', the ultimate end of mysticism being to establish a partial coincidence with the creative effort which life manifests. Such inherent creativity can appear as mental pathology, and Bergson takes time to spell out the differences between the symptoms of genuine mental transcendence and those of simple insanity.[54] Mental imbalance, we saw already, is frequently regarded by Bergson as an excess of mental power rather than a deficiency: the usual restrictive role of the brain has been weakened to allow a greater degree of consciousness to flood the subject. The weakness of such disorder lies in an inability to restore equilibrium between this new surplus and the surrounding environment.[55] The mystic achieves this restoration: he or she has travelled the same route as the madman but has also discovered the way back.[56]

So, what is moral action? Oddly enough, what allows the hero to act as a model for others is described as a type of passivity before life. It entails 'the complete and mysterious gift of self'.[57] What is termed 'complete mysticism' is wholly for the other rather than self-absorbed: 'True, complete, active mysticism aspires to radiate, by virtue of the charity which is its essence'.[58] How it actually radiates is through the contagious properties of a genuinely creative emotion: 'For heroism itself is a return to movement, and emanates from an emotion – infectious like all emotions – akin to the creative act'.[59] But again, the etymology of emotion should be taken into account: Bergson is not endorsing some private ecstasy but a type of movement rich in meaning, a movement of openness. In one very interesting analysis, Bergson describes Socrates as a mystic and religious hero as well as a philosophical model. When philosophers constructively engage with society, they do not follow the Socratic archetype so much as actualise the Socratic-movement and thereby make him live again.[60]

This idea is worth some pause for thought as it indicates a point of contention between *TSMR* and *CE*. In neither book does Bergson support Lamarckism – acquired characteristics do not alter our nature. Yet *CE* did propose that humanity could continue to evolve beyond its current form, only it never specified what type of process might be involved.[61] It seems as though *TSMR* has found that process, only it does not work through physiological mutation but, at a cultural level, through the contagious activity of moral renovation:

> If we went down to the roots of nature itself we should perhaps find that the same force which manifests itself directly, rotating on its own axis, in the human species once constituted, also acts later and indirectly, through the medium of privileged persons, in order to drive humanity forward.[62]

Not that this implies a dualism between nature and culture. Rather, in terms of process, the movements required in cultural and biological evolution are exactly the same, only they are operating at different levels. Other philosophers have tried to explain cultural change using biological models – Dawkins' theory of the meme and Dan Sperber's epidemiological concept being two that come to mind – but Bergson's 'contagion' theory of cultural diffusion is not meant to operate fundamentally at some brute material level subtending cultural phenomena: when operative at all, what is essentially vital in evolution works at every level in the same way.[63] Monism equals pluralism.

Yet what is truly significant about such contagious emotion is not simply that it is more a matter of ethics than it is of psychology, but, we should also remember, that this emotion is 'more metaphysical than moral in its essence'.[64] Following this allusion to the metaphysical basis underlying an ethical phenomenon, the object of Chapter Five will be to uncover what ethical resonance there may be amongst the various levels of Bergson's other work in the metaphysics of time, mind and biology that we have so far examined. Moreover, we will see this line of inquiry open up new dimensions for our own continued attempts to understand Bergson's thinking beyond dualism.

NOTES

1. *TSMR*, p. 33 [*OE*, p. 1002]. Quotation omits original form of rhetorical question.
2. See Scharfstein 1943, pp. 104–5n10, 125–6; *TSMR*, pp. 104–5 [*OE*, pp. 1063–4].
3. Scharfstein 1943, pp. 125–6. In *The Open Society and its Enemies*, Karl Popper credits Bergson as the first to use the now hackneyed terms 'open' and 'closed society'. Despite 'a certain similarity', there is still 'a considerable difference' between them, however, namely that Popper's dyad depicts a rationalist distinction, the closed society being irrational, the open rational. Bergson's is a religious distinction; see Popper 1966, vol. 1, p. 202n. Indeed, for Bergson, it would be a contradiction in terms for an open society to regard itself as having any enemies.
4. Hartshorne 1987, p. 379.
5. See *TSMR*, p. 100 [*OE*, p. 1060].
6. See *TSMR*, p. 117 [*OE*, p. 1074] which says that individuals may already be societies or 'aggregates of aggregates'.
7. *TSMR*, pp. 177, 116 [*OE*, pp. 1125, 1073].
8. *TSMR*, pp. 101, 91–2 [*OE*, pp. 1061, 1052–3].
9. *TSMR*, pp. 161, 81, 24 [*OE*, pp. 1112, 1043, 994].
10. See Jacques Chevalier, *Entretiens avec Bergson*, pp. 75, 154–5, 159, cited in Gallagher 1970, p. 98.
11. *TSMR*, pp. 269, 68, 85, 89 [*OE*, pp. 1204, 1033, 1047, 1050–1].
12. *TSMR*, p. 90 [*OE*, p. 1051].
13. *TSMR*, p. 47 [*OE*, pp. 1014–15].
14. *TSMR*, pp. 43–4, 45 [*OE*, pp. 1011–12, 1013].
15. *TSMR*, p. 257 [*OE*, p. 1194].
16. *TSMR*, p. 234 [*OE*, p. 1174].
17. *TSMR*, p. 96 [*OE*, p. 1057].
18. See *TSMR*, pp. 9, 13–14, 26–7 [*OE*, pp. 981, 984–6, 996–7].
19. Borch-Jacobsen 1991, p. 69.
20. *TSMR*, pp. 27, 21 [*OE*, pp. 997, 992].
21. *TSMR*, pp. 32, 18–19, 30, 31 [*OE*, pp. 1001, 989–90, 1000, 1001, 1002].
22. See the various writings collected together in Clarke and Linzey 1990.
23. Balibar 1991, p. 50.
24. *TSMR*, pp. 39, 205–7 [*OE*, pp. 1007, 1150–1].
25. *TSMR*, p. 36 [*OE*, p. 1005].
26. *TSMR*, pp. 17, 33–4 [*OE*, pp. 988, 1003].
27. *TSMR*, p. 38 [*OE*, pp. 1006–7].
28. See *TSMR*, pp. 52, 39, 254–5 [*OE*, pp. 1019, 1007, 1191–2].

29. *TSMR*, pp. 51, 84 [*OE*, pp. 1018, 1046]. This personal element of open morality, its necessary embodiment in an individual, will require an examination of Bergson's idea that it is only in imitating the heroic that a movement of closure can be transformed into one of openness.

30. *TSMR*, p. 96 [*OE*, p. 1057], my italics.

31. See *TSMR*, pp. 84, 213 [*OE*, pp. 1046, 1156].

32. See *TSMR*, pp. 32, 38, 59 [*OE*, pp. 1001–2, 1007, 1025].

33. See *TSMR*, pp. 69–79 [*OE*, pp. 1033–41].

34. Cited in Rachels 1991, p. 223.

35. *TSMR*, pp. 300–5 [*OE*, pp. 1231–5].

36. *CM*, p. 128 [*OE*, pp. 1364–5].

37. Cited in Singer 1981, p. xiii.

38. Ibid. p. 50.

39. Ibid. p. 9.

40. Sober 1993, p. 150.

41. Singer 1981, pp. 19–20. Of course, animals don't actually calculate the proportions of shared genetic heritage, they simply act *as if* they do; see ibid. pp. 13–14.

42. *TSMR*, p. 37 [*OE*, p. 1006].

43. Moore 1996, p. 137: Bergson's sociobiologism is certainly not formed from hard-wired instinct or genetic reduction.

44. Singer 1981, pp. 96–9, 106, 113, 142.

45. *TSMR*, pp. 90–1 [*OE*, p. 1052].

46. *TSMR*, p. 269 [*OE*, p. 1204].

47. See *TSMR*, pp. 79–80 [*OE*, pp. 1041–3].

48. *TSMR*, pp. 282, 283 [*OE*, pp. 1215, 1216].

49. Critchley 1992, pp. 209, 240.

50. See *TSMR*, p. 80 [*OE*, p. 1042].

51. *TSMR*, pp. 34, 49, 68, 84, 278 [*OE*, pp. 1003, 1016, 1032, 1046, 1212].

52. Nonetheless, religious dynamism needs static religion for its expression and diffusion (*TSMR*, p. 179 [*OE*, p. 1127]), and the two are not at all opposed in their common origin, which Bergson once again alludes to mysteriously as 'some intermediate thing' (*TSMR*, p. 178 [*OE*, p. 1126]). The object of dynamic religion is also its source: the generative action of life, which Bergson periodically describes as 'God', though this is clearly an immanent and suprapersonal divinity; see *TSMR*, pp. 53, 252–62 [*OE*, pp. 1119–20, 1189–98].

53. *ME*, p. 32 [*OE*, p. 834].

54. See *TSMR*, pp. 220, 228ff [*OE*, pp. 1162, 1169ff].

55. See *ME*, pp. 153–5 [*OE*, p. 910–11].

56. See *TSMR*, p. 228 [*OE*, p. 1169].

57. *TSMR*, p. 225 [*OE*, pp. 1166–7]. Bergson is here quoting N. Soderblom.

58. *TSMR*, p. 309 [*OE*, p. 1138]. Hude 1989–90, vol. I, p. 149, cites a lecture course on ethics where Bergson advises that in the resolution of moral conflicts we should opt for that action which involves 'the greatest sacrifice, give that which costs you the most'.

59. *TSMR*, p. 53 [*OE*, p. 1119]. In *L*, p. 141 [*OE*, p. 454], an emotion is said to be dramatic and contagious when all the harmonics in it are heard along with the funda-mental note.

60. See *TSMR*, pp. 61–2 [*OE*, p. 1026–7]. Bergson sees Socratic rationalism as a reaction against the moral empiricism of his day.

61. See *CE*, pp. 285–6 [*OE*, pp. 724–5].

62. *TSMR*, pp. 50–1 [*OE*, p. 1017].

63. Dawkins' meme is described as a 'unit of information residing in a brain'. The phenotypic effects of such memes may be in the form of 'words, music, visual images, styles of clothes, facial or hand gestures, skills such as opening bottles in tits, or panning wheat in Japanese macaques' (Dawkins 1982, p. 109). The spread of a meme does not depend on intrinsic fitness but also on opportunities such as other amenable memes already residing in the environment; they are also less immune to the causal agency of acquired characteristics than are genes: organisms can make a difference (ibid. pp. 110–12). At face value, Sperber's epidemiological model resembles Bergson's more, though in the end, the 'spread of disease' image rests on a reductionist materialism consisting of an understanding of public representations ('narratives'), mental representations ('stories'), and the causal chains of transmission between them (mostly by imitation and communication) purely in terms of the 'material interaction between brains, organisms and environment' (Sperber 1996, p. 26). At least in this model the transmission is also intrinsically transformative (with incidental replication) rather than essentially replicative (with accidental mutation) as is the case in Dawkins' theory (see Sperber 1996, pp. 101–3). Also, there is no linear parental influence or line of descent, but a wide range of phenomena influencing, or rather attracting minds to an idea in the success (spread) of the representation (ibid. pp. 104–6).

64. *TSMR*, p. 234 [*OE*, p. 1174].

5

The Ethics of Durée

My books have always been the expression of a discontent, of a protest.[1]

ETHICS AS FIRST PHILOSOPHY

Walter Benjamin speaks of Bergson's work in general as one which strived to resist the increasingly 'blinding age of big-scale industrialism'.[2] This has been a common enough assessment: that Bergson wrote at the turn of the twentieth century – the consummate age of mechanical reproduction and artifice – is thought to have left its own mark on his thought. Profoundly conscious of the fact that he was seeing what has been termed 'the evolution of mind in crisis',[3] Bergson was part of a movement that saw in this growing homogenisation and habitualisation a genuine 'fear of life'.[4]

Certainly, we saw that even his first thoughts in *TFW* protested against the increasing loss of our subjectivity through the encroachment of the public, spatialised realm. In the course of his work, Bergson extended his understanding of this withering subjectivity to a varied set of concepts: movement, *durée*, virtuality, *élan vital*. Each term is connected with a specific area of the objective's incursion into privacy: psychophysics (movement); determinism (*durée*); mind–body reductionism (virtuality); biological mechanism (*élan vital*). It has been said that Bergson's interest in these areas of advance is philosophical: 'His attitude is metaphysical... given true duration, how does it come about that we so distort it?'[5] Thus far, we ourselves have asked questions of this ilk too. But others go further: given the continual invasion of mechanism, Bergsonism forwards a moral judgement: 'There is an ethical quality in Bergson's thought on this, since it becomes an imperative to retain as great a degree of consciousness and freedom of action as possible'.[6]

That Bergson's work is driven by ethical motives certainly seems confirmed when one reads him making pronouncements such that, for him, 'automatism is the enemy'.[7] But *TSMR* has added a new dimension to this ethical enterprise. By writing of an ethical emotion – openness or love – which is 'more metaphysical than moral in its essence', it looks as though his thought may not merely be animated by a certain moral outrage, but that ethics itself may comprise its content in some form. As we put it in our introduction: Bergsonism may best be read as an ethics of alterity fleshed out in empirical concerns.

This may not be so surprising in that, unlike much Anglo-American thought, Continental philosophy has long shown little aptitude for the 'dissociation of ethics from metaphysics'.[8] The Spinozist adage that we can only begin to answer the question 'How should we act?' by first answering the question 'What are we?' is taken seriously: our metaphysics conditions our morals.[9] Yet there is a strain of Continental thought which takes things still further, not merely tying metaphysics and morals together by deriving the latter from the former, but reversing this hierarchy, positing ethics as first philosophy in place of metaphysics altogether. Emmanuel Levinas is the exemplary case of this: 'Morality is not a branch of philosophy, but first philosophy', he declares, and his work follows this maxim in moulding secondary disciplines – ontology, epistemology, aesthetics – according to axiological criteria.[10]

Levinas is a phenomenologist in his methodology, but he promotes the realm of appearances in a most unusual manner: rather than studying perceptual awareness, he makes his foundation that most subjective act, moral responsibility. The demand for justice is the basis to all relatedness, linguistic, conceptual and ontological. The ethical relation between humans is the 'irreducible structure upon which all the other structures rest'. Because epistemology and ontology rest on ethical ground they both lose their respective claim to first philosophy in favour of ethics: the love of wisdom becomes the wisdom of love and truth itself is renamed 'justice'. Levinas rejects the requirement of an ontology to constitute the things that are related; the ethical relation is prior to any thing: 'Being *is* not *first*'.[11]

According to his view, Western philosophy has been dominated by the idea of totality, of securing knowledge of the whole of reality, consuming it in a concept. It has thus privileged ontology and epistemology throughout its history. But for Levinas, this exposes its essence as a philosophy of power, 'an appropriation of what is, an exploitation of reality'.[12] It is a philosophy of injustice, of mastery. As ontology, then, philosophy reduces the other to the same, it homogenises reality. This 'philosophy of the same', as Levinas can call it, works hand in hand with epistemology: 'Knowledge is re-presentation, a return to presence, and nothing may remain *other* to it'.[13] In his own ethical thought, Levinas attempts to bypass moral philosophy in its traditional garb which has always played a subordinate role to either epistemology or ontology: 'The ethical relationship is not grafted on to an antecedent relationship of cognition; it is a foundation and not a superstructure'.[14]

So what is this ethics which Levinas proposes in place of philosophy's traditional values? For a start, it is not a theory of action, set of rules, type of reasoning or description of language. What Levinas constructs is a pre-rational ethics as a positive and grounding phenomenon rather than a mere irrationality. This is a proto-ethics sustaining the possibility of any actual decision-making process in ethical matters. A *source* of ethics. As he understands it, this source is simply 'The calling into question of my spontaneity by the presence of the Other'. It is firstly the critique of my own power and of all that issues from it. What I possess is placed in question by my obligation to justice. But this is not an abstract and impersonal justice: it is the absolute justice owed to the singular 'Other'. Levinas runs together themes from Jewish and phenomenological traditions centring on the individual's encounter with the Other, not as a threat to oneself, but as a call to moral responsibility. This pre-theoretical ethics is not a type of economics where we calculate our obligations according to some measure of the Other's worth in terms of need, potential for reciprocity or even sentience. My debt to the Other is absolute and infinite, transcending my own power of judgement: 'The pure passivity that precedes freedom is responsibility. But it is a responsibility that owes nothing to my freedom; it is my responsibility for the freedom of others'.[15] The other is the prime source of infinity read as ethical responsibility. The candidates for paradigmatic alterity (or the first revelation of alterity) have varied along Levinas' philosophical evolution: the feminine, existence, time, language. Underlying this development, though, has always been a humanist concern: the alterity is that of another human being – the gender, being, time or speech of a human person.

There is much we could discuss in this curious philosophy which seems to have taken the most unsustainable of theses for its own: that Being comes after responsibility. It is as though relationship could be prior to the things related. Our interest, however, must limit itself to the fact that Levinas has been clearly influenced by Bergson in a good deal of this.[16] *TSMR* would be too obvious a starting point to begin exploring this inspiration: as a work in proto-ethics which argues that morality does not equal reciprocity, it is clearly a forerunner to much in Levinas' thought. Rather, because it is Bergson's metaphysics that is said to have influenced Levinas most, and because we wish now to focus on that metaphysics, we shall instead turn to Bergson's other writings. It has been claimed, for instance, that the *élan vital* itself is but another way of thinking about alterity.[17] This is unquestionably the case once we again reiterate the fact that the significance of its so-called vitalism resides ultimately in a theory of time. Certainly, what Levinas has done is to take Bergson's philosophy of novelty and moralise it: 'the absolutely new' becomes the Other.[18] In his book *Time and the Other*, Levinas outlines the philosophical debt owed to Bergson thus:

> It is important to underline the importance of Bergsonism for the entire problematic of contemporary philosophy; it is an essential stage of the movement which puts into question the ontological confines of spirituality. It no longer returns to the assimilating act of consciousness, to the reduction of all novelty – of all alterity – to what in one way or another thought already supported, to the reduction of every other to the Same. It is no longer what one could call the thought of the equal, a rationality revealing a reality which keeps to the very measure of a thought...Priority is given to the relations traditional philosophy always treated as secondary and subordinate...In this reversal – the priority of duration over permanence – there is access to novelty, an access independent of the ontology of the Same.[19]

Specific points of contact between the two philosophies of Bergson and Levinas are not hard to find. In *TFW* there is an extended argument showing why it is impossible to gain a total knowledge of the other. The specificity of the time of the other, every detail of his or her *durée*, requires one actually to become that other person as part of what it is to know him or her totally. In other words, so long as there is any temporal distance or separation between self and other, that will ensure that the other *as other* remains unknowable in absolute terms.[20] Moreover, in the effort to represent the other, one eventually sacrifices this desire to know so as simply to become him or her instead, but with that, the ability to re-present at all is lost as well. Here is an irreducible dilemma: how can one represent fully those whose features include not representing themselves? To know all about him or her, a necessary (though not sufficient) condition is that one be that other, yet in doing so one must consequently lose one's desire to be the one who represents the other.[21] *CE* showed that 'the natural function of the intellect is to bind like to like'; in representation, therefore, we can only build upon similarities, repetitions and abstract generalities: genuine difference is off-limits.[22]

This enforced passivity as regards knowledge is the direct product of *durée*: as *CE* also tells us, it is simply time itself which 'obliges me to wait, and to wait for a certain length of psychical *durée* which is forced upon me, over which I have no power'.[23] It is this that has led readers of Levinas to describe his notion of alterity as 'an ethical *durée*'.[24] But rather than explore this comparison between these philosophies further, it is their difference that we should ponder. Despite the views mentioned above, it remains that Bergson's philosophy of life is still too ontological for Levinas, too creative and active.[25] Creation itself presupposes something more fundamental, according to Levinas, namely the revelation of human alterity. The philosophy of the *élan* is flawed because it 'tends toward an impersonal pantheism'.[26] This charge is undoubtedly true: Bergsonism is not a humanism but is primarily a philosophy of time extended to all being. Levinas' humanism is wrapped up in his phenomenology, for he clearly views time anthropologically in its essence, and it is noteworthy in this respect that he regards *TFW*, Bergson's most psychologistic work, as his primary text.[27] Without being rationalist, Levinas' primacy of the subjective still remains classical in as much as it disregards the value of non-human forms of life. As we will see, however, Bergson's anti-reductionism extends his version of ethical irreducibility beyond the human psyche towards anything that genuinely endures.

For now, we hope to show that Levinas' assertion that there is an ethical obligation towards another perspective also proves that a materialist monism cannot succeed to a total view of reality. The very existence, even if only theoretical, of such an ethic topples it from its pedestal of first philosophy. This ethical permutation of anti-reductionism, however, comes to light first in some of Bergson's lesser-known early works, written some thirty years before *TSMR*.

LE BON SENS

In 1901 the French Philosophy Society met to discuss the significance of Bergson's treatment of the mind–body problem. At one point in the debate, Bergson's interlocutor, Gustave Belot, commented upon the purely hypothetical nature of the address Bergson had presented to the Society, each of his conclusions having begun with the conditional 'if'.[28] In a reply that has struck one commentator as 'astonishing', Bergson countered Belot's observation by claiming that the conditional had nothing to do with any hypothetical nature of his argument, he himself was 'convinced' of its truth.[29] Rather, the conditionals were concerned with the nature of its presentation.[30] He had no right, he said, to speak as if he had convinced others; the 'if' is one of what he calls '*politesse*', politeness rather than hypothesis. It is a *politesse* towards those who would eventually challenge his point of view, a recognition of this future difference.

This remark belies a significant philosophical point concerning more than just civility, for six years earlier Bergson had already delivered a speech on '*la politesse*' that gave it an application going far beyond the meaning associated with its English equivalent of 'politeness'.[31] *La politesse* firstly concerns an equality of relation, of justice; it is the ability to show another 'the regard and consideration which he deserves'. But it also goes beyond a theoretical justice, being a love for the other that exists 'almost before knowing him'. Such a love consists of handling the sensibilities and sufferings of others with care; it is the faculty 'of putting oneself in the place of others... and of forgetting oneself'.[32]

The issue of the other also emerges in a lecture given in 1895 on what Bergson now terms the faculty of good sense, '*le bon sens*'. While the other senses place us in relation with things, *le bon sens*, he observes, 'governs our relations with people', orienting our attention 'in the direction of life'. It is again the principle of social justice, though it is a justice 'living and acting' rather than 'theoretical and abstract'. *Le bon sens* is first and foremost a 'strength of feeling' of which theoretical justice is a derivative form. It is also described as an attention to life, though this attention is neither an extended experience, more exact deduction, nor rigorous logic: it remains a spirit of justice. Nevertheless, *le bon sens* also has an intellectual role, demanding the sacrifice of our firmest convictions and best explanations in order to preserve us from 'intellectual automatism'.[33] Such beliefs must be made provisional if we are to remain open to the opinions and solutions of others. As one critic describes it: 'Good sense demands both flexibility and perpetual readaptation of means to ends: in a word, it demands open-ness'.[34]

It is when *le bon sens* is addressed under the alternative designation of 'common sense' that this notion enters the foreground of Bergson's thought. Now it is no longer only an attention to the sensibilities of human beings, it is an attention to otherness as such before the bifurcation between the enduring and the inert has been performed. An enduring reality, writes Bergson, is what is given immediately to our mind, and it is common sense that is said to endorse this truth.[35] The introduction to *MM* openly equates the picture it will draw of the physical, that of an existence 'placed halfway between a "thing" and a "representation" ', with the common sense conception of the material world.[36] Admittedly, Bergson also writes much in condemnation of the illusions and false problems common sense can lead us into: our confusions of quantity for quality, simultaneity for succession, immobility for movement, and homogeneous space for time are obvious examples.[37] Bergson's philosophy, therefore, is not a commendation of common sense pure and simple: it endorses one

type of common sense.[38] In fact, the type concerned is part of the Bergsonian project of reclaiming an individual's vision of reality.[39] Common
sense becomes a trap when it is no longer a good sense, but is instead
what only emphasises the common. By this we mean that the good common sense, *le bon sens* directed towards otherness as such, seems to retain
the proportionality required to temper its own perspective with that of the
other, whereas the bad common sense enforces the sacrifice of its own
alterity to the communal view: self-homogenisation. *Le bon sens* is thereby
the sense that equally demands that we adopt a position that will always
and necessarily be ours alone.[40]

In that he equates this good sense with a form of common sense, it is
arguable that Bergson is here establishing a pragmatism with moral over-
tones, and Chapter Eight will examine what Bergson writes on pragmatism
that might bear this out. Even more radically, though, in as much as *le bon
sens* is a sense at all, Bergson has given ethical scope to perception as such.
By examining *DS* next, we hope to provide a case study that will help to
substantiate this contention.

THE DURATION OF THE OTHER

DS, which sets out the differences between Bergson's theory of time and
Albert Einstein's, characterises the Special Theory of Relativity (STR) as
an attempt to give a representation of the world 'independent of the observer's point of view'. Indeed, seeing that STR's attempt to eliminate the
observer is also an attempt to provide '*absolute relations*' for the experience
of all possible observers, its title of 'relativity theory' is actually a misno-
mer: its account of individual differences is motivated by the desire to create an absolute account of all difference: to be 'everywhere or nowhere'.[41]
Not that Bergson rejects STR out of hand: it cannot express all of reality,
but, as he admits, 'it is impossible for it not to express some'.[42] It is its
ambition to account for every level of time that Bergson wants to curb.
His aim is not to refute STR but, as always when engaging with scientific
research, to 'establish the philosophical signification of the concepts it
introduces'.[43]

At the heart of his disagreement with the common interpretation of
STR is a difference in attitude towards the 'twins paradox' first put forward by the physicist Paul Langevin. This concerns a thought-experiment
where one individual, Paul, sends his twin brother Peter off in a rocket at
a speed just less than that of light. After a year, the rocket turns around
and heads back to earth at the same velocity. Peter gets out after his two-
year journey in the rocket only to discover that Paul has aged two hundred
years whilst waiting for him on earth. This paradox represents one of the

hypothetical outcomes of STR's thesis concerning multiple relativistic times and what are called the 'Lorentz transformations'. We can thankfully dispense with any of the technical details. What is relevant is that STR assumes that it is possible to position oneself arbitrarily within different reference frames; thus, in the twins paradox, as well as experiencing our own time here on earth with Paul, we can also imagine the experience of another's time such as that of Peter, the hypothetical space traveller.

But Bergson's commitment to the irreducibility of lived time challenges the position which says that there are no privileged reference frames and that any one perspective can be represented totally by another. In his mind, the paradox is predicated upon an impossibility: that of Paul fully representing the experience of Peter. There is more to Peter's movement than how it is seen from Paul's or any other perspective for that matter: experience is more than the representation of experience.[44] For one to represent fully another's lived time, one must experience it in every detail. But this is impossible without being that other person: 'If I want to actually measure Peter's time, I must enter Peter's frame of reference; I must become Peter. If I want to actually measure Paul's time, I must take Paul's place'.[45] Images and representations, being symbolic, are necessarily more general and less individual. Symbols will not suffice to represent the totality of another's experience: one must become the other. But as we will see, in becoming the twin in space, some startling results ensue.

Bergson's complaint is that STR does not go far enough: it, or at least some popular interpretations of it, still holds on to an absolute point of reference, thus leaving STR as what Bergsons terms a 'half', 'single' or 'unilateral' relativity:

> His gaze [the physicist's] never leaves the moving line of demarcation that separates the symbolic from the real, the conceived from the perceived. He will then speak of 'reality' and 'appearance', of 'true measurements' and 'false measurements'. In short, he will not adopt the language of relativity. But he will accept its theory.[46]

In the twins paradox then, what Bergson queries is whether we on earth, representing the flight of the twin through space, should take our frame of reference as the immobile point of reference. Why is the earth's frame of reference privileged? If we take relativity theory to its full extent, we would find that the twin in space should reciprocate our actions and take his frame of reference as the static one. But if that were the case, then it would be we who are travelling at near the speed of light relative to him, and it would be we who have aged two years as compared with his two hundred years.

Bergson's project, therefore, is to relativise relativity. But doing so lets Bergson emerge with what he calls a 'full-relativity' that actually reinstates a new absolute. For, if each perspective takes its own frame of reference as an absolute, then everyone, relative to the other's point of view, travels and ages at the same altered rate, which is to say that everyone ages and travels at the same rate. Thus a new absolute is restored: 'The hypothesis of reciprocity gives us at least as much reason for believing in a single time as does common sense'.[47] But this is unlike the absolute of half-relativity, for the latter alters the temporal conditions only for the perspective of the other as we represent him or her. Bergson's new absolute takes account of the other's own tendency to repeat the very same operation on us, that is, to imagine a half-relativity that would alter our experience of time. Taking account of the other's reflection of our own intolerance, so to speak, actually offsets the activity of both: our equal unequal treatments of each other balance themselves out.

Against this analysis, various experimental results have been cited by Christopher Ray in his reassessment of Bergson's argument.[48] He talks of mu-mesons travelling at .99 times the speed of light, with their atomic half-life lasting nine times longer than normal as a result. Another experiment established that clocks on aeroplanes operate slower than clocks on land. The results from these researches are said to be valid in relation to the twins paradox 'since a person is, in an important sense, no more than a biological clock'.[49] Consequently, Bergson got it wrong on relativity:

> Bergson argued that the travelling twin would be no more than a phantom in the physicist's imagination and that on his or her return to Earth ages and clocks would all agree. We can now see why STR does not support such a view.[50]

But the problem with Ray's critique is that firstly, Bergson would not see a person as 'no more than' a clock in any sense, and secondly, even if that were all a person is, a clock is still not time – it is a measurement of time. The public time measured by a clock (be it biological or non-biological) is calibrated according to one series of events, the clock's. But *durée* is multiple: what applies to the clock-events does not necessarily hold for the events comprising a subject's experience of *durée*. To reiterate Bergson's point: if I want to measure Peter's time, I must become Peter. And of course, this is impossible whilst retaining the ability to represent Peter. Peter, in all his alterity, is beyond representation. The desire to subsume him within a concept is self-defeating, for it must incorporate the being of Peter that consists precisely in not desiring to subsume him so.

Ray goes on to assert that all that can be concluded from the fact of reciprocity is that neither account, the earth-bound physicist's, nor the space-travelling twin's, is the correct one. But after this nod to true relativism, he immediately states that we can 'appeal to geometry to resolve the "paradox" – to the geometrical ideas of spacetime paths and world lines which present the motion of objects in the only way possible in STR: within the union of space and time'. Thus, after admitting that different points of view cannot be reduced to each other, he posits a true 'view from nowhere' to resolve the paradox. He appeals to homogenised space (geometry) to provide the 'mechanism by which we can overcome our locally bound perspectives'.[51] But such an appeal only ignores the very level at which the paradox occurs for Bergson: that of perceiving, living subjects, not that of a geometrical vision of the space they traverse. Yet, as Bergson laments: 'This tendency [to spatialise *durée*] simply expresses our inability mathematically to translate time itself, our need to replace it, in order to measure it, by simultaneities which we count'.[52] We already saw, however, that Bergson had smashed the illusion that there is any God-given simultaneity or 'now' which contains us all, no matter how accurate the clock used to measure it: to a microbe, our absolute simultaneity would be its relative one, while what appears as an absolute simultaneity to a giant's perspective would be merely relative for us.[53] If perfect simultaneity is gone all the way up and down, then half-relativity has nothing left to push against: only multiple, lived simultaneities are left.

This examination of the latent absolutist tendencies in STR is not without precedent in Bergson's work on the philosophical form of relativism, despite his own careful nuancing of the differences between the two.[54] For Bergson, there is a definite connection between relativism and absolutism, or, rather, between relativism and absolutism of a certain sort. He regards the motive behind Kant's Copernican Revolution as itself a symptom of an absolutist intellect having failed in its attempt to totalise or subsume the world and that turns instead to a humble relativism that dismisses the possibility of finding any absolutes whatsoever.[55] In fact, one could look upon Bergson's philosophy in general as a reversed Kantianism: '*The whole* Critique of Pure Reason *rests also upon the postulate that our thought is incapable of anything but Platonizing*, that is, of pouring the whole of possible experience into pre-existing molds'.[56] This relativism starts from the same assumption as dogmatic absolutism: that our understanding begins with '*rigidly defined concepts*'.[57]

If Kant banished metaphysics and with it the absolute, Bergson sees it as his task to reinstate them both, only now in a newly redeemed understanding rather than in the form in which Kant uncovered them. His new abso-

lute is not lost or found through rigid Kantian concepts or the geometry
of STR. It is grounded on the recognition of our selectivist *tendency* to
centralise our own point of view by making everything else move relative
to it, to be private Ptolemaicists. The plurality of STR's half-relativity is a
spurious one which 'looms up', as he puts it, 'at the precise moment when
there is no more than one man or group to *live* time'.[58] In contradistinc-
tion to this, Bergson's plurality recognises, in the modern parlance, 'the
otherness of the other' by not reducing it to the convenience of one point
of view's representation of it. While Bergson's is a real pluralism, the multiplicity of times posited by STR is a mathematical fiction. Of course, the
physicist may deny that he or she does ever centralise his or her own
frame of reference, but Bergson refutes this:

> When the physicist sets his system of reference in motion, it is
> because he provisionally chooses another, which then becomes
> motionless. It is true that this second system can in turn be mentally
> set in motion without thought necessarily electing to settle in a third
> system. But in that case it oscillates between the two, immobilising
> them by turns through goings and comings so rapid that it entertains
> the illusion of leaving them both in motion.[59]

It might sound here as if Bergson himself is trying to imagine another's
experience, in this case, the physicist's. But this is exactly what he is not
doing. It remains true that it is impossible to measure the profundity of
Peter's *durée* without being Peter. Bergson, on the other hand, is only imagining a superficial and transferable aspect of another's experience, namely
how they themselves imagine the experience of others: it is a second-order
intolerance towards intolerance, so to speak, or full-relativism in other
words. What he rejects is the strategy in STR which pretends to undo the
opposition of symbolic and real while in actual fact maintaining them in a
relativism that only selectively reduces the real to the symbolic; it reduces
the experience of the other alone.[60] Bergson maintains these distinctions
but only by taking relativity to the limit. It is as though the sceptic, being
sceptical even about his or her own scepticism, has created an alternative,
non-dogmatic place for belief.

As the analysis of *le bon sens* described, giving due regard to the experience of the other is part of what it is to understand and reclaim one's own
alterity. Rather than an isolation, such subjectivity is a genuine sociability
for it balances its own acts with those of the other. The name *TSMR*
gives to this communal recognition of otherness is fraternity or love: the
delicate and continually adjusted balance between the forces of egoism (liberty) and altruism (equality). The 'absolute' simultaneity STR relativises

was never a singular absolute but a creation by another real absolute, though one of another order: life itself.[61] For behind the 'single time' reinstated by Bergson lies the source of this pragmatic absolutism: it is our mirrored intolerance. A reciprocal closure (the desire to totalise the other in a representation), combined with the recalcitrant alterity of the other which refuses to allow that closure to succeed, ensures that a certain balance is maintained, a tension between the forces of liberty (the self asserting its power of representation) and equality (intolerance mirroring intolerance). As a result, simultaneity is inadvertently stratified through a set of psycho-ethical acts blind to their own combined effects. Bergson's *philosophy* of full-relativism, on the other hand, can consequently be read as a process of proliferation that extends relativism beyond its false, egocentric humility to every possible perspective, irrespective of its 'content'. An absolute is rehabilitated. In place of simply a mirrored intolerance (full-relativism *per se*), a *cognisance* of this reflection leads to a new level of tolerance or balance between intolerances. An equality amongst inequalities.

As such, the Bergsonian absolute is far from dogmatism: it has only the ethical force of openness. But similarly, its affirmation of multiplicity is not an endorsement of relativism either. Partial knowledge is one thing, relative knowledge something else again.[62] As we have already seen in *MM*, while the relative implies a lost absolute, the part opens itself up to the whole. The only hierarchical scale to be found in Bergsonism, as we will see when we return to *CE*, pertains to the degree in which we recognise the value of that alterity which extends beyond us. This new absolutism arises out of a full-relativity that takes the value of otherness as its sole directive. One commentator has said that Bergsonism, 'without being a philosophy of judgement', is nonetheless animated by the 'fundamental concern' of recreating the 'accord' between spirits.[63] We would extend this idea and say that any hierarchy in Bergsonism must not be directly grounded on a principle of nature above us or below us ('onto-theology'), but on our own greater or lesser neglect of the alterity of others around us. Another interpreter has written that Bergson can only talk of 'greater' or 'lesser' if he has some notion of a limit.[64] The limits of a pure openness and closure come to mind in this respect, and it will be our task to show further how these notions generate a hierarchy.

THE DUPLICITY OF MOVEMENT

Integrating elements from Bergson's other works into this ethical reading of openness/closure poses relatively less difficulty. The whole idea of homogeneous space in *TFW* is built around exclusion: 'Externality is the distinguishing mark of things which occupy space'. The sign of a quantitative multiplicity is reciprocal closure and impenetrability: that of two mutually exclusive positions in desiccated space. Via the process of endosmosis, the scheme of closure and containment extends itself throughout the mind, such that it now seems as if the body contains consciousness, a strong affect potentially contains a weak affect, and, of course, time itself is simply a container of events. Subsequently, part of *MM*'s object is to break down the dichotomy of inside and outside by showing how space is as much within us as it is without. Instead of the static modes of being on either one or the other side of a closed container – space, time, body – this second work puts the whole scheme into motion: it becomes a progress *towards* closure: 'The distinction between inside and outside will then be only a distinction between the part and the whole – ... The whole subject becomes clear if we travel thus from the periphery to the center'. In principle, perception does not extend from my body outward to other bodies: it begins, Bergson claims, 'in the aggregate of bodies, then gradually limits itself and adopts my body as its center'. The physical basis of my personality, the image of my body, is found through a movement of closure, an ostracisation in which two worlds are created: the world as it is and the world as it refers to me. After this, the body and its brain are both instruments of selection, exclusion and discrimination.[65]

In what follows, *TSMR* expands on this genesis of our carnal chauvinism:

> For if our body is the matter to which our consciousness applies itself it is coextensive with our consciousness, it comprises all we perceive, it reaches to the stars. But this vast body is changing continually, sometimes radically, at the slightest shifting of one part of itself which is at its centre and occupies a small fraction of space. This inner and central body, relatively invariable, is ever present. It is not merely present, it is operative: it is through this body and through it alone, that we can move parts of the large body. And, since action is what matters, since it is an understood thing that we are present where we act, the habit has grown of limiting consciousness to the small body and ignoring the vast one ... If the surface of our organised small body ... is the seat of all our actual movements, our huge inorganic body is the seat of our potential or theoretically possible actions.[66]

The body is a centre of action, be it either the actual activity of the smaller organic body or the possible actions of our vast anorganic body. This larger body – the aggregate of all images *MM* begins with – 'reaches to the stars'. But nonetheless, in actuality it cannot behave as though it embraces the universal, and the reason for this is simple: survival. The organic body has certain needs the fulfilment of which entails that it treats its 'vast body' (the universe) as though it were other to it: it must consume other beings in order to live. Containment becomes incorporation. *MM* describes how the body has to immobilise the living and require its death:

> This body itself... is led by its various needs to distinguish and consti-
> tute other bodies. In the humblest living being nutrition demands
> research, then contact, in short, a series of efforts which converge
> toward a center: this center is just what is made into an object – the
> object which will serve as food. Whatever the nature of matter, it
> may be said that life will at once establish in it a *primary discontinuity*,
> expressing the *duality* of need and that which must serve to satisfy
> it.[67]

It is the 'fundamental needs of life', Bergson continues, which generate the 'first subdivision of the real': here we have a pragmatic and vital origin to dualism.[68] Furthermore, if the body homogenises in order to survive, this is not simply in virtue of reasons essential to its constitution but accidental to its being; the body *is* this continuing act of consumption:

> Our needs are, then, so many searchlights which, directed upon the
> continuity of sensible qualities, single out in it distinct bodies. They
> cannot satisfy themselves except upon the condition that they carve
> out, within this continuity, a body which is to be their own and then
> delimit other bodies with which the first can enter into relation, as if
> with persons. To establish these special relations among portions thus
> carved out from sensible reality is just what we call *living*.[69]

One reader has found a circular reasoning in this passage: 'Our needs carve out a body – but how do we have the needs unless we already have a body?'[70] But such apparent circularity can be dissolved once we understand the 'body' as a substantialisation of need, as one phase of a process. The body is an item in continuous transformation: it has desires, but it was itself created from desires. The sociologist Ann Game has rightly said that Berg-son, like Michel Foucault, understands the body as a 'site of forces. As soon as a subject is immobilised, to use a Bergsonian term, there is, for Foucault, no play of power, but violence, slavery'.[71] The discovery of our small organic body is a centripetal rather than centrifugal movement; it progresses from an indiscriminate 'aggregate' of anorganic images to the 'privileged' image of the organised body, and it makes this progression at the behest of our most pressing needs.[72] This movement from the vast body to the 'inner and central' one is the ongoing expression of a desire: to consume others and with that forge a closed body of increasingly self-identical nature from another, open body embracing a universe of difference. As Levinas would phrase it: 'Nourishment...is the transmutation of the other into the same'.[73]

At one point in *TSMR* Bergson calls the 'logic of the body' an 'extension of desire'.[74] In our biology, there is an imprinted tyranny; the others who are fortunate enough to be treated as 'Other' are simply those whom, at the crudest level, we do not eat. On account of their status as foodstuff, there are many individuals who will never enter the omnivorous society no matter how just and egalitarian the latter might think itself. As *TSMR* would argue, a completely open society is a contradiction in terms, in that every in-group must have its own particular out-group. Nourishment is the first cause of this primary division and duality of inclusion–exclusion. To be open, one must occupy a position to be open from, and it is a necessary fact that every occupied territory is someone else's past, present, or future home. One must contain a space. Again, to conclude using Levinas' words:

> My being-in-the-world or my "place in the sun", my being at home, have not these not also been the usurpation of spaces belonging to the other man whom I have already oppressed or starved, or driven out into a third world.[75]

ELAN D'AMOUR

Between *TFW* and *MM* we have seen a static containment develop into a dynamic closure. But it was *CE* that explained how the opposite movement was possible. It contrasts vital organisation with artificial manufacture as two opposed movements, the former operating dissociatively in a centrifugal direction, the latter working associatively in a centripetal direction.[76] It claimed that matter itself, however, had merely the *tendency* to constitute closed systems, adding that material systems were *completely* closed only by science and only in theory: in reality there never is complete closure. The reason why is simply because matter endures, and so is both partly open as a state and hence open also to the influence of life as a process. In their common origin, the emergent states of matter and life are simply tendencies, forces or modes of organisation. Their only difference is that they move in opposite directions, from order to chaos (matter) and from chaos to order (life).[77] In their actual form, they interpenetrate as a result of being an accommodation between these two forces.

Openness is represented in *CE* primarily in its non-teleological conception of evolution. Having no objective *telos* for life makes Bergsonian evolutionism radically non-hierarchical, positing, as *TSMR* says, a 'discontinuous evolution which proceeds by bounds, obtaining at each stopping-place a combination, perfect of its kind'.[78] Just as *TFW* argued that grey is not a variation upon white, neither is *Homo sapiens* nor any other species a variation upon a transcendental theme. Nonetheless, there is a scale amongst the living, but only an immanent, self-referential one set by the respective capacity of each species to continue openly evolving – it concerns nothing else. It is sometimes phrased as the differing ability with which organisms accumulate and dissipate energy, with more mobile, explosive animals taking a stand over vegetable forms of life, the latter not having 'the same power to evolve'.[79] Openness and closure are here naturalised as dissipation and accumulation respectively.

More often though, openness is expressed as a kind of 'attention to life'. Indeed, attention to life can appear in *CE* as nature's sole imperative. If there are any hierarchies to be found, then they are created immanently within life when each species falls into self-absorption and a disregard for 'almost all the rest of life'. The lower form of life is the species and individual who 'think only of themselves', behaving as if 'the general movement of life stopped at it instead of passing through it. It thinks only of itself, it lives only for itself'. Bergson also describes this disregard through which a hierarchy of the living is instituted as 'a partial sleep': whichever species manages to retain the greatest degree of wakefulness automatically attains superiority.[80]

CE eventually sees the evolution of different social forms as the best illustration of the contrast between the open and closed. This is not because society is an end in itself for life, but because life contains within itself two originary and conflicting ideals with implications for social evolution: equality and liberty. They conflict simply because equality can be oppressive and liberty can be divisive. The different forms of society found amongst insects and humans manifest this clearly:

> The former are admirably ordered and united, but stereotyped; the latter are open to every sort of progress, but divided, and incessantly at strife with themselves. The ideal would be a society always in progress and always in equilibrium, but this ideal is unrealizable.[81]

Behind this social duality (fully expounded only in *TSMR*) are two powers which *CE* describes as 'immanent in life and originally intermingled, which were bound to part company in course of growth'. Consequently, the evolution of life in the twin direction of individuality and association has nothing accidental about it, being due 'to the very nature of life'.[82]

But what is truly remarkable is not only that hierarchy is immanent to life, but that it concerns the question of hierarchy itself *qua* social form. The evolutionary scale does not ultimately concern rationality, complexity

or language *per se* (though these may be by-products of an underlying hierarchy). The hierarchy pertains to different levels of change and of openness
to other forms of life. The creation of an unfounded hierarchy through
self-absorption is symptomatic of a closure that consequently feeds back to
form a *well-founded* hierarchy with, all else being equal, the self-absorbed
species at the lowest point on the scale. This is the great irony of the little
teleology posited by Bergson: it involves the ability (always at issue and
never secure) to evolve towards further evolution, to remain open, and
this openness has as much meta-ethical import as it has biological significance. The hierarchy entails an openness towards the open as well as a
closure before the closed.

   TSMR elaborates on this import further, with explicit references to
moral openness and closure. But both these moralities rest in turn on types
of transcendental emotion: hatred or the movement of exclusion in one
case, and love or the movement of openness in the other. The emotion of
love is explicitly drawn in terms of a movement outwards, a centrifugal
progress and hence an opening. But again, these are ideal limits; in reality,
there is only the process of movement between the extreme 'attractors', so
to speak, of complete openness and closure: 'Between the closed soul and
the open soul there is the soul in the process of opening'.[83]

   In his methodological writings (which we will soon be examining), this
process of opening can be seen in an ameliorated attitude towards the
environment. In order to see reality as it is rather than as we would wish
it to be, Bergson believes that we must transform our perception from a
calculative interrogation of nature to an assumed passivity before it: we
must aspire to look at the object 'for itself', 'for nothing, for the pleasure
of doing so'.[84] Our practical needs homogenise nature: distancing ourselves
from the immediate demands of survival may help to restore to our eyes
some of nature's lost heterogeneity (how we go about doing this will be
discussed in Chapter Seven). Without any thought of measurement, relation or comparison, we can be in 'sympathy' with reality. In fact, Bergson
describes metaphysics as a *'sympathy* with reality' entailing the ability 'to act
and suffer in imagination with the object studied'. He contrasts this with
the method of analysis or instrumental reasoning required by science.
Indeed, if metaphysics involves something like openness, then science,
which must aim at control and mastery, represents a type of closure. Bergson tells us that the 'rule of science' concerns obedience and command:
the scientist makes nature 'submit...to the action of man'. The true philosopher, on the other hand, 'neither obeys nor commands; he seeks to be
at one with nature'.[85]

CONCLUSION

Having run through the ethical dimensions of Bergson's studies of time, mind and life, a return to the issue of Bergson's dualism would seem appropriate at this concluding stage. What we have seen has certainly not been a naturalised ethics: there is no question here of deriving a moral code from a set of biological facts (open morality is necessarily too vague for such a task), so Bergson has not fallen foul of any fallacy of reasoning in that regard. Quite the converse, far from trying to derive a prescriptive ethic from nature, he seems to have discovered an ethical intensity original to natural forces. The vital order of accumulation and dispersion emerges from the original conflict of tendencies within life between liberty and equality. But lest this be seen to fall into some type of idealism, Bergson does not say that ethics is first philosophy with Levinas: life is a type of emotion, but its essence remains more metaphysical than moral. Bergson does not embrace the complete inversion of philosophy that places ethics over ontology (though as Chapter Eight will explain, not for reasons of any apparent consequential absurdity). As such, we are still in search of a bridge between two poles, though now the dyad in question is neither space and time (*TFW*), material *durée* and mental *durée* (*MM*), nor virtual organisation and dissociated nature (*CE*): presently, the pair encompass the higher-order dualism of ethics and metaphysics itself. But we must be careful how we approach this metaphysics if we are to avoid simply repeating ourselves in what remains of this study. The interface between ethics and Bergson's metaphysics of space and time is made visible when we re-read liberty and equality in terms of heterogeneity and continuity, or in other words, *durée*. The homogeneity of space has its source in the tendency towards equality in the origin of matter. The heterogeneity of time has its source in the tendency towards liberty in the origin of life. But the crucial point is that matter and organic life share the same origin. Ethics meets the metaphysics of space and time. This interface becomes clearer still, however, if we interpret matter and life with respect to two ontological categories, namely, repetition and difference. Our next chapter will take this ontological turn, tackling *durée* itself from the vantage point of its own ontological problematic: how can repetition or continuity be reconciled with difference or heterogeneity? How can an ontology of process be sustained without a concept of substance? What is the difference between qualitative difference and quantitative difference? Such questions will raise our investigation of Bergsonian duality to a level of abstraction hitherto untouched. Exploring this territory will firstly reveal another source of Bergson's ethical enterprise, this time one which is situated squarely at the centre of ontology: his critique of nothingness.

NOTES

1. De La Harpe 1943, p. 359.
2. Benjamin 1992, p. 154.
3. Barron 1987, p. 221.
4. Gross 1985, p. 372.
5. Scharfstein 1943, p. 38.
6. Pilkington 1976, p. 165.
7. *M*, p. 495.
8. Sprigge 1988, p. 247.
9. Of course, there are also some Anglo-American thinkers, such as Roger Sperry, who readily admit that 'doctrine regarding ultimate values is closely tied to beliefs about the properties of the human psyche or conscious mind and its relation to physical reality'. See Sperry 1983, p. 20. Others who show the same connectivity in their thought include Derek Parfit, T. L. S. Sprigge and Ted Honderich, to mention just three.
10. Levinas 1969, p. 304.
11. Ibid. pp. 79, 203, 215.
12. Ibid. p. 46.
13. Levinas 1989; see also Levinas 1987a, p. 50.
14. Levinas 1987a, p. 56.
15. Levinas 1969, p. 43; Levinas 1987a, p. 135.
16. Cohen 1987, p. 11. Levinas remarks on the strong influence Bergson had upon him in Kearney 1984, p. 49.
17. Trotignon 1991, p. 288.
18. Levinas 1969, p. 219.
19. Levinas 1987b, p. 132.
20. See *TFW*, pp. 185–9 [*OE*, pp. 121–4].
21. The similarity between this idea and Thomas Nagel's thesis concerning the ineffability of what it is to be like another organism is not incidental and will be examined later.
22. *CE*, p. 211 [*OE*, p. 665].
23. *CE*, p. 358 [*OE*, p. 782].
24. Critchley 1992, p. 175.
25. See Llewelyn 1995, pp. 11, 13.
26. Levinas 1987b, pp. 80–1, 92.
27. See Levinas 1985, p. 37.
28. See *M*, pp. 464–5.
29. It is André Robinet (1965, p. 169n1) who finds the following response astonishing.
30. *M*, p. 473.
31. The lecture was first delivered in 1885, then in 1892 in amended form; we will be referring to both versions as contained in *M*, pp. 317–32. On p. 319 civility and *politesse* are said to have little in common, for the former is often no more than a ceremonial varnish.
32. *M*, pp. 320, 322, 326, 328.
33. *M*, pp. 361, 363, 364, 371, 362.
34. Gunter 1995, p. 393. It should be no surprise that later in *TSMR* Bergson will attribute '*un bon sens supérieur*' to the mystics (*OE*, p. 1183 – though it is translated as 'common sense' in the English at *TSMR*, p. 245).
35. See *CM*, p. 188 [*OE*, p. 1420].

36. *MM*, pp. xi–xii [*OE*, p. 161]; see also *MM*, p. 80 [*OE*, p. 219].
37. The very first page of *TFW* castigates common sense for confusing quality with quantity; see also *CE*, pp. 9–10 [*OE*, pp. 501–2]; *CM*, pp. 126, 127 [*OE*, p. 1363]; *TSMR*, p. 272 [*OE*, p. 1207].
38. See Fabre-Luce de Gruson 1959, p. 198.
39. See Jankélévitch 1959, pp. 51–2, 17 who describes it as a 'learned naïvety' and 'ingenuous simplicity'.
40. See *M*, p. 362.
41. *CM*, p. 301n5 (hardback edition) [*OE*, p. 1280n]; *DS*, p. 184n [*M*, p. 237n].
42. *DS*, p. 64 [*M*, pp. 117–18].
43. Bergson 1969b, p. 133.
44. 'Peter' may even represent an anticipation of Peter about himself at a future date.
45. Bergson 1969a, p. 174.
46. *DS*, p. 109 [*M*, p. 163].
47. *DS*, pp. 77–8 [*M*, p. 131].
48. See Ray 1991, pp. 25–6, 44–5.
49. Ibid. p. 24.
50. Ibid. p. 44.
51. Ibid.
52. *DS*, p. 60 [*M*, p. 113].
53. See *DS*, pp. 56, 86 [*M*, pp. 109–10, 140].
54. See *CM*, p. 301n5 (hardback edition) [*OE*, p. 1280n1].
55. See *CE*, pp. 216, 379–80, xi [*OE*, pp. 669, 798–9, 490–1].
56. *CM*, p. 197 [*OE*, p. 1430]; see also Barthelemy-Madaule 1966; Jankélévitch 1959, pp. 47, 225; Heidsieck 1957, p. 90.
57. *CM*, p. 190 [*OE*, p. 1421].
58. *DS*, p. 80 [*M*, p. 133].
59. *DS*, p. 41 [*M*, p. 95].
60. Of course, there are arguments from Einstein's General Theory of Relativity (GTR) that purport to undo Langevin's paradox. Einstein's incorporation of force (acceleration and gravity) into the theory shows why the twin travelling in space could not reciprocate and take his own frame of reference as absolute, in that only he goes through the various physical forces of deceleration and acceleration as his rocket turns around to head back to earth. However, Bergson rejected these arguments as presented in examples concerning forces experienced on moving trains or cars (see *DS*, pp. 173–6 [*M*, pp. 225–9]; Bergson 1969a, pp. 179–82). His response was that they tend to conflate one system of reference, a person's body or the point of view of an objective observer outside the car, with that of another: the subject's. In general, most commentators look upon this part of *DS* as a failure because it does not recognise that GTR, far from continuing the spatialisation of time in STR, actually moves towards the 'dynamisation of space' (Čapek 1952, p. 345). Consequently, this work is regarded as minor within the Bergsonian corpus, the significance of its notion of full-relativity being missed (though see Herbert Dingle's introduction to *DS* (Dingle 1965) for a modern defence of Bergson against GTR's supposed final settlement of the matter).
61. See *DS*, pp. 102, 118 [*M*, pp. 156, 171–2].
62. See *M*, p. 774.
63. Fabre-Luce de Gruson 1959, p. 198.

64. See de Lattre 1990, p. 76.
65. *TFW,* pp. 99, 89 [*OE,* pp. 67, 60–1]; *MM,* pp. 47, 61 [*OE,* pp. 44, 64]; *CM,* p. 153 [*OE,* p. 1388].
66. *TSMR,* p. 258 [*OE,* pp. 1194–5].
67. *MM,* p. 261 [*OE,* pp. 333–4], my italics.
68. *MM,* p. 262 [*OE,* p. 334].
69. *MM,* p. 262 [*OE,* p. 334].
70. Lacey 1989, p. 139.
71. Game 1991, p. 45.
72. See *MM,* p. 44 [*OE,* p. 196]. The parallels with Deleuze and Guattari's idea of the Body without Organs are obvious: for a discussion of them see Mullarkey 1994–5.
73. Levinas 1969, p. 111.
74. *TSMR,* p. 167 [*OE,* p. 1117].
75. Levinas 1989, p. 82.
76. See *CE,* p. 97.
77. Remember that 'chaos' here refers to a material form of order rather than pure randomness.
78. *TSMR,* p. 127 [*OE,* p. 1082].
79. See *CE,* pp. 265–6, 124 [*OE,* pp. 708–9, 595].
80. *CE,* p. 135 [*OE,* p. 604]; *CE,* p. 53 [*OE,* pp. 537–8]; *CE,* p. 268 [*OE,* p. 711]; *CE,* pp. 135–7, 142 [*OE,* pp. 604–5, 610].
81. *CE,* p. 106 [*OE,* p. 580].
82. *CE,* pp. 140, 275 [*OE,* pp. 608, 716]. Most probably, this same conflict has relevance for concrete biological reproduction, the relativity of terms like individual, identity, dependency, integrity, part, whole and containment bearing the brunt of much controversy in moral debates over abortion, for instance. Doubtless, these words could be read as cognates of either liberty or equality.
83. *TSMR,* p. 63 [*OE,* p. 1028].
84. *CM,* p. 138 [*OE,* p. 1374]. Bergson is fond of using this quote from Victor Hugo's *Marion Delorme* ('*pour rien, pour le plaisir*'); see also *L,* p. 106 [*OE,* p. 437]. At *ME,* p. 31 [*OE,* p. 833] nature too 'seems to create lovingly, for nothing, for the mere pleasure of it . . '.
85. *M,* p. 1550; *CM,* p. 305n20 (hardback edition) [*OE,* pp. 1392–3n]; *M,* p. 978; *CM* p. 38 [*OE,* p. 1279]; *CM,* p. 126 [*OE,* p. 1362]. Bergson does not hold, therefore, with the distinction between applied and pure knowledge: 'Science may be speculative in form . . . [but] it is always . . . practical utility that science has in view. Even when it launches into theory, it is bound to adapt its behaviour to the general form of practice'. (*CE,* p. 348 [*OE,* p. 773]).
    Of course, in contrast to this egalitarian environmentalist ethic, both *CE* and *TSMR* claim that humanity may possibly embody the reason for the existence of all living things (see *TSMR,* p. 257 [*OE,* p. 1194]; *CE,* pp. 281, 195 [*OE,* pp. 721, 652]). This extreme humanism would certainly seem to place humanity above and outside the rest of nature. But Bergson admits that considering humanity the reason for the rest of life is just 'a manner of speaking'. In reality, there is 'only a current of existence and the opposing current; thence proceeds the whole evolution of life' (*CE,* p. 195 [*OE,* p. 652]). He explains that *Homo sapiens* is more of a place-holder for a particular moral role than a hallowed essence. The successful line of evolution giving rise to *Homo sapiens* might have been pre-empted by other lines leading to equal success. Yet

none of these hypothetical species would inevitably be our ancestors (see *TSMR*, p. 273n [*OE*, p. 1207n]). There is simply a 'vague and formless being', which may be *Homo sapiens* or 'a being who morally must resemble him' (*CE*, p. 281 [*OE*, p. 721]). Saying that humanity can be the meaning of evolution indicates the ability of the form it takes to instantiate an ethical state: the type of movement epitomised by life, that of openness. In fact, *TSMR* amends one aspect of the humanism in *CE* when it ackowledges that humanity, as a species, is but one more cul-de-sac in life's evolution. As a species, we can no longer evolve. But as individuals, it is said that the mystics' movement of openness allows the *élan* to flow forward again: the movement is no longer explained by a so-called terminus in humanity *per se*.

6

Ontology

Yes and *no* are sterile in philosophy. What is interesting... is *in what measure?*[1]

FROM NOTHINGNESS TO CONTRA-DICTION

Bergson's renowned critique of the idea of nothingness first appears in the final chapter of *CE*. The motivations behind it go back to his reading of the Ancients. Bergson explains how change was then regarded as a secondary phenomenon no less than mechanistic philosophy today sees it as a reducible 'higher-level property'. The Ancient strategy in achieving its reduction was to explain the emergence of change as a product of the addition of nothingness to what is essentially an immutable reality: 'In that consists the Platonic "non-being", the Aristotelian "matter"– a metaphysical zero which, joined to the Idea, like the arithmetical zero to unity, multiplies it in space and time'.[2] Change or creation emerges as a mere multiplication or repetition '*ex nihilo*'. The concept of nothingness, therefore, sustains the ontological priority of unchanging reality, and with that, reductionist thought from Ancient Greece to the modern era. Hence, the need for a critique of this concept as it has been employed by traditional philosophy: creation *ex nihilo* is precisely the image of creation Bergson will resist in favour of creation *de novo*.

His argument pursues a clear objective: that of exposing the confusion latent within the ontological question of why being rather than nothing exists.[3] The confusion is similar to that which posits the antecedent reality of possibility, for it will only appear as a question if one posits nothingness first and being second (just as one might erroneously think that a possibility pre-exists the real action that retrospectively creates it). But nothingness is not only secondary to being; be it imagined or conceived, it is also secondary to the act of negation (which Bergson calls 'suppression'): the former derives from the latter.

Moreover, at the heart of negation itself there is something else again: the emotions of desire and regret. The startling notion that there might have been or could be nothing rather than something pertains to no more than 'what we are seeking, we desire, expect'. Our desires lag behind reality and are only interested in what might have been. What should be an acceptance of what is, becomes instead a desire that this reality be something else: 'suppression thus means substitution'. But metaphysics falls into absurdity when it attempts to universalise nothingness as the idea that there might not have been anything at all. If negation is substitution, then a negation of everything would be a complete substitution, but for what? There is nothing left to substitute for being. The idea has all the 'emptiness of its dissatisfaction' rather than the 'fullness of things'.[4]

R. M. Gale's masterly treatment of Bergson's critique points up two interesting facts. The first is that Bergson holds to a redundancy theory of existence, in which case, any attempt to represent nothingness will necessarily represent an existent and thereby fall flat on its face.[5] Gale believes, however, that the consequences of this thesis are also devastating for Bergson's main assertion that all nothingness is at base suppression. If nothingness is merely suppression, combining this with the redundancy thesis consequently leads to the conclusion that 'every negative existential judgement would turn out to be necessarily false' (a finding which Gale regards as 'absurd'). This is all the more interesting when one notes, as Gale states at the outset of his analysis, that the aim of Bergson's critique is not simply to deny the existence of the idea of absolute nothingness alone, but also to argue against 'partial' or 'relative' nothings or privations.[6] In Bergson's defence, however, if partial nothings are denied, then it is certainly not simply absurd but actually consistent that every negative existential judgement should be false.

But if one denies a denial, what is the status of one's own denial? There is something paradoxical about Bergson's critique of nothingness, for in denying its existence he is himself attributing nothingness to it. The concept of nothingness, say the critics, is one of those 'negative factors against which he directs nihilating arguments; yet negativity is, in his philosophy, *denied*'.[7] If this is the case, then surely Bergson would have been wiser to model his thought on the relativisation of relativity in *DS* and critique his own critique of nothingness. The idea of nothingness would not *not* exist, it would simply exist less. And absurd though this notion may also seem, its presence too has been observed already within Bergson's critique.

This brings us to Gale's second point, which is that Bergson appears to assume 'that *existence* is a vague term that admits of degrees, so that one thing can have more existence than another'.[8] Yet, what Gale sees as a vice – he adds that this is certainly not 'our' ordinary concept of existence – can also be seen as a virtue, provided that one realises that it is not a matter of a quantitative scale. There are no degrees of the one 'Being', for there is no one Being at all, simply different beings. As Frédéric Worms writes, Bergson has created a true '*metaphysics of degrees of reality*, on condition, however, that one specifies that it is not a question of the "same" reality, but of *different* realities'.[9] Bergson does not hold to an 'ontological difference' between beings and Being. He rejects the Platonist idea that 'Being was given once and for all, complete and perfect'.[10] Being is a developing, unfolding process: a multiplicity rather than a singular abstraction. Gilles Deleuze states Bergson's case emphatically: 'There are differences in being and yet nothing negative'.[11] Becoming does not require an immobile *nihil* to start from or an immobile Being to aim for: becoming, like movement, exists for itself.

So with the denial of negativity there comes almost axiomatically the affirmation of multiplicity and plurality, of *types* of reality. The differences of *durée* cannot be reduced to not being something else, they are their own foundation.[12] Though Bergson never desists from using the term 'being' in his work, he uses it in a non-oppositional sense. Various interpreters have commented on this pluralism, writing that Bergson's is a 'philosophy of *planes of reality*' and that 'a description of his metaphysics in terms of reality and appearance is certainly not a happy one'.[13] Bergson's thought, it is said, posits each reality as 'an irreducible "excess-being" that cannot be explained by mechanisms proper to the previous plateau'.[14] One illustration of this pluralism would be the vehicle of specifically cultural evolution in *TSMR*, for instance (the contagion of emotion), which need not be reduced to a physical substratum in the brain or genetic programming: it embodies the movement of evolution through its own specific cultural modes. The planes of memory in *MM* which constituted a non-quantitative scale of being with different levels of *durée* would be another, earlier version of this multiple reality.[15]

In conclusion, then, whenever (and if ever) we deny, we must not assert a non-existence but simply a lesser existence (though just what 'more or less' means here will be discussed later). All thought, even 'erroneous' thought, stands for something. 'Error itself', Bergson writes, 'is a source of truth': '*yes* and *no* are sterile in philosophy. What is interesting... is *in what measure?*'[16] The best interpretation can only be a question of fixing something's just place in the whole.[17] The objection to this that says that one can deny the content of another's belief without necessarily denying the belief itself as a belief, misses the point. The belief *is* the belief in the veracity of its content, and it is an acknowledgement of this veracity that is demanded. In the context of our broader analysis, the other's point of view, even if that other is an earlier version of oneself, is irreducible and undeniable; it exists and as such has a reality. The being of even our most ephemeral moments of belief and opinion cannot be denied, and any philosophy that recognises 'an effective action and a reality' to every level of *durée* has to realise this.[18]

AGAINST MISREPRESENTATION

The question for the advocate of absolute truth and falsehood, as a consequence, must be the origin of erroneous experience. Two thinkers with interesting ideas on this front are Fred Dretske and Jerry Fodor. Dretske has been immensely influential in popularising causal accounts of mental content which utilise the information processor model of the mind. The problem with these naturalistic accounts, however, is that they only rely on correlations between events: when there is a correlation, it can be said that one event transmits information to the other. The difficulty is that while correlations can be strong or weak, they can never instantiate a '*mis*-correlation'.[19] As Dretske puts it: 'natural signs . . . are powerless to *misrepresent* anything. Either they do their job right or they don't do it at all'.[20] So how do we explain the origin of misrepresentation?

A naturalistic account, of course, entails that any error in representation must not involve or be parasitic upon '*our* interpretative intentions and purposes'.[21] We need an explanation of what counts as the 'optimal' circumstances for a correlation – but the optimum specified must be natural, that is, ultimately physical.[22] It is easy enough to imagine an organism misrepresenting the absence of x (food, for instance) for its presence, but it is much harder to explain how one presence could be confused for another, that is, a genuine case of misrepresenting x as y.[23] To escape from this dilemma, Dretske proposes that only the more complex organisms possess such misrepresentational capabilities, ones with some form of 'associative learning' capacity.[24] In respect to his critique of nothingness, Bergson would agree: only an organism with memory, and so the ability to anticipate and regret, can negate its present.[25] However, the flaw in this solution is that, once memory is introduced into a materialistic explanation of misrepresentation, our suspicions will be raised that the consequent descriptions in terms of information processing and engrams will assume the presence of a homunculus in one form or the other.

Alternatively, Jerry Fodor speculates that an old ontological distinction could be invoked to separate truth from falsehood within a fully naturalistic scheme. It has often been remarked by philosophers that falsehood is dependent on truth: the first emergence of representation must have been veracious, that is, it had to work on the basis of *x* newly playing the role of *truly* meaning *y*. Infidelities are parasitic on fidelities. If a parallel for this ontological dependency could be discovered in the biological evolution of representation, then naturalistic mechanisms may be found that distinguish truth from falsehood and so explain the existence of misrepresentation.[26]

However, no matter what these mechanisms might be, one could still wonder, on ontological grounds, how such an offspring of errors as such could be engendered in a materialist's universe. Whereas it is obvious that perspectival errors concerning colour-facts can arise in a world of colours, or even that non-existent objects like unicorns and golden mountains can exist in a world where horses, horned beasts, gold deposits and mountains are all readily available, it is not so clear how an essentially objective, material and extended cosmos could ever give birth to such a radically different ontological category of existent as that of a subjective, immaterial and unextended perspective. Individual errors may be explicable in complex mechanical terms. But the vehicle or carrier of such errors, perspective as such, is of another class of entity altogether. How can there be perspective, that is, a blindness, within a cosmos of light at all? This emergent property seems to go too far beyond anything that ought to exist in a physicalist's universe. It would be easier to envisage the Kierkegaardian absurdity of an infinite being made simultaneously finite than this immaculate conception.

The crux of this 'error problem' facing materialist accounts of misrepresentation is even more fundamental: if materialism is true, then there is no obvious naturalistic basis for misrepresentation. But if the materialist were to accept that no such basis could be found, he or she would inevitably be led to either a relativist or a pluralist position. Yet then materialism, being a monistic philosophy, would be rendered false for the very fact that it is *ex hypothesi* exclusively true. Thus, when materialism is true it would also be false. Clearly, to avoid such paradox materialists must be desperate to discover a physical basis to legitimate the truth of the idea that non-materialists can be (and are) in error.

An alternative escape from this predicament that might salvage some degree of the materialist's position would involve reconfiguring our understanding of mind and world: both could be understood as processes, a view which would admit a pluralistic theory of truth. The belief in erroneous thought as a simple mistake of speculative mind is part of the belief in non-being. Erroneous thought is deemed to belong to non-being in that error is a non-correspondence with reality and a correspondence with nothing. The speculative or informational model of thought puts a gap between the mind and the world that allows one to confine to 'error', 'prejudice' or 'falsity' the philosophies at variance from one's own. But if the so-called 'content' of thought is itself a process that comes out of a world made of processes, is a part of the world (which contains no gaps or voids), then it is neither absolutely true nor false but simply there as one of the many types of worldly process.

THE ETHICS OF PERSPECTIVE

To bring this discussion back to our exploration of ethics, it is worth turning to the ideas of Thomas Nagel with respect to representation and subjectivity. As a major proponent of anti-reductionism, a recurrent theme of his work concerns the inherent tension between an objective description of the world and the fact that there can exist such irreducible things as '(a) oneself; (b) one's point of view; (c) the point of view of other selves, similar and dissimilar; and (d) the objects of various types of judgment that seem to emanate from these perspectives'. In *DS*, as we saw, Bergson also tackles what it is to be a subject of experience *per se* as well as the more characteristically Bergsonian theme of time. And it is interesting to note that Nagel himself also connects the problem of perspective with that of the reality of subjective time:

> The temporal order of events can be described from no point of view within the world, but their presence, pastness, or futurity cannot... The tenseless description of the temporal order is essentially incomplete, for it leaves out the passage of time'.[27]

Having so clearly advocated an A-theory of time like this, it is not surprising to find Richard Rorty linking Nagel's name with Bergson's as follows:

> For Bergsonians and other process philosophers, the sheer *whooshiness* of motion is simply ignored by modern science, just as for Nagel the sheer what-it-is-to-be-likeness of consciousness is ignored. In the end, Bergson thought, motion can only be understood from the first-person point of view – by actually whooshing about a bit, in order to remind oneself what it is like. Whereas Aristotle had contrasted natural and violent motion, Bergson made his point by contrasting absolute with relative motion... Bergson applies the same relative-absolute distinction to express Nagel's distinction between third- and first-person points of view.[28]

Given Bergson's current low standing in some quarters, as a reductionist Rorty is probably engaged here in a strategy of guilt by association against Nagel. A more serious critique of Nagel comes at the hands of Christopher Peacocke, however. It is not, he writes, that there is a distinct reality to subjective knowledge, but only that there are distinct '*ways of conceiving* of the world'. Admittedly, there are indexical and demonstrative forms of thought about the material world, but it nonetheless remains the same material world as when it is thought of in a non–indexical manner. Nagel's error is to move 'directly from forms of understanding to differences in reality ... from modes of description to the things described'. His position is an attempt to bridge this gap between description and reality, but he cannot succeed unless some state or object is presented that can only be thought of at a relatively subjective level and no other.[29] This he fails to do.

The weakness of this critique is its conflation of the question of perspectivism as presented in Nagel's *The View from Nowhere* with the arguments for subjective knowledge in his earlier essay, 'What is it Like to be a Bat?' The barrage of criticisms that followed the first essay turned mostly on whether *qualia* could provide us with privileged knowledge: can only the experience of red give us true knowledge of red, for instance? The response to Nagel's 'argument from knowledge' then claimed that the perspectival nature of these experiences only pertained to a certain practical knowledge involved, and not at all to any knowledge of a theoretical kind (this alone of the two being of importance for an objective description of the world).[30] The dispute boiled down to the question of whether or not *qualia* could be categorised as facts. It is true that Nagel's earlier essay does invite this treatment by continually referring to the 'facts of experience' or the 'existence of facts beyond the reach of human concepts'.[31] Yet there is a defence of Nagel that does not see his position as one concerning facts at all, but one of the ontological status of perspective.[32] *The View from Nowhere* is the clearer expression of this: the question no longer hinges on whether what is known to the subjective view is true or false (that is, on whether it is real knowledge), but on the very existence of this perspective right or wrong. The real issue may not be an affirmation of the absolute truth of subjective content so much as the fact that we have a point of view at all, an otherness which cannot be negated by the same.

The ethical nature of negation is even more striking when seen in the light of Bergson's discussion of its social and affective origins: negation 'is of a pedagogical and social nature', being to 'warn others or warn ourselves'. This corrective element may appear positive, but all the same, its desire remains to expel, 'an *exclusion* of this particular object'. Bergson also calls it an act of 'expulsion'. The echo of closed morality is audible here. For every group identity too an exclusion is required. Admittedly, where the affective source of closed morality lies in hatred, that of negation lies in the weaker sentiments of regret and desire. Still, the purpose of negation is to take account only of replacement, substitution and exclusion.[33] The contrast with the absolute affirmation of open morality is stark: instead of an immediate embrace of the universal, negation involves the absolute denial of whatever faces it. A part (the judgement of one point of view) pretends to be the whole by exclusion rather than by integration, that is, it makes a totalising judgement against the other.

We saw above how the affirmative spirit of openness is evident in Bergson's own pluralism: denial pure and simple is uninstructive, it is the proportionality of truth that should interest the philosopher. However, lest we fall into paradox, perhaps it should be conceded that the one error that may not be instructive at all is the one that denies the existence of something absolutely. To deny such an absolute negation is what Bergson called in an essay from 1911, a positive 'intuition', a 'no' that resists the power of dogma: the negation of negation becomes an affirmation.[34] Between openness and absolute denial, Bergson's non-quantitative scale of beings can be constituted. The uttered negation is a social act of ostracisation and, when absolutely condemnatory, must be absolutely condemned. But this is really only to reflect its own negativity back on to itself. Its negativity is self-referential.

THE PROBLEM OF RADICAL NOVELTY

Such a *laissez-faire* approach is not without its own perils, however. One consequence of it is whether or not we should simply accept uncritically the irreducibility of difference on which it rests in spite of an inherent weakness in this concept. The matter is best illustrated with Bergson's valued idea of novelty. Fundamental to his conception of time is its essential creativity: *durée* is described as 'the uninterrupted up-surge of novelty' and is continually evoked in terms of 'radical novelty', 'the radically new' or 'complete novelty'.[35] But in order for any novelty to be recognised as new, it must firstly be recognised as such, there must be something familiar about it. 'Absolute novelty' seems like a contradiction in terms: it has nothing with which to contrast or stand out as new. This is exactly what one critic has highlighted in saying that Bergson does not give sufficient stress to the 'recognition of Form and structure' in his theory of *durée*.[36] In other words, novelty appears to be in need of some form of generality or continuity. Indeed, that our memories of early childhood are often so sparse and incoherent has been explained in terms of the paucity of 'general knowledge schemas' with which young children can interpret, organise and stabilise their early autobiographical memories.[37] It would be ironic if memory, one of the prominent features of the depiction of *durée* in *MM*, should prove in need of exactly that degree of generality that would negate *durée*'s purported radical novelty. In fact, such radical novelty would actually negate the possibility of memory.

The same problem affects cognate notions such as 'pure heterogeneity' in *TFW*.[38] But, in his defence, does not Bergson equally call *durée* a 'heterogeneous continuity' and with that also introduce precisely the degree of structured generality required by a sustainable concept of novelty? Alas, this apparent concession to criticism has alienated as many critics as it has placated. A large body of commentary has attacked Bergson for placing too much emphasis on continuity in his depiction of time![39] A good deal of Gaston Bachelard's early career, for instance, was preoccupied with anti-Bergsonian works denouncing the lack of any discontinuity within *durée*. For Bachelard, time is essentially imbued with various 'rhythms' and 'lacunae'.[40] What Bachelard sees as Bergson's 'intuition of global homogeneity' would be less a living reality than a morose, torpid non-existence.[41] But isn't Bachelard here confusing continuity with homogeneity? Surely, he has now lost sight of the place for heterogeneity and novelty in Bergson's *durée*? Bergson never simply asserts a continuity *simpliciter* but always a mutable continuity of some sort: 'A *moving continuity* is given to us, in which everything changes and yet remains the same'. Likewise, *TFW*'s early analysis of a being's psychological *durée* denoted it as 'ever the same and ever changing'.[42]

A related problem has been the issue of what type of structure *durée* really has, if any at all. As early as 1922, the critic Karen Stephen argued that not only is there no 'now' in *durée*, there are no real divisions of time whatsoever, be they days, weeks or years.[43] *Durée* on this view is absolutely indivisible, a continuous flow of interpenetrating shades of time. But others such as Milič Čapek depict Bergson's view of reality as one which 'grows by concrete drops of novelty; hence the *pulsational* character of time'.[44] This view is sometimes called a 'pulsational' but more often an 'epochal' theory of time. Epochal theorists point to the evidence of internal difference or novelty in time where non-epochal interpretations emphasise its continuity. Whoever is right, the stakes are very large for Bergson either way. The integrity of novelty is essential to his work, not only as a defining metaphysical characteristic of *durée* but also in his empirical critiques of quantitative intensive magnitudes in psychophysics and gradualism in evolutionary biology: novelty underpins both the *qualia* of experience and the speciation of life. Yet, it is no less essential that this novelty should not bury continuity either: *MM*'s theory of memory consists of a infinite set of planes wherein our lives are repeated differently: each plane is different from the other, yet each is a repetition of the other too.[45] In like manner, the sources of life and morality are supposed to embody an accommodation between the forces of creative novelty and integrative continuity. Ann Game has described *durée* as 'a conception of difference in repetition', but how these two can be reconciled remains to be seen.[46]

The issue dividing these sets of critics boils down to their need to know exactly what is the defining characteristic of *durée*: is it continuity or heterogeneity? The two concepts do not seem to hang well together; the slogan 'ever the same and ever changing' is as epigrammatic as it is immediately incomprehensible. But perhaps the problem lies mostly with the critical desire to pin down the nature of *durée*. Returning to our initial problem of radical novelty, Gilles Deleuze's work has long pursued the goal of establishing a cogent philosophy of pure difference. In his attempt, Deleuze introduces a number of commentaries on Bergson that show a strong kinship between difference and novelty in terms of both their common features and shared problematic. Indeed, Deleuze paints Bergson as an early philosopher of '*différence*':

> Duration is always the location and the environment of differences in kind; it is even their totality and multiplicity. There are no differences in kind except in duration – while space is nothing other than the location, the environment, the totality of differences in degree.[47]

What Deleuze writes about Bergson here is no distortion. In *TFW* homogeneous space is indeed described as 'a principle of differentiation other than that of qualitative differentiation',[48] and the similarity between the two philosophers has led many writers to describe Deleuze as the 'disciple of Bergson' or as the 'embattled heir' who embodies a 'New Bergsonism'.[49]

Like Bergson, and also like Levinas, Deleuze sees the failing of philosophy in its prioritisation of the same over the different, a weakness which he traces back to Plato. The whole economy of self-identical Forms and derivative copies is symptomatic of a philosophy of the same that has relegated most subsequent thinking about difference to a secondary position. A counter-philosophy of difference endeavours to 'reverse Platonism' by showing how pure difference acts as the 'groundless ground' on which sameness rests. Difference is the new absolute. The same, however, or, as it is also called, 'repetition', is not unreal: productive repetition – as opposed to a bare, material or unproductive repetition – has genuine being because it is a species of becoming. Nevertheless, the being of all repetition ultimately depends on the priority of pure difference. This assertion of dif-

ference over repetition echoes Levinas' prioritisation of (ethical) relationship over the beings related in his own attack on the philosophy of the
same. In each case, the primacy of relationship or difference entails a
demotion of the identical or repetitious. When looking at Bergson and
Levinas earlier we stepped back from taking Bergson in this direction, but,
perhaps, utilising a strategy we can borrow from Deleuze, giving such pre-
eminence to novelty over continuity may allow us to fashion a reconciliation between these two concepts in the only way possible: by giving
novelty the upper hand. This would also fit with Bergson's pluralist position in ontology in defence of which, we recall, we heard Deleuze endorse
Bergson's critique of nothingness: 'There are differences in being and yet
nothing negative'.[50] Like difference, novelty is non-oppositional: neither
requires an immutable self-same continuity to oppose as they both exist for
themselves.

To start with, such an inversion aids in removing the need to think of
novelty in terms of absolute creation *ex nihilo*. Traditionally, the choice for
a philosophy of creative change has been between either that or falling
back into thinking of the new as a rearrangement of the old, that is, of
pre-existing entities. Novelty is simply a new combination of the elements,
a shuffle of the cards, a quantitative event. Of course, this is precisely how
the intellect operates, according to Bergson. Its natural function is 'to bind
like to like' as it can only understand the new as a variant of the old: the
new must somehow be contained in the old.[51] Hence the mysterious quality of the phenomena of emergence which have made such an impact in
the sciences of complexity. In certain schools of biology today, emergence
is regarded as the rule rather than the exception.[52] Concepts such as self-
organisation, feedback, autocatalysis and non-linear change facilitate the
emergence of real novelty: where sexual reproduction, for instance, was
understood on the older model of the selfish gene as essentially replication,
with novelty just an accidental error in self-copying, in the new thinking
it is seen as a genuinely creative event.[53] Niles Eldridge sees reproduction
as a 'more making': organisms make more of themselves rather than simply
replicate.[54] Similarly, animal behaviour too is regarded as an emergent
order that is not imposed by programming but generated through powers
internal to collections of organisms.[55] These developments are part of a
holistic approach to nature that need no longer rest more on impressionis-
tic language than 'hard' evidence: the data from computer models, field
research and laboratory experiments bear out a picture of laminated reality,
with not one level wholly explaining the next. Attention is focused, not
on the fine details of isolated small-scale systems as is the tendency for
reductionists, but on phenomena at every level – micro, macro and cosmic

– with a view to discovering 'large-scale patterns, rules, meta-rules'.[56] So the picture now appearing is of a material reality comprising a plurality of independent levels of behaviour. Presaging these ideas, Roger Sperry writes:

> Although the causal forces at the lower quantal, atomic, molecular levels in the infrastructure continue to operate in full force as usual, they are enveloped, encompassed, overwhelmed, superseded, super-vened, and outclassed by the new causal properties that emerge in the whole.[57]

Bergson in his day characterised the enduring mind as the 'faculty of drawing from itself more than it contains'.[58] The ability to create a new thought, new emotion or new way of perceiving cannot be reduced to the one and the same physical substratum each time and *in toto*. In the following quotation, Bergson enunciates this principle by opposing a philosophy of emergence to the monolithic Kantian and scientific worldview prevalent when he was writing:

> If there is *one* science of nature (and Kant seems to have no doubt of it), if all phenomena and all objects are spread on one and the same plane, so as to produce a unique, continuous experience that is entirely on the surface (and such is the constant hypothesis of the *Critique of Pure Reason*), then there is only one type of causality in the world, all phenomenal causality implies rigorous determination and it is necessary to search for freedom outside of experience. But if there is not *one* science but several *sciences* of nature, if there is not *one* scientific determinism but several scientific *determinisms* of unequal rigor, then it is necessary to distinguish between different *planes of experience*; experience is no more simply on the surface, it also extends into the depths . . . .[59]

Classically, to conceive the new or emergent one had to make recourse to the image of nothingness – otherwise change is simply rearrangement. But we have seen Bergson remove that option for both him and those materialists who would wish to explain the emergence of higher-level properties from lower-level realities. To think instead of creation *de novo*, 'from the new', signifies the irreducibility of novelty, the reality of emergence as an aspect of nature. Though the two paradigms of the rearranged and emergence *de novo* may seem to converge at the level of everyday appearances – where the motto 'nothing new under the sun' would hold – the difference between them remains essential: the first sees the mundane as the basis on which all more extreme instances of change should be understood.

All novelty can ultimately be traced to pre-existing entities. By contrast, the Bergsonian paradigm, like Deleuze's groundless ground of pure differ-ence, sees the new as an autonomous realm *down from which* we should think of the lesser surprises of our normal day-to-day existence. In other words, a greater novelty is not a creation modelled upon or formed through the association of smaller novelties; rather, lesser moments of upheaval are formed through the dissociation of a more general source of transformation: '*change has no need of support*', Bergson proclaims, it emerges *de novo*.[60]

Finally, such a shift in thinking about novelty also puts paid to one of the oldest arguments used against process philosophy. It is the problem of how any process can be sustained as a process without some element of substance: what is it a process of? In the end, it is claimed, some notion of substance must be retained to support a process for, otherwise, we could not identify one process from another with each merging into a monoto-nous undifferentiated unity. The answer now, as it always was for Bergson, is that substance has never been sacrificed but simply reconfigured: the meaning of substance is what is always open to interpretation, and for Bergson a substance is a complexity of change. In other words, processes are processes of other processes, all the way down. Nicholas Rescher puts the case for this view succinctly:

> How can a process preserve its own self–identity in the face of altera-tion – how it can [*sic*] be one particular item and yet change? The answer lies in a single factor: internal complexity. A process does not change as such – as the particular overall process at issue – but any such process can incorporate change through its unifying amalgama-tion of stages or phases (which may themselves be processes).[61]

Bergson's favourite example of pure change is the melody: 'When we lis-ten to a melody we have the purest impression of succession we could possibly have'.[62] But this is not to say that everything must change like a melody or not change at all, as some seem to think. A. R. Lacey, for instance, insists that many phenomena do not have the temporal character-istics of a melody.[63] And, of course, it is clear that objects like buildings and cricket balls do not alter in the same way as a melody, but this does not obviate the fact that they can still be regarded as a condensation of many different changes that could be illuminated by an attentive percep-tion. The truth is, however, that direct perceptual interaction with the mutable character of all the processes surrounding an organism would be both useless and possibly dangerous for it. We need to immobilise in order to survive. But just because our mundane powers of perception are normally closed to what is ongoing in our environment, it does not follow that there is nothing there.

DIFFERENCE OVER REPETITION?

Deleuze, like Bergson, fleshes out his own ontology of difference through a series of analyses in the mathematical and empirical sciences that add weight to this autonomy of pure difference. This is what makes Deleuze's version of a philosophy of difference unique, for he seeks the principle of difference not just in language and signs, but even more so in applied mathematics (the differentiation of calculus), biology (epigenetic 'differenciation') and physics (differential energy, potential and temperature). However, as a metaphysical move, the enthronement as such of difference is non-verifiable: it boils down to a choice between two options that Deleuze pictures as follows:

> Let us consider the two formulas: 'only that which resembles differs' and 'only differences can resemble each other'. These are two distinct readings of the world: one invites us to think difference from the standpoint of a previous similitude or identity; whereas the other invites us to think similitude and even identity as the product of a deep disparity.[64]

Deleuze opts for the 'deep disparity': pure difference is the groundless ground that sustains notions of the same, the similar, identity, and repetition: 'Resemblance subsists, but it is produced as the external effect'.[65] Placing this dual option before Bergsonism and choosing in a similar manner, one could write that novelty or heterogeneity is the ground on which continuity is built and subsequently try to justify this preference (as it cannot be verified) through the added weight of empirical evidence as we began to do in the last section. Indeed, we have seen Bergson write that immobility itself is the effect of a complex interaction between mobilities (as the impression of motionlessness is derived from two trains in motion at the same velocity and in the same direction). In a similar vein, stability is deemed a 'complexity of change'.[66]

The problem, however, is that immobility in Bergson's philosophy is not analogous to the role given to repetition or the same in Deleuze's. Its place within Bergson's system is higher than that of productive repetition, but not because it is not derivative; rather it is because *both* pure mobility and immobility are derivatives for Bergson: 'Radical instability and absolute immutability are therefore mere abstract views taken from outside of the continuity of change'.[67] In one respect, the opposition Deleuze constructs between the two slogans that only different things can be the same and only similar things can be different is comparable to the opposition between Heraclitus and Parmenides: either everything is really in flux or nothing is. But Bergson would rather have neither hold the transcendental ground. He clearly renounces the label of Heraclitanism that has so often been attached to his philosophy.[68] This may sound astonishing coming from someone purporting to be a process philosopher, but it is actually consistent with a 'full-process' theory, so to speak, which can never allow itself the title of an eternal truth. Both mobility and immobility are derivative, or, if you prefer, neither is: the issue of transcendence, of which principle gains eternal pre-eminence, is problematised in a full-blown philosophy of change where even the content of that philosophy can be in motion. As he relativises relativity, so too Bergson's philosophy of change cannot allow itself to stand outside of the flux to gaze in detachment at the immutable verities.

THE CIRCLE OF QUALITY AND QUANTITY

We are now on the brink of moving from ontology into the paradoxes of metaphilosophy, for it is certainly paradoxical to say that process philosophy, if true, must render its own status as true unfounded. Examining these issues in our final chapters will bring us into territory dealing with the expression of Bergson's philosophy, its understanding of truth, and its attitude towards philosophy as such. For now, let us return to the dispute between the two ideas that only differences are similar or only resemblances can differ. Where Deleuze opts for one pole or phase of this closed circuit, Bergson moves instead between the poles, between difference and repetition. In that he refrains from prioritising pure difference, it should not be thought, though, that Bergson could ever allow pure repetition the upper hand as a result. The primacy of such a bare repetition is, in fact, an axiom of reductive materialism and the ontological basis for favouring dissociative thought over associative thought that we discussed in Chapter Two. But for Bergson, both repetition and difference have equal status, which is why he could never say either that materialism is absolutely true or that it is absolutely false (at least as a process of materialisation).

The picture of a resistance on Bergson's part to tethering his philosophy to the pre-eminence of any one principle is revealed in the complex relations between quality and quantity in his writing. Qualitative change is read by Deleuze as pure difference while quantitative change is interpreted as repetition. There is no need to mention how fundamental this opposition is in Bergson's thought, for it recurs again and again in both his negative critiques and his own positive philosophy.

Now, a first reading of Bergson could give the impression that qualitative change is indeed dominant, with quantity itself being described as actually revealing a 'nascent quality'.[69] Below repetition, difference. This is certainly the theme of the phenomenological orientation in *TFW* that argued that 'it is through the quality of quantity that we form the idea of a quantity without quality'.[70] But even by the time we get to *MM* the relation between the two seems less straightforward, perceived qualities being analysed now as condensations of 'repetitions and changes'.[71] Suddenly, in Bergson's later work it is quantity which seems to subtend quality, with degrees in difference having the ability to generate a difference in kind: 'From the fact that we pass from one thing to another by degrees it does not follow that the two things are of the same nature'.[72] Indeed, part of Bergson's main objection to reductionism is its assumption that the failure to establish a qualitative difference between two phenomena can license the disregard of all quantitative difference, no matter what its degree between them. Sometimes a difference in degree can be so immense that it creates a difference in nature.[73]

Yet, Bergson still believes that there remains an irreducible difference between quality and quantity despite these relations of production between them.[74] If we look more closely, though, we will see that the two constitute a paradoxical pair when we consider what differentiates them from each other. After all, what is it that differentiates qualitative difference from quantitative difference? It may well be impossible to answer or even ask such a question, that is, to state what type of difference, of degree or in kind, differentiates the set of all differences in kind from the set of all differences of degree (short of saying that one or the other does not exist – a reductive strategy that simply denies the question's intelligibility). This is a type of Russellian paradox. To attempt an answer would be to cite a difference that must fall into one of the two sets rather than a third which separates them. Any form of difference that exists belongs to one or the other of the two.

In what we take as his answer to this paradox, Bergson looks to the notion of 'qualitative multiplicity'. We should not let the first word in this term tempt us into opposing it to a simple quantitative multiplicity as happens in *TFW*. This phrase is employed by Bergson from *TFW* onwards, but it only comes in for closer scrutiny in *CE* and *CM*. In Bergson's later work, it takes on the mantle of both quantity and quality. *CE* characterises it as 'a unity that is multiple and a multiplicity that is one'.[75] Some solutions to a paradox only rephrase the puzzle in a less perspicuous language rather than really explaining it, and one might be forgiven for thinking that such is what Bergson is offering us here. But what qualitative multiplicity actually proposes is quite appropriate to the Russellian form of this paradox: it represents a higher-order difference which separates and subsumes quality and quantity, one which cannot be conceived in terms of either and yet which generates both. The quality of the multiple and the quantity of the one or same are mutually implicative, despite operating at different levels. Likewise, difference and repetition are not identical, but necessarily held in a relationship of reciprocal dependency. These are internal dichotomies rather than external dualisms of dominator and dominated.

In his later work, this inherently dualistic term, qualitative multiplicity, is present in a number of analyses. It acts as a principle of complimentarity facilitating an inescapably double-sided approach to reality. Physics, he finds, by treating matter as both 'wave and...corpuscle' – as a mobility and as an immobility, in other words – is itself rediscovering this duplicitous reality. That the mental and life sciences too can render consciousness and evolution either into the solid substances of molecular chemistry or into emergent, creative complexity (depending on the methodology used), is another aspect of this complimentarity. Furthermore, *durée* itself is described at this stage as a 'continuity which was neither unity nor multiplicity' but potentially both.[76] Yet it is in *CE* that we find the *élan* exemplifying best this Janus-faced principle, being a source which is 'neither pure unity nor pure multiplicity' but which generates both in its actualisation. Reproduction as such can be seen as a qualitative multiplicity in action, where something is both one and many.[77]

The later, ethical turn taken in this line of thinking is embodied in the figure of the mystic. Open morality is said to work best as the 'multiplicity and generality of its maxims merge more completely into man's unity and individuality'.[78] Qualitative multiplicity is embodied in the individual, the singular universal. Our last chapter tried to show how, going back again to the start of Bergson's thought, *durée* was always already ethical in import, a point which the work of Henri Gouhier has also tried to reveal from a religious perspective. The metaphysical description of *durée*, he writes, undoes the classical opposition of same and other in virtue of the fact that, 'because duration is memory, I am not other; because it is creation, I am not the same'.[79] Generality and novelty are subsumed in the conjoined ethical and metaphysical significance of time, a point we hope our investigation into the ethical basis of full-relativity brought out earlier.

LEVELS OF CLOSURE

In moving from the last chapter to this, we sought first to understand what Bergson meant by a creative emotion that was more metaphysical than moral in essence, for it seemed to be the key to all the other dichotomies in his work. We have looked at the ontological issues that arise from an ethics of open emotion, especially as they are crystallised in the pluralism of full-relativity and the problem of radical novelty. The problem of novelty led us to the question of Bergson's metaphilosophical abnegation of any eternal principles in his thought and so to the complex relationship between quality and quantity. An answer to our first question may now emerge in the manner in which quality is transformed into quantity and vice versa. The irreducibility between the two does not concern their own immutable status (which is clearly dispelled) but rather the irreducibility between the levels of reality in and through which they can be transformed from the one into the other. Once again, it is a question of vital action and metaphysical levels. The clue to this answer comes from a striking passage in the introduction to *CM* which begins by asserting that 'all the categories of perception...correspond, on the whole, to the choice of a certain *order of size* [*grandeur*] for condensation', and continues as follows:

> The world in which we live, the actions and reactions of its parts upon each other, is what it is by virtue of a certain choice in the scale of size, a choice which is itself determined by our power of acting. Nothing would prevent other worlds corresponding to another choice, from existing with it in the same place and the same time....[80]

This thought, of course, could be contrasted with how *TFW* focuses on the impossibility of any two things occupying the same place simultaneously in homogeneous space.[81] Just as we earlier saw Bergson multiply the present in different rhythms of *durée*, it now seems that our world is at least potentially multiple: any one world is the sum or level of existence we choose to condense or contain in an act of perception. Admittedly, Bergson has often said already that our perception is a condensation of the quantitative changes around us.[82] Hence, time is serialised, tiered or stratified in a set of nested *durées*, the temporality of each individual rhythm of past, present and future being a contraction of other such rhythms. But it is the footnote attached to the passage above which makes a truly remarkable admission. In it, Bergson suggests that by this act of containment, an indeterminate world is transformed in our gaze into a determinate one, and that this occurs in order that we can live:

> One might ask himself if it is not precisely to pour matter into this determinism...that our perception stops at a certain particular degree of condensation of elementary events. In a more general sense, the

activity of the living being leans upon and is measured by the necessity supporting things, by a condensation of their duration.[83]

In Chapter Five, we saw *MM*'s portrait of the duplicity of organic life in
its exploitation of others: in order to live, one must consume the living.
Now this seems to be confirmed at a more general level still, with each
plane of living reality having to treat other planes of existence as inert in
order to support their own vitality. This support is not just a matter of
survival mechanisms – nourishment – but a question of what gives life its
identity. The world of the living is thus one that must choose to en-close
and exclude at the most metaphysical level: what is called quantitative
'matter' is the most excluded. Its own level of indetermination, and so of
durée, and so also of quality, becomes the ultimate out-group 'lent upon' to
constitute the identity of the in-group we call 'life'.

But if this is a question of choice, it is not a wholly ethical issue all the
same, for that choice is itself 'determined by our power of acting' – the
two agencies are run together: which level of *durée* we exist at dictates our
power of action (metaphysics); that power determines our choice of condensation (ethics); that choice configures our perceived place in the scale
of *durées* (metaphysics). What seems like circularity is more probably a
deliberate con-fusion of ethics and metaphysics. Bergson believes that our
power of perception is elastic to a certain degree, but, at the level of the
species, our thresholds of perception represent our degree of closure to
other species and the enduring world. *CE* describes specific versions of this
containment as it operates at different levels.[84] Extensive movements, evolutionary movements, qualitative movements: each of them is condensed,
diminished or contained at some level, and yet each is also a partial condensation itself of other planes of existence. We are shown a tiered reality
with qualities subtending quantities themselves subtended by their respective elementary components, and so on all the way down, existences at
each level denuding the next lowest of what *durée* they have. Fundamentally, one's threshold of perception, type of condensation or place in the
scale of being is determined by a stand taken by 'life' so-called, over 'matter' so-called. Clearly a 'choice' cannot be determined but, if one regards a
species as a particular ongoing and, to some extent, dynamic accommodation between equality and liberty, openness and closure, or heterogeneity
and continuity, one can begin to see how choice and determination can be
fused together.

We must remember that Bergson rejects the priority both of ethics over
metaphysics and of metaphysics over ethics. Both are subsumed by creative
emotion:

Antecedent to the new morality, and also the new metaphysics, there is the emotion . . . neither has its metaphysics enforced moral practice, nor the moral practice induced a disposition to its metaphysics. Metaphysics and morality express here the self-same thing . . . .[85]

This chapter has only begun to unearth just what that expression might be beyond Bergson's simple reference to creative emotion. In doing so, however, we have been brought to the edge of what can be intelligibly expressed, to paradoxical concepts and to layers of apparent contradiction. Chapter Seven will take up this discussion on the plane of just what can be coherently asserted in Bergson's thought, his approach to language and his renowned concept of intuition. But, in doing this, it will not only investigate his methodology but continue the research into his dualism as well for, at a number of specific points in *TSMR*, Bergson also calls this creative emotion 'intuition'.[86] Indeed, such metaphilosophical matters will direct the course of our thinking through dualism from this point forwards.

NOTES

1. *M*, p. 477.
2. *CE*, p. 334 [*OE*, p. 762].
3. The *locus classicus* of Bergson's critique of nothingness is the fourth chapter of *CE*, pp. 288–314 [*OE*, pp. 726–47], though it is repeated in *CM* (pp. 96–8 [*OE*, pp. 1336–8]), where it is subsumed under the more fundamental critique of possibility. We will be examining it mostly in the terms set by the later presentation.
4. *CM*, pp. 97, 98 [*OE*, pp. 1337, 1338].
5. See *CE*, pp. 300–2 [*OE*, pp. 736–7].
6. Gale 1973–4, pp. 287, 272.
7. Gunter 1992, p. 240.
8. Gale 1973–4, p. 288n17. If there seems to be an inconsistency in making existence pertain in degrees while denying, *à la* Kant, that it is a predicate, it should be noted that even when making the point about redundancy, Bergson says that to assert P is to assign it 'a *certain* reality', not just existence *simpliciter* (*CE*, p. 300 [*OE*, p. 736], my italics).
9. Worms 1997a, p. 256.
10. *CM*, p. 104 [*OE*, p. 1344]. His critique of nothingness actually counters Being as well and consequently, as Jacques Maritain bemoaned, 'strikes a blow at all metaphysics' (or at least a certain type of metaphysics); see Maritain 1968, p. 316.
11. Deleuze 1988, p. 46.
12. Deleuze 1956, p. 96.
13. Jankélévitch 1959, p. 103; Herman 1980, p. 54.
14. Cariou 1990, p. 64.
15. See *MM*, p. 275 [*OE*, p. 342].
16. *M*, pp. 331, 477.
17. See Frank 1943, p. 193.
18. *CE*, p. 17 [*OE*, p. 508].
19. Fodor 1987, pp. 102–3.

20. Dretske 1990, p. 131.
21. Ibid. p. 135.
22. Fodor 1987, pp. 102–3.
23. Dretske 1990, p. 137. Though, in our opinion, even the first case could be inter-
    preted in terms of a seeing *as*.
24. Ibid. pp. 129, 141.
25. See *CE*, p. 298 [*OE*, p. 734].
26. Fodor 1987, pp. 107–8.
27. Nagel 1986, pp. 27, 57n1.
28. Rorty 1982, p. 182.
29. Peacocke 1989, pp. 68, 69.
30. See, for example, Churchland 1995, p. 199; Nemirow 1990; Lewis 1990, pp. 516–17.
31. Nagel 1979, pp. 172, 171.
32. See Tallis 1991, pp. 149–55; Searle 1992, pp. 116–18.
33. *CE*, pp. 304, 307, 301, 310 [*OE*, pp. 739, 741, 736, 743].
34. *CM*, pp. 109–10 [*OE*, pp. 347–8].
35. *CM*, pp. 18, 99, 35 [*OE*, pp. 1259, 1339, 1276]; *CE*, p. 173 [*OE*, p. 634].
36. Hausman 1975, p. 82.
37. See Cohen et al. 1986, p. 53.
38. *TFW*, p. 104 [*OE*, p. 70].
39. See Serres 1977, p. 134; Merleau-Ponty 1962, pp. 79n, 415; Blanché 1969, pp. 110–
    11.
40. See Bachelard 1963, pp. vii–ix, 1–30.
41. See ibid. p. 24. Soulez 1984, p. 204 points to the oddity of Bachelard contrasting his
    'rhythm-analysis' with the supposed continuity of Bergson's *durée* when in fact rhythm
    is so important to Bergson's understanding of *durée*. Bergson even cites Bachelard's
    work favourably on the quantum mechanical fusion of wave (continuity) with corpus-
    cule (discontinuity) at *CM*, p. 304n11 (hardback edition) [*OE*, p. 1313n4].
42. *MM*, p. 260 [*OE*, p. 333]; *TFW*, p. 101 [*OE*, p. 68].
43. Stephen 1922, p. 98.
44. Čapek 1987, p. 139.
45. *MM*, pp. 222–3 [*OE*, p. 309].
46. Game 1991, p. 94.
47. Deleuze 1988, p. 32; see also pp. 31, 38, 93.
48. *TFW*, p. 95 [*OE*, p. 64].
49. Descombes 1979, p. 26; Deleuze 1995, p. 184n3; Rose 1984, pp. 87–108.
50. Deleuze 1988, p. 46.
51. *CE*, p. 211 [*OE*, p. 665].
52. Cohen and Stewart 1994, p. 436.
53. Goodwin 1994, p. 163.
54. Eldridge 1995, pp. 180–1.
55. Goodwin 1994, p. 178.
56. Cohen and Stewart 1994, p. 391.
57. Sperry 1983, p. 117–18.
58. *ME*, p. 27 [*OE*, p. 831]; see also *M*, pp. 887, 1064.
59. *M*, pp. 493–4.
60. *CM*, p. 147 [*OE*, p. 1382].
61. Rescher 1996, p. 39.

62. *CM*, p. 149 [*OE*, p. 1384]; see also *CM*, p. 19 [*OE*, p. 1261]; *TFW*, pp. 100–1, 111 [*OE*, pp. 67–8, 74].
63. See Lacey 1989, p. 97.
64. Deleuze 1990b, p. 261; see also Deleuze 1994, p. 116 and Deleuze 1995, p. 156: Deleuze credits Claude Lévi-Strauss with the formulation of this dichotomy. Deleuze 1994, p. 76 phrases it as follows: '*Difference lies between two repetitions.* Is this not also to say, conversely, that repetition lies between two differences...?' Our point will be that it is indeed true that saying one is also saying the other so that priority can be given to neither.
65. Deleuze 1990b, p. 262.
66. *CM*, p. 88 [*OE*, p. 1328].
67. *CM*, p. 156 [*OE*, p. 1390].
68. See *CM*, p. 305n23 (hardback edition) [*OE*, p. 1420n].
69. *CM*, p. 191 [*OE*, pp. 1422–3]; see also *CE*, p. 223 [*OE*, p. 674].
70. *TFW*, p. 123 [*OE*, p. 82].
71. *MM*, p. 277 [*OE*, p. 343].
72. *CE*, pp. 74–5 [*OE*, p. 555].
73. See *TSMR*, p. 10 [*OE*, p. 982].
74. *MM*, p. 268 [*OE*, p. 338].
75. *CE*, p. 272 [*OE*, p. 714].
76. *CM*, pp. 72, 14 [*OE*, pp. 1313, 1256].
77. *CE*, pp. 275, 15 [*OE*, pp. 716, 506].
78. *TSMR*, p. 35 [*OE*, p. 1004].
79. Gouhier 1987, p. 59.
80. *CM*, pp. 59–60 [*OE*, p. 1301], translation altered.
81. See *TFW*, p. 88 [*OE*, p. 60].
82. See *CE*, p. 317 [*OE*, p. 749].
83. *CM*, p. 303n6 (hardback edition) [*OE*, p. 1301n].
84. See *CE*, pp. 320–1, 332 [*OE*, pp. 751–2, 761].
85. *TSMR*, p. 49 [*OE*, p. 1016].
86. *TSMR*, pp. 46, 64 [*OE*, pp. 1014, 1029].

7

Methodology

An idea, no matter how flexible we may have made it, will
never have the same flexibility as a thing.[1]

At the heart of this chapter lies a puzzle over the very status of Bergson as
a philosopher of time. The problem is this: according to everything Bergson seems to write about language, thought and philosophy itself, it is far
from evident how he, or anyone for that matter, could ever have been
able to write genuinely about time at all. This puzzle, which one commentator has dubbed the 'Bergson paradox', arises from the Bergsonian
dichotomy between homogeneous space and time.[2] Spatialisation is the
enemy of true time, or *durée*. Yet whenever we philosophise about time
we inevitably confuse this space with time – thinking and talking about
time distorts it: 'We cannot measure time, we cannot even talk about it,
without spatializing it'.[3] To philosophise about time we must resort to
thought and language, that is, we must utilise some form of representation,
and it is precisely this unavoidable requirement of philosophy, and indeed
of all conceptual endeavour, which undoes any true understanding of time
as a process of continuous novelty. *TFW* sets out his predicament well in
terms of psychology: 'I said that several conscious states are organized into
a whole, permeate one another ... but the very use of the word "several"
shows that I had already isolated these states, externalized them in relation
to one another ... '.[4]

   Of course, there would still remain a possible recourse to the metaphysical intuition of *durée*; but while this would allow us a means of 'grasping'
real time immediately, it seems that it could only do so 'over and above all
expression, translation or symbolic representation'.[5] An immediate grasp of
the temporal that is itself inexpressible would hardly seem to be a good
place to begin one's philosophy.

For Bergson, then, time is something which we simply 'cannot think', as he puts it. In Chapter One we noted his view that thought about time inevitably becomes 'lodged in concepts such as duration, qualitative or heterogeneous multiplicity, unconsciousness – even differentiation'. It is significant that all the concepts he lists are peculiar to the Bergsonian philosophy of time. Even *durée* itself is described as a notion that fits none of our 'categories of thought'.[6] Indeed, it could be said that irrespective of the specific language used, be it the B-theorist's vocabulary of 'before, simultaneous with, and after' or the A-theorist's vocabulary of 'past, present, and future', to some extent each will always homogenise time into a linear, contained and calculable entity. Even 'time' itself, *qua* concept, is a representation and as such a spatialisation.[7] But the abolition of time by representation is not simply the representation of a time abolished: representation is that abolition itself. With this representation, perceptions, novelty, alterity and difference are all entered into an indifferent and homogenising schematism. Differences become differences *of* some unchanging substance: of the world, of the present, of memory, of the past and so on. Representation kills time, or rather, 'time' kills the non-symbolic or non-conceptual intuition it is meant to express, for what would an unrepresented time be for any theory, save nothing that could be called a theory of time at all?

The reason for this pessimism, we know, rests with Bergson's view of conceptualisation itself and the tenet of his philosophy that 'our concepts have been formed on the model of solids'. Hence, it is apparently impossible to think about time in any authentic, that is, non-spatialising, fashion: 'To think an object, in the usual sense of the word "think", is to take one or several of these immobile views of its mobility. It is, in short, to ask oneself from time to time just what it is, in order to know what to do with it'. The intellect is simply 'not made to think *evolution* . . . that is to say, the continuity of a change that is pure mobility'. So where the philosophical origin of our distortion of time is found in Plato, this is not to say that such a corruption could have been avoided or might be subsequently overcome. The Greeks' dissociation of reality into sensuous change and eternal intellectual form, Bergson writes, is 'the natural metaphysic of the human intellect'.[8]

The dilemma, then, is quite simple: despite having questioned the possibility of both talking and theorising about temporality, Bergson, with a whole body of work devoted to the philosophy of time, has either kept something back from us on the subject of language and conceptuality or shown an extraordinary ability to live with the most intrusive of inconsistencies. The answer to the riddle will be a species of the former explanation, though it is not so much what Bergson has kept back on the topic of language as what we, his readers, have missed in his writing. The apparent inconsistency leading to the 'Bergson paradox' belies other realities: it is not that Bergson abandoned all hope for a language of time, for he actually left the way open for a language that might instantiate it.

One early reviewer of *CE* rounded on Bergson for trying to make thoughts not merely know but be the things for which they stand.[9] The same might also be said of Bergson's use of language. He wants it less to stand for a thing than to become the thing or, at least, to become some type of reality. This last qualification is central to any proper grasp of this area of Bergson's thought. Too often it has been understood that Bergson wants his concepts to be like 'real' objects, that the concept of 'mobility' is culpable for not moving, just as the concept of 'quadruped' must be chastised for not having four feet.[10] But this is to assume a certain understanding of what a 'real thing' must be and, as such, the criticism misses the whole point of a process philosophy such as Bergson's. His aim is not to have thought and language correspond to an immobile thing, but to recreate the movement of things and, by that, render them a part of process-reality. We must create new concepts, ones that are enlarged, more flexible and so fitted to the specificity of each individual movement. Such concepts would not be wholly non-iconic either, but would be a type of 'image' described as 'almost matter...and almost mind'.[11] If this is mimesis, then it is mimesis with a new meaning: language imitating reality by being real itself, this being achieved by giving language a certain *élan*, a movement of reality.[12] In fact, mimetic art itself does not aim, says Bergson, to reproduce either the 'abstract type' or conception of its model, or the 'materiality' of the model: it recreates the 'characteristic movement' that animates its lines. So when Bergson famously asks for a metaphysics that would *'dispense with symbols'*, it is really a question of what type of symbolism that is at stake.[13]

THE LANGUAGE OF PROCESS

It has been suggested that if Bergson is a neglected philosopher today 'It is because language plays a minor role in his conception of the world'.[14] It would be truer to say that, while language has little thematic import in his work and a certain type of concept and a certain type of word are without doubt treated with a vehemence, the work language does within his writing is still very large. Orthodox representative conceptuality and language are condemned by Bergson, but they are also replaced with a novel use of simile, comparison and metaphor. Bergson speaks of metaphysics working best not so much when it dispenses with concepts as when it 'frees itself of the inflexible and ready-made concepts and creates others very different from those we usually handle, I mean flexible, mobile, almost fluid representations'.[15] A metaphor, for example, is one such fluid concept with boundaries as yet unfixed. In itself, it imitates a style of nature and its ongoing dynamism.[16] Without falling into the trap of seeing metaphor as some sort of 'peephole on the nature of transcendental reality', Bergson nonetheless exhorts us to 'use metaphors seriously'.[17] Literally, or rather, statically speaking, life is not the 'immense wave' that some passages of *CE* imply; but the process or specific movement an immense wave typifies may suggest what life is to us.[18] In mimicking the processes of reality, the metaphorical imagery Bergson employs can be partly real itself, because every reality is a type of process or style of movement. As Gilles Deleuze would say, metaphor equals metamorphosis.[19]

We noted above that art does not imitate either an abstract idea of its object or its materiality, but rather the movement animating its lines: this point is vital. What, otherwise, would the replication of one movement in another be if not simply the creation of another just like it, or in other words, repetition? Likewise, if we abstract what, say, life and waves have in common in their movement, surely we are only picturing an impoverished perception of both? What Bergson presents is an understanding of movements which are individuated by their embodiment in certain actualisations but which are nonetheless resonant on account of what is supra-individual about them without simply being abstract. A specific movement pre-exists both the wave and life as objects. What is 'imitable' is not formed associatively by abstraction or bare material repetition: it is the imitable which forms what imitates it in a dissociative action – the virtual capacity underpins the actual performance rather than being derived from it. For instance, we saw in Chapter Five that one of the movements of life is centrifugal and that one of those in morality is also centrifugal. This is not to say that life imitates morality or that morality imitates life: instead, both instantiate and imitate a movement which is beyond biology and morality but nevertheless actualisable in either form.

The fluid imagery Bergson uses to describe *durée* may appear metaphorical to some, yet it is, he says, the only precise manner in which we can express it.[20] It is precise in virtue of the fact that it instantiates something of what it is trying to express. Though the difference may only be a matter of degree between orthodox conceptuality and the alternative espoused by Bergson, it is in view of the former's supposedly rigid representational quality that Bergson condemns it outright. If the concept is to be a fixed picture of reality, then Bergson wants no part of it. The inflexibility of the ready-made concept carries within it a 'practical question' which can only be answered by reality with a yes or a no.[21] All that can follow is never-ending dialectic and the various oppositions of philosophy: phenomenon and noumenon, substance and accident, being and appearance.[22] But the bivalency of the answer is merely the necessary response to the narrowness of the question: what is missed entirely between the two is the polyvalency of a reality that does not allow for such rigid antitheses. The static representational concept requires a separation between knower and known. A different type of knowledge, on the other hand, may 'coincide with the generative action of reality', as Bergson asserts.[23] But 'coincide' here does not mean 'correspond'. The relationship is one of membership, of belonging to the same process-reality, not one of representation between rigid concept and fixed referent.

And yet this picture is not wholly faithful to Bergson's thinking either. It is only the bivalent realism found in certain forms of imperious representationalism that worries him. In one sense, Bergson is really against metaphor altogether. The so-called 'clear and distinct' concepts of scientific realism (read 'materialism') and the vague and indistinct concepts of *durée* are both literally true when applied in their own categories and only metaphorical when placed in the wrong category. Hence, it is no less figurative to speak of consciousness as a mechanical process than it is to think of matter as a form or symbol of spirit. Both materialism and idealism are equally wrong because they are equally totalising in their attempt to subsume all reality under one all-encompassing explanation. From this perspective, Bergson is thoroughly classical, retaining a realist view of truth as correspondence. His originality lies in advocating a different type of (mobile) reality and so a different type of concept to correspond-coincide with this reality.

Nevertheless, we should not lose sight of how far Bergson has extended language and conceptuality: if the language of process corresponds to process-reality that is because it also proceeds as a process-reality, rather than because it is a static image of it. Likewise, even though we have used the verb 'to express' in referring to Bergson's ameliorated view of language, all of the foregoing should lead us to an understanding of the term 'expression' far from its usual representationalist roots. As Jeanne Delhomme has argued, Bergsonian expression does not signify the representation of a hidden meaning so much as the relationship that a work of art can have with its artist. She explains the meaning of this expressionism for us thus:

> Expression is self-expression, not the expression of something hidden behind the self; exactly as music and painting are expressions of themselves and not of a psychological or ontological ulterior world; expres-

sion is its own movement, incarnation is its own progress. In the full rigour of the term, there is nothing to express, nothing to incarnate.[24]

In Bergson's work, artistic expression becomes a paradigm through which we can reform our understanding of what language can and cannot achieve. The imagery used in Bergson's writing is 'not an ornament' he says: it reveals a language of process that does not obfuscate its subject matter through spatialisation so much as instantiate it through its own temporality.[25]

THE IMPURITY OF PURITY

In the first chapter of *MM* it is claimed that there is never any 'image without an object' in perception, whilst in the introduction Bergson writes of each object as a 'self-existing image'.[26] It was not without some controversy that Bergson chose the word 'image' as his designation for every type of perception in *MM*, and a good deal of that controversy stems from the impression that each image is also a type of object: there is never an image that is not in some way objective.[27] It is here where we find an ontological basis for a conceptuality that can be a part of reality rather than solely an image of it. At the same time, Bergson's theory of the image gives us a thoroughgoing anti-representationalism opposing any exclusively cognitivist understanding of thought as well as a presentation of material reality in quasi-phenomenological terms.

That anti-representationalism, we saw, stems from a critique of the portrait of perception as a cognitive instrument which must either double, mimic or reproduce the world in an immaterial or informational manner. Bergson arrived at his view by examining both the evidence from evolution and the structural development of the nervous system. In doing so, he found that the nervous system is basically a facility for exchanging movement: it adds nothing to what it receives; its function is simply to allow a communication or to delay it. Perception is not a new emergent quality but rather, *de jure*, the product of an elimination: '*there is in matter something more than, but not something different from, that which is actually given*'.[28] In one of *MM*'s thought-experiments, Bergson attempts an exorcism of all that might make perception subjective in order to elaborate on its relationship with the world. He constructs a 'pure' perception that belongs neither to any subject nor to any body-subject, but instead to a mathematical point perfectly mirroring the universe.[29] The body literally becomes a point perspective. Along with the banishment of the body goes memory, as memory too, both bodily and intellectual, lends perception its usual subjective character. This ultra-objectivism will be an absorption in a timeless present wherein we are 'actually placed outside ourselves; we touch the reality of the object in an immediate intuition'.[30] This is the principled perception, discussed earlier, which operates at the object rather than in the brain.

Yet Bergson realises that even this anonymous perception will never achieve its desired objectivity in full. What is given in this pure perception as a 'presence' is still not the entirety of the object. The '*present* image' or 'objective reality' is never fully present, remaining always partially obscured. All that is given is what interests our body, even though it is a body without extension. Simply because it has to be located, perception cannot fail to be perspectival and as such, cause the suppression of those parts of the object hidden from its perspective. The images of objectivity may be fully present to each other, but they can only be known under pain of diminution or a certain condensation: 'Pure perception, in fact, however rapid we suppose it to be, occupies a certain depth of duration'.[31] This supposed 'view from nowhere' too is a contraction, a glimpse rather than a panopticon. Pure perception itself becomes a type of 'representation': indeed, it can never escape representation, for all perception entails the reduction of a presence. In this presence too, moreover,

> Representation is there, but always virtual – being neutralised, at the very moment when it might become actual, by the obligation to continue itself and to lose itself in something else. To obtain this conversion from the virtual to the actual, it would be necessary, not to throw more light on the object, but, on the contrary, to obscure some of its aspects, to diminish it by the greater part of itself, so that the remainder, instead of being encased in its surroundings as a *thing*, should detach itself from them as a *picture*.[32]

Yet this is not meant to signal the ascendancy of idealism: Bergson's respect for the natural sciences was too great for him to have ever implied that, and he states explicitly that 'an image may *be* without *being perceived*'.[33] The lesson emerging from Bergson's thought-experiment, therefore, does not cast doubt on whether the objective world actually exists but simply cautions us that it can never be fully given to any perspective, including the scientific one. The world is not a state to be known but a process to be a part of. This is simply one more facet of Bergson's critique of simultaneity. The world can only be experienced piecemeal through the succession of its various aspects, not all at once in a simultaneous vision. Gilles Deleuze puts it as follows:

The Whole is never 'given'... This is the constant theme of Bergsonism from the outset: The confusion of space and time, the assimilation of time into space, make us think that the whole is given, even if only in principle, even if only in the eyes of God.[34]

As far as our *knowledge* of the world is concerned, we cannot escape from representations: 'We are always more or less in idealism'.[35] But Bergson is still no idealist as regards ontology, the 'more or less', the desire to reach beyond to what a certain system of images might signify is essential. It defines the difference between solipsism and what we saw him elsewhere describe as *le bon sens* or full-relativity. Objectivity exists, but it is not as we might think it to be: it is less an entity than an aspiration, an attitude towards alterity. Objectivity can obviously be identified easily with a certain homogeneous physical reality. But as Bergson sees it, this is merely the cancelling out of perspectival differences 'where everything balances and compensates and neutralizes everything else': representation made the same, muted or virtual.[36] In fact, this is actually an ephemeral picture of the physical; a substratum that symbolises power, resistance and impenetrability alone: 'Humanity [is] generally accustomed, whatever it may say, to accept as existing only what it can see and touch!'[37] But there is another picture of the physical that would accommodate itself to the multiplicity of perspectives rather than expunging them. This would be an objective physical. Unlike the homogeneous, which can only belong to everyone on pain of self-impoverishment to the lowest common denominator, this physical would be given to no one as a reality but to everyone as a potential aspiration. The ethics of representation would here be reintegrated with its metaphysics.

METAPHYSICS AND INTUITION

Remoulding our use of language and concepts is only one half of Bergson's attempt to show how our notions of mind and reality can be reconnected: the other requirement is a new picture of reality itself. We have already examined this world in some detail in terms of the qualitative and mutable texture of the living body, biological evolution and physical time. But before moving to Bergson's method of engaging with this world philosophically through intuition, we must note how he reshapes the traditional understanding of the discipline that purports to address any reality directly, that is, metaphysics. Bergson's main goal in this conversion is to bring metaphysics down from the supersensuous heights where Plato deposited it: metaphysics becomes, in Bergson's hands, a remedial technique in perception, not a form of ethereal contemplation.

In his 1903 essay 'Introduction to Metaphysics', Bergson talks of the
object of perception as a 'metaphysical object'. He goes on as follows:

> A true empiricism is the one which purposes to keep as close to the
> original itself as possible, to probe more deeply into its life, and by a
> kind of spiritual *ascultation*, to feel its soul palpitate; and this true
> empiricism is the real metaphysics.[38]

He adds that this real metaphysics focusing on singularity would be as
equally distant from the 'transcendent speculations of certain German
Pantheists' as it would be from the 'so-called' empiricism of contemporary
figures like Hyppolyte Taine: as equally static and abstract depictions of
nature, the two are in fact far closer to each other than either might
think.[39] Milič Čapek has argued that Bergson practised a 'radical empiricism' before William James had even coined the term.[40] This radical
empiricism has two primary features, one negative and one positive. The
negative element is what distinguishes it from a false empiricism which
consists, Bergson claims, 'in seeking the original in the translation where it
naturally cannot be, and in denying the original on the plea that one does
not find it in the translation'.[41] Gilles Deleuze has echoed this criticism of
mundane empiricism as that which simply replicates the empirical as its
own condition of possibility: true or 'transcendental' empiricism, by contrast, is neither a dogma concerning the origin of knowledge nor a demar-
cation of all possible experience. Radical experience can neither be
'induced' nor 'traced' from the ordinary empirical forms of common sense,
it is rather the being of that which can only be sensed.[42] Similarly, Bergson
argues that true, metaphysical empiricism is not a fall into the passivity of
experience but an effort to create experience, to perceive what can *only* be
perceived rather than what is a mixture of abstraction and everyday experience: as such, 'metaphysics will then become experience itself'.[43] This
effort is its second, positive facet: radical empiricism is metaphysical to the
extent that it focuses on the individual specificity of its object – the singularity of the individual that can only be sensed rather than imagined. Metaphysics is not the contemplation of an alternative reality but the perception
of a heightened reality, a perception Bergson eventually calls 'intuition'.

Pinning down the meaning of this intuition requires a little detective
work into Bergson's thought. Intuition, like instinct, is described initially
as a sympathy that seems to imply some type of immediate consciousness;
yet, intuition is clearly distinguished from immediate knowledge, being
described elsewhere as a search requiring prodigious effort.[44] It can also be
'supra-intellectual' or 'ultra-intellectual' – Bergson might even have chosen
to name this faculty 'intelligence' instead of intuition.[45] By about the year

1911, though, there is a significant harmonisation in Bergson's writing, its broad import being that 'in order to reach intuition it is not necessary to transport ourselves outside the domain of the senses'. The 'superior intuition' that Kant thought necessary to ground any would-be metaphysics, Bergson (unlike Kant) does hold to exist. But it exists, he says, as the '*perception* of metaphysical reality'. It is only because Kant pictured this intuition as 'radically' different 'from consciousness as well as from the senses' that he dismissed its likelihood so quickly. Bergson not only accepts its reality, he bases it on the primacy of perception. Rather than attempt to 'rise above' perception as philosophers since Plato have wished, sensuous intuition must be 'promoted', he writes. He encourages us to 'plunge' and 'insert our will' into perception, 'deepening', 'widening' and 'expanding' it as we do. A higher intuition would not be a piling up of newer generalities but an illumination of 'the detail of the real' – a superior empiricism.[46]

Indeed, this plasticity of perception can explain the fact that intuition is so difficult to demarcate, that it is exactly what excludes, in the words of one commentator, '*the idea itself* of definition'.[47] Bergson believes that there is no 'simple and geometrical definition of intuition': a changing reality requires 'views of it that are multiple, complementary and not at all equivalent'.[48] Intuition entails whatever is required by a subject in a particular context to adjust to the full alterity of that situation as it extends beyond the confines of his or her perspective. This adjustment, however, is dynamic: it is an attempt to enter into the flux of *durée* rather than escape into eternity. Consequently, the demands on intuition will be as varied as the changing reality into which it enters us.

In terms of origins, the relationship between intuition and instinct is as complex as the one we discovered between life and matter. It is usual amongst interpreters to follow Bergson's most famous characterisation of intuition as an instinct 'that has become disinterested, self-conscious, capable of reflecting upon its object and of enlarging it indefinitely'.[49] These additional four features all stem from *CE*'s depiction of intellect so that it seems right to say that intuition represents a synthesis of all that is best in instinct and intellect: it has inherited instinct's attunement to life along with intellect's potential for continual evolution. This dual heritage allows it to avoid both the threat of closure through fixation on any one life-form and the emptiness of pure change or difference with no interest in the world at all. Instead, intuition has 'life in general' as its object, only not as a theoretical abstraction: it signifies a genuine openness to the universal: 'Detachment from each particular thing would become attachment to life in general'.[50] Here we have once more the ethical turn in Bergson's thought made explicit, this time in virtue of intuition revealed as a redemptive attention to life.

However, it can also appear to the reader that intuition is not the product of a synthesis between instinct and intellect but the remnant of a dissociation. We have already noted how Bergson equates creation itself with intuition read as an ethical emotion. *CE* adds to this picture, saying that 'intuition is mind itself, and, in a certain sense, life itself: the intellect has been cut out of it by a process resembling that which has generated matter'. Now it looks like intuition is a basic ingredient in a process rather than the result of one. But if intuition is the source of intellect so also must it lie at the origin of instinct, for both intellect and instinct are said to be cut from the one 'common origin'.[51] This duplicity of intuition, existing both at the source of intellect and instinct and at their prospective union is explicable, however, when one turns to Bergson's methodological use of intuition.

Sometimes the method of intuition can sound like some form of mind-expansion technique opening the doors of perception to altered states of consciousness and experience. If the metaphysics of *durée* is nothing less than 'experience itself', these new-age clichés may have some basis in Bergson's thesis of the plasticity of perception. But the technique involved is not psychopharmacological: intuition utilises the native resources of the mind alone in an attempt to change our place in reality rather than escape from it. Artistic perception is often invoked as a model. Art is not an act of imagination fancifully creating *ex nihilo*: it is rather a restoration of a world that our normally practical, narrowed and impoverishing perception has destroyed. It is a way of seeing.[52] The artist, likewise, is not qualitatively different from the non-artist: each of us can create *de novo* by altering our vision. Hence, intuition can act as a resource, the excavation of which can lead to new inventions, art forms, theories and emotions.

All the same, when Bergson does describe his more common intuitive method it is frequently in terms of psychology rather than aesthetics. In the 'Introduction to Metaphysics' it is described as a 'reversal' of the mind's normal direction of thought, so that we seem to be talking in terms of movements again.[53] We know that the natural bent of the mind is to work associatively and centripetally. Intuition could rightly be seen as reflection therefore: literally, 'to bend back' and so to turn back. This would be to think dissociatively, that is, in terms of the destruction of a unity rather than its creation. Another name for this way of thinking about intuition is 'qualitative integration', which Bergson describes as '*one of the objects of metaphysics*'.[54] This is no rationalist reconciliation of thesis and antithesis through teleological mediation.[55] It is an attempt to place oneself into the process that brought about a particular dichotomy, thought put into '*reverse*', or attention turned '*back*'.[56] Intuition here is a rethinking of dichotomy in terms of the mutual opposition of its elements. This rethinking cannot take place, however, on the level of associative and associating intellect, but only through intuiting original unities long dissociated. The method of intuition, then, recombines the virtues of instinct and intellect only by undoing the bifurcation that rendered them separate and opposed. It is as much an act of re-integration as of integration, coming both before and after instinct and intellect.

CE hinted at the effort intuition might involve by referring to philosophy as an act of violence on the mind.[57] Nonetheless, what this effort consists in – mental reorientation or perceptual awareness – remains ambiguous for reasons we gave above. Intuition is probably a mixture of both, Bergson refusing to compartmentalise the mind: a reversal of thought *is* an expansion of perception. As for its ethical aspect, *TSMR* compounds what is written about 'attention to life' in *CE* by bringing the ethical dimension of this effort further to light. As intellect proceeds 'in the opposite direction' to the one 'whence that [vital] impetus came', it is only by 'turning back' in intuition that an individual can follow the line of life and therewith 'give itself to society'.[58] We should also remember the relationship between intuition and negation: here its mode of reversal becomes a moral resistance, an expression of intellectual discontent in the face of absolutist dogma.[59]

THE ANTI-NOUMENON

Alongside integration, Bergson asserts that the other purpose of metaphysics is '*to operate differentiations*'.[60] In this respect, intuition can be looked on, in part, as a method of multiplication. Put at its simplest, this is something of a reversal of Ockham's principle, '*Entia non sunt multiplicanda praeter necessitatem*'. Instead of emphasising the fact that the best solution is often the simplest one, the Bergsonian rule states that false problems most often ensue whenever we simplify too much in the face of a true, though unpalatable, multiplication of entities. Of course, our intelligence 'loves simplicity': but, 'while our motto is *Exactly what is necessary*', Bergson claims that nature's motto is frequently '*More than is necessary* – too much of this, too much of that, too much of everything'.[61] Bergson's working hypothesis is one of disunity in the active sense of that term: a dis-uniting of the ego, of the present and even of being. To escape from a false problematic we must multiply the number of variables at work within it. Indeed, the problems of philosophy, in Bergson's view, most often stem from a set of confusions about which version of an entity one is discussing.

However, we would be wrong to view Bergson's alternative call for multiplicity as a gratuitous predilection for the baroque: the importation of wholly new entities in his method is not being endorsed. On the contrary, it is a sensitivity towards certain subtle differences pertaining to what is already within the ontological economy of the problematic which is at issue: 'variations on a theme', so to speak. Thus, we have all the famous dualities and pluralities at work in Bergson's thought: types of time (*durée* and spatialised); types of memory (virtual, habitual and representational); types of relativity (half and full); types of morality (open and closed); types of religion (static and dynamic); and even types of multiplicity itself (qualitative and quantitative).

This method of multiplication can also be read as a corrective against the presence of any absolutes in philosophy, that is, any principles that are either universal or eternal with no potential for mutation. One instance of this that we have already encountered is Bergson's critique of Kant's treatment of space and time. According to Bergson, Kant had to hoist any objective space and time out of the conceivable (and thereby existence, from the Kantian perspective) only because he thought that there was one type of space and time alone for our knowledge, one which is clearly dependent upon mind rather than vice versa. While allowing that there are different ways of knowing our own actions, through pure reason where they appear to be determined, and through practical reason where we infer their freedom, no similar multiplicity is predicated of space and time. Freedom is lucky enough to be hauled up out of pure reason into the noumenal realm.[62] But forms of space and time other than those conceived by pure reason, on the contrary (and there is only one form of each conceived by it), are removed to oblivion. As a result, any absolutes that might have been directly perceptible had to be conjured off to the noumenal. Kant's error was one of degree, having mistaken a plurality for a singularity.

In sharp contrast to this, the essence of the Bergsonian method is the attempt to expand our perception, to see something other than we do before reaching a verdict on whether a being can be known or not. Thus, before we pronounce in favour of the existence of nothingness, we must try to see another being than the one expected. Before pronouncing in favour of the existence of absolute chaos, we must try to see another order than the one desired. And before pronouncing in favour of the noumenal, we must try to perceive differently to the way we do and, with that, to see a different spatiality to the one we do. In each case, Bergson's anti-noumenalism utilises the method of intuition to enact a simultaneously perceptual, mental and ethical opening in order to dispel the image of any absolutes in philosophy. In the next and final chapter we shall look at this strategy working in his approach to philosophy itself and see how a type of metaphilosophical dualisation operates against all forms of absolutism in thought, both monistic and dualistic. In fact, the challenge of going beyond dualism will no longer pertain to a 'fundamental' understanding of Bergsonian physics, psychology or biology such as we have sought thus far, so much as his philosophical thought of duality *per se*.

NOTES

1. *CM*, p. 206 [*OE*, p. 1438].
2. Wagner 1983, p. 275.
3. *DS*, p. 150 [*M*, p. 205].
4. *TFW*, p. 122 [*OE*, p. 81].
5. *CM*, p. 162 [*OE*, p. 1396].
6. *CE*, p. 173 [*OE*, p. 634]; *CM*, p. 35 [*OE*, p. 1275]; *CM*, p. 14 [*OE*, pp. 1255–6].
7. See Giroux 1971, p. 21: 'Represented time (or the time of "reflective consciousness")...is really space'. See also *TFW*, pp. 90, 91 [*OE*, pp. 61, 62] for Giroux's reference to 'reflective consciousness'.
8. *CE*, p. ix [*OE*, p. 489]; *CM*, p. 183 [*OE*, p. 1415]; *CE*, pp. 171, 344 [*OE*, pp. 633, 770].
9. See Loveday 1908, p. 408.
10. See Maritain 1968, pp. 138–9, 162.
11. See *CM*, pp. 29, 45, 175, 118 [*OE*, pp. 1270, 1288, 1408, 1355].
12. See Jankélévitch 1959, p. 289; see also Santoro 1993 on mimesis as an imitation of style rather than substance.
13. See *CM*, pp. 230, 241, 162 [*OE*, pp. 1460, 1470–1, 1396].
14. Lecercle 1991, p. 197.
15. *CM*, p. 168 [*OE*, pp. 1401–2].
16. See *M*, p. 501.
17. Nowottny 1965, p. 87; *M*, p. 980.
18. *CE*, p. 280 [*OE*, p. 720].
19. Deleuze 1973, p. 47.
20. See *CM*, pp. 42–3 [*OE*, p. 1285].
21. See *CM*, p. 189 [*OE*, pp. 1420–1].
22. See *CM*, pp. 176–7 [*OE*, p. 1409]; Delhomme 1960, pp. 52, 56.
23. *M*, p. 773.
24. Delhomme 1954, p. 172.
25. *M*, p. 960.
26. *MM*, pp. 39, xii [*OE*, pp. 193, 162].
27. See *CM*, pp. 77 [*OE*, pp. 1318].
28. *MM*, pp. 19, 78 [*OE*, pp. 180, 218].
29. See *MM*, pp. 24ff [*OE*, pp. 184ff]. Despite describing the body of pure perception as a 'mathematical point' at *MM*, p. 310 [*OE*, p. 363], elsewhere (*MM*, p. 83 [*OE*, p. 221]) Bergson's concentration lapses and pure perception is described in terms of 'organs' and 'nerve centers'. Perhaps we should read these lapses as representative of a *purer* perception (memory would still be held in abeyance) if not a perfectly pure perception.
30. *MM*, pp. 80, 84 [*OE*, pp. 220, 222].
31. *MM*, pp. 28, 75 [*OE*, pp. 186, 216].

32. *MM*, p. 28 [*OE*, p. 186].
33. *MM*, p. 27 [*OE*, p. 185].
34. Deleuze 1988, p. 104. See *CE*, pp. 39–41 [*OE*, pp. 526–8], where Bergson reproaches those who believe that '*all is given*'; see too Game 1991, p. 100: 'With his conception of differentiation, Bergson disputes any idea of a whole as given'.
35. *ME*, p. 248 [*OE*, p. 970].
36. *MM*, p. 293 [*OE*, p. 353].
37. *TSMR*, p. 316 [*OE*, p. 1245].
38. *CM*, p. 175 [*OE*, p. 1408].
39. *CM*, p. 175 [*OE*, p. 1408].
40. Čapek 1971, p. 193.
41. *CM*, p. 173 [*OE*, p. 1406].
42. Deleuze 1994, pp. 143–4; Deleuze 1972, p. 164.
43. *CM*, pp. 175, 18 [*OE*, pp. 1408, 1259].
44. See *CE*, pp. 185, 186 [*OE*, pp. 644, 645]; *CM*, pp. 161, 32, 87–8, 30 [*OE*, pp. 1395, 1273, 1328, 1271].
45. See *M*, p. 1322; *CE*, p. 380 [*OE*, p. 799].
46. *CM*, pp. 127, 139, 140, 134 [*OE*, pp. 1364, 1374, 1375, 1370]; *CE*, pp. 380, 384 [*OE*, pp. 799, 801].
47. De Lattre 1990, p. 261.
48. *CM*, p. 34 [*OE*, p. 1274].
49. *CE*, p. 186 [*OE*, p. 645].
50. *TSMR*, p. 212 [*OE*, p. 1156]; see also *TSMR*, p. 214 [*OE*, p. 1157]; *CE*, p. 187 [*OE*, p. 646].
51. *CE*, pp. 282, 142 [*OE*, pp. 722, 610].
52. See *L*, pp. 150ff [*OE*, pp. 458ff].
53. *CM*, p. 190 [*OE*, p. 1422].
54. *CM*, p. 191 [*OE*, p. 1423]. The analogy with infinitesimal calculus is intended, Bergson being among those philosophers who see in calculus a special mode of thought: in his case, he cites it as one example of what intuition can achieve as we try to think in duration.
55. See Mourélos 1964, p. 160.
56. See *CM*, pp. 190, 138 [*OE*, pp. 1422, 1373].
57. *CE*, p. 31 [*OE*, p. 519].
58. *TSMR*, p. 212 [*OE*, p. 1155].
59. See *CM*, pp. 109–10 [*OE*, pp. 1346–7].
60. *CM*, p. 191 [*OE*, p. 1423].
61. *CM*, pp. 209, 210 [*OE*, pp. 1440, 1441].
62. See *TFW*, pp. 232–3 [*OE*, pp. 151–2].

8

Metaphilosophy

What is absurd in our eyes is not necessarily so in the eyes of nature.[1]

ON A CLEAR DAY . . .

In our introduction we heard Bergson's proclamation that he has never tried to produce a philosophical system. The *'esprit de système'* found in so much philosophy and science foolishly tries, he says, to 'embrace the totality of things in simple formulas'. Such vanity is shunned not for reasons of false modesty on Bergson's part so much as its simple futility. Quoting Claude Bernard, Bergson clearly endorses the view that the one thing we can be certain of when we produce a general explanation 'is that all these theories are false, absolutely speaking. They are only partial and temporary truths . . .'. We have already noted that Bergson never began a new work without also forgetting his previous positions and demanding what he termed a new effort of research. This lack of system and transferable method is actually meant to match a lack in nature, the fact that reality is not a 'systematic whole' which we can 'reconstruct by thought with the resources of reasoning alone . . .'.[2]

But where is the evidence for this anti-system? After all, hasn't the language of *durée*, novelty and freedom continually reappeared under the various headings of psychology, biology, physics, morality and sociology in Bergson's work? Yet, the preponderance of these terms belies the fact that they are all rather vague or indefinite in Bergson's employment of them. Aside from the difficulty of interpreting these expressions *vis-à-vis* a single reading of Bergsonism, a difficulty we ourselves have spent a considerable time examining, Bergson actually insists that they must be inherently vague. Beginning with freedom, his first book asserts that the relationship between the subject and the free act it performs is 'indefinable, just because we *are* free'.[3] Likewise, in his work on the mind – body relation, consciousness cannot be defined so much as simply characterised as memory.[4] When *CE* extends this research into biology, Bergson tries to take an intermediate route between radical finalism and mechanism by integrating these partial views in a larger, though thereby less definite perspective. His explanation of life will be necessarily indefinite, he says, because it is holistic; at best, it will seek '*dynamic* definitions'.[5] Finally, we have just seen how Bergson's method of intuition itself, as an attempt to adjust dynamically to reality, entails that no 'simple and geometrical definition of intuition' is possible.[6] With this conceptual indefinability has followed a certain reorientation (or 'inconsistency') in how these same terms are deployed across different texts such that, to take an obvious case, the *durée* of *TFW* is quite distinct from the *durée* of *MM*.

The definitions Bergson avoids pertain to what we should call 'stipulative definitions' – assigned meanings to which we must adhere. The ocular and spatial connotations of the word 'definition' should also be kept in mind when considering why he normally rejects it. An explicative definition, on the other hand, might truly be welcomed by Bergson for the simple reason that a definition in terms of the indefinite could suggest a positive understanding of the phenomenon in question. As we saw, Bergson explains open morality as an attention to life 'in general'; but he also explains pure memory as a retention of the past 'in general' and the *extensive* as 'things in general'.[7] But these generalities are not intended as logical abstractions; nor do they prove that Bergson has reneged on his philosophical duty to explain things precisely: they simply indicate a positive vagueness in reality itself when taken as a whole: 'Metaphysics has nothing in common with a generalization of experience, and yet it could be defined as the whole of experience (*l'expérience intégrale*)'.[8] Bruno Paradis has referred to the vague or fuzzy nature of Bergson's concepts. He also points to an indetermination of conceptuality or 'inexactitude' in Bergson's work.[9] A technical discussion here of the logic of vagueness would bring us far off the point, but the fact remains that Bergson clearly uses the notion of the undefinable and the indefinite, not in an attempt to perpetuate mystery, but to point to a genuine feature of the world. Indeed, the opening paragraph of *MM* tries to make it obvious that we are all of us 'in the presence of images, in the vaguest sense of the word'.[10] This vagueness is not a question, he asserts elsewhere, of giving up all logic whatsoever, but it does indicate a need to 'extend it, make it more supple, adapt it to a duration'.[11]

The very first sentence of *CM* shows Bergson's total commitment to precision in philosophy, but what that precision entails need not be the usual examples of clear and precise ideas so beloved of modern thought.

We saw already that Bergson takes the use of metaphors in philosophy seriously as the only precise manner in which the enduring aspect of reality can be expressed. In fact, he claims that when the sciences take abstraction into the realm of life it is they that are left floundering in metaphor, here understood negatively as merely figurative language: 'science is less and less objective, more and more symbolical, as it goes from the physical to the psychical, passing through the vital'.[12]

Bergson's strategy here in avoiding the dichotomy of woolly metaphor and clear concept is to divide and conquer: throughout his work, he multiplies the number of variables at play on both sides of the divide. Alongside metaphor, one could equally call into question the understanding of simplicity, clarity and unity as received values in philosophy. There are, for example, two types of clarity, according to Bergson, the first instantaneous and deductive, the second a generative *'becoming-clear'* which, while comparatively slow to emerge, is all the more enduring as a result.[13] He also speaks of types of simplicity – the one based on experienced immediacy, the other on definitional implication – and similarly one encounters types of unity, multiplicity and even alterity and sameness.[14] In each case of this multiplication, a vital, changing variety is contrasted with a rigid, inert one.

SOLID LOGIC

This emphasis on the dynamic in Bergson's conceptuality is one facet of his broader position as an evolutionary epistemologist. In place of thinking that 'the mind fell from heaven with a subdivision into psychological functions whose existence simply needs to be recognized', for Bergson, 'one must refer to the fundamental exigencies of life to explain their presence'.[15] We have already looked at his sociobiology in *TSMR* as well as the metaphysical origin of intellect in *CE*. Here we are concerned less with ontology and more with psychology and logic: the particular form our intellect takes. For Bergson, this form cannot emerge *ex nihilo* but must be given its 'proper place back in the general evolution of life' in that it corresponds primarily to 'vital needs'.[16] That form or 'subdivision' is generated, we learnt already, alongside a certain type of spatiality: 'Concepts, in fact, are outside each other, like objects in space; and they have the same stability as such objects . . '..[17]

Such a lashing together of form and content will strike many as pure psychologism, but the subtleties of Bergson's position remain to be seen. They come to light best if we examine the interrelationship between space and mathematics in Bergson's philosophy of number as set out in *TFW*. The essential aspect of his theory of number is that counting is inseparable from homogeneous space.[18] Homogeneous space is the ideal and necessary medium through which we effect any arithmetical collective. Bergson's theory is therefore constructivist to the extent that it agrees with the Kantian view that numerical distinctions involve a juxtaposition of spatial entities. Here is Milič Čapek with a synopsis of Bergson's view:

> He pointed out first that a mere *enumeration* or listing of members of a certain class is not counting. When we really count instead of mere enumerating, for instance, when we count sheep in the herd, we deliberately disregard individual qualitative differences between them; in considering their number we even disregard their common features which makes them to [*sic*] belong to the same species and treat them as homogeneous units each of which is qualitatively identical to other [*sic*] and each of which still remains distinct from other [*sic*]. What differentiates such qualitatively undistinguishable units must be *a principle of differentiation other than qualitative* and this is precisely space.[19]

Through this 'principle of differentiation' a quantitative multiplicity is effected. But before such a multiplicity can be created through the agency of space, there must firstly be given the unity to be quantified, namely a qualitative multiplicity.[20] Bergson provides the example of a clock striking four times. The series of four strokes are said to interpenetrate 'to give the whole a peculiar quality, to make a kind of musical phrase out of it'. Of course, apart from creating a musical whole, the strikes also represent the number four, but it is a *type* of the number four. It is a qualitative instance of it that (to a certain degree) is specific to its individual context. Because the states of a qualitative multiplicity are indivisible, they cannot be quantified, or, rather, when they are quantified, the qualitative multiplicity they formerly composed changes in kind as this happens.[21] It changes from a particular degree of quality to one of quantity.

   Naturally, most anti-psychologistic philosophers will vigorously oppose nearly all of these ideas. Bertrand Russell, for example, believed it was Bergson's (purportedly) strong tendency to visualise that led him to think that space and number are intimately linked. According to Russell, we could only know the twelve apostles, tribes of Israel, months of the calendar and signs of the zodiac as twelve in number if the number twelve were something abstract and separate from each of these collections and not if it were some property possessed in common by them all. It is possible to group these four collections with each other rather than, say, a cricket eleven only because 'What different collections of twelve units have in common...is something which cannot be pictured because it is abstract'.[22]

But Russell is mistaken in his presentation of Bergson as a strong visualiser. Homogeneous space, and this is stated explicitly by Bergson, is simply a 'principle of differentiation' and not the locale for some visual scene.[23] However, it must be admitted that, even as a principle, this homogeneity does have some intrinsic spatial increment to it, for why otherwise would a form of space be the primary site of homogeneity? As H. W. Carr says in his defence of Bergson against Russell, it is immaterial whether the image underpinning number is visual, auditory or motor, 'The essential thing is that it is spatial'.[24] But this would not be a fatal blow to Bergson's argument, for Milič Čapek has shown that the increasingly imageless nature of modern mathematics does not preclude the existence of '*far more subtle and more elusive elements* [of spatiality] *even in the most abstract mathematical and logical thought*'.[25] One might ask, for instance, to what degree the logical continuity of a mathematical series is free from our understanding of a spatial continuum. In a similar vein, the mathematical intuitionist L. E. J. Brouwer believed that the principal of the excluded middle arises in part out of 'an extensive group of *simple every day phenomena*'.[26] The metaphorical status of 'logical space' in Wittgenstein's *Tractatus* is also clearly open to interrogation on this account. If it is merely a metaphor, why has the particular metaphor of space been chosen?[27] According to Čapek:

> There is a perfect isomorphism between physical atomism and the logical atomism of Wittgenstein: the objects of *Tractatus* are as immutable, discontinuous, indivisible and simple as the indivisible and homogeneous particles of classical physics. In both kinds of atomism, change is reduced to the changing 'configurations' ... of these ultimate units.[28]

The modern champion of anti-psychologism was, of course, Gottlob Frege, whose understanding of number shares the same Platonic premises with Russell's. Significantly, Frege also posited a number of 'reefs' upon which he thought any psychologistic conception of number would inevitably founder. Most important for our purposes is the first of these reefs, concerning the differentiation of number: how the sameness of the units is reconciled with their distinguishability.[29] With this proposed obstacle to psychologism, Frege places Russell's reservations with the Bergsonian theory of number in an explicitly philosophical context of the sort Russell failed to provide. Perhaps, then, we can estimate whether Bergson's conception really is psychologistic by considering how his philosophy would have fared against this reef.[30]

Bergson's answer to the problem of differentiation is clear: homogeneous space provides just the right medium to synthesise the one (the sameness of the units) with the many (their distinguishability).[31] Now, Frege also notes that the correct degree of abstraction is 'difficult to hit'.[32] It must be enough to form a genus but not so much that the particularity of the species to be numbered under this genus is dissolved. It is only a difficulty, however, if it is deemed to be a mental act of abstraction. Now, according to *TFW*, it is we who form homogeneous space. But though this medium may be an abstract conception that also supports further acts of abstraction, it is not itself formed by an act of abstraction: it is formed through an intuition (in a sense of that term quite different to how Bergson will develop it later).[33] Furthermore, in his later thought in *CE* it is matter itself which is given the ability to stretch itself towards homogeneous space as a limit: 'Matter has a tendency to constitute *isolable* systems, that can be treated geometrically'. In neither case, then, is this space a mental creation involving fallible volition and deliberation.[34] Indeed, this process-matter, being able to form itself into what can be a repository of number for us, would seem to indicate a Bergsonian analogue for the objectivity Frege had to seek in his other-worldly 'Third Realm'.[35]

In connection with this last point we can also draw the following parallel between Frege's platonic recourse to a Third Realm and Bergson's anti-noumenalism in regard to Kant. Kant characterised things-in-themselves as unknowable in virtue of what was for Bergson his impoverished conception of understanding and the perception of space and time. Bergson rematerialised these noumena through the widened perception of a non-homogeneous spatiality. In like manner, Frege had to make his Third Realm extra-sensory for reasons similar to Kant's. For Frege, however, this was because he did not see how spatiality, this time moving in the opposite direction, could form itself into a greater level of homogeneity than that to be seen in such usual empirical givens as those listed by Russell against Bergson: the twelve apostles, the twelve tribes of Israel and so on. From the Bergsonian point of view, number and homogeneous space are objective, but by 'objective' we should not understand something bereft of subjectivity, nor something that cannot evolve into something else less objective. Space exists in many forms in the Bergsonian account, tending both towards and away from those things we call either the subjective or the objective. The banishment to an otherworld of either the things-in-themselves or all mathematical objects is founded upon a vision of the physical as something simpler than it is. A plurality of entities will only be regarded as incommensurate with our worldly reality if one's picture of this reality is impoverished.

As a consequence, we ought to amend our earlier judgement that dubbed Bergson a constructivist. The constructivist holds that spatial configurations underlie numerical distinctions, that mathematical activity is a creativity of the mind and that mathematical objects are creations of the mind. As regards numbers, then, this view is idealist. It is usually contrasted with the Platonist's position (such as Frege's or Russell's), which is a realist conception of number, seeing abstract objects (mathematical ones included) existing independently of the mind apprehending them. Given the orthodox meaning of both mind and matter, and what we have learnt above, it would be better if Bergson's theory were described as being intermediate between these two positions. His so-called psychologism could just as well be redubbed a physicalism, though neither term would be wholly faithful.

Of course, the mathematical Platonist could reply that it was the very formulation of multiple spaces by thinkers such as Reimann and Hilbert that led to a mathematics divested of any reference to the actual world and becoming instead a pure science of numbers (that might possibly exist in a Third Realm).[36] However, it is arguable whether Riemann's non-Euclidean space, for example, constitutes a truly new space as opposed to what would be for Bergson a mere reformulation of Euclid's homogeneous medium. This was certainly his opinion of Hermann Minkowski's spatial interpretation of STR.[37] Moreover, Bergson asserts that the natural geometry he speaks of is not that of Euclid or any mathematician: 'prior to the science of geometry, there is a natural geometry'. Indeed, the existence of this form of universal natural geometry probably explains the levels of good success with which different mathematical systems can be applied to real space – matter inclines in certain directions, but mind can complete it variously.[38]

POSSIBILITY

The mutable physicality of psycho-logical content is given further emphasis in Bergson's treatment of possibility. We first looked at possibility when examining Bergson's refutation of determinism in *TFW*. It is odd in itself that the modality Bergson most rigorously contrasts with the novelty of *durée* should be neither necessity nor probability but possibility. In another philosopher's hands, possibility would be the hallmark of novelty, futurity and freedom. Not so in Bergson's case. Possibility is compared negatively with *durée*. And yet the two are not simply opposites either, but co-engendered opposites. In the introduction to *CM*, Bergson spells out his view that in a creative evolution 'there is perpetual creation of possibility and not only of reality'. *Durée* is both the mark of reality, he claims, and the agency behind our illusions concerning what makes any one reality possible. Real *durée*, being prior rather than subsequent to the possible, actually creates the latter retrospectively. For example, French nineteenth-century

Romanticism was supposedly made possible because of the preceding conditions created by French Classicism. But, asks Bergson, was it not the romanticism of a Chateaubriand, Vigny or Hugo that really created the supposed nascent romanticism of the earlier classical writers in whose lineage the Romantics are assumed to be? Romanticism, by its very coming into existence, retroactively created both its own prefiguration in the past and, by that, the causal explanation of its emergence.[39]

In a sense, Bergson's thesis on possibility amounts to a broadening of the *post hoc ergo propter hoc* fallacy: the duplication of the present as a past spuriously set up to explain the origins of this present.[40] According to his view, it is extremely hard for us to acknowledge that each present is really something radically new. Our inveterate logic of retrospection perpetually recreates the present with elements of the past: meaning is reconstituted from words that are already meaningful, melody is reconstructed from notes that are already musical. In each case, it is because we know the result that we can so easily reverse engineer some mechanism as its causal past.

But there appears to be something peculiar about this doctrine. According to Bergson, we can contrive to have any new present causally linked with earlier states out of which it will be said to have emerged. Another illustration of this concerns the relationship between the colours red, yellow and orange.[41] Imagining that our experience was such that we had had no perception of strong red or yellow but only various hues of orange (through living in a certain environment perhaps), Bergson asks whether orange would then be composed of those two colours as we consider it to be currently. His answer is no. Simply by coming into being, red and yellow create a new possibility (the derivative nature of orange) in supposedly antecedent states of affairs (the combination of red and yellow). Previously there was only orange in the orange, now there is the admixture of red and yellow. What was a simple state is now compound and what was something genuinely new is now a mere consequent. And yet Bergson is not only talking here about our beliefs concerning orange, red and yellow: he is also talking about the colours themselves. An analysis of orange similar to this occurs in *TSMR*, and it is not surprising that at least one commentator has found it 'strange', not knowing whether its significance is epistemological or more than that.[42]

The reason why it is strange is this. Talk of possibility can mean many things. We can refer to physical possibility; metaphysical possibility (is it metaphysically possible for minds to exist without a body?); logical possibility (can the same mind exist both with and without the same body at the same time?); and epistemic possibility (situations left undecided within some body of knowledge).[43] Yet Bergson makes no such distinctions as these, preferring to speak simply of possibility in general, especially in cases when he would normally be expected to distinguish between logical and physical possibility in particular. But we have seen that Bergson makes no such distinction because logic has its roots in the physical. And even more radically, as we will see, Bergson asserts that logic is not merely physical in its origins, but, as an aspect of process reality, it is physical *tout court*.

Conflating logical possibility with physical possibility would also seem to add a degree of reality to the modality of the possible that Bergson had seemingly revoked when contrasting it with *durée*. However, there is an ambiguity as to the illusory status of the possible throughout Bergson's work. At times he does not deny the possible outright but only its existence now in order to predict the future.[44] The present reality can be said legitimately to create the possible, but solely when it is as a means to explain that present. Therefore, the possible does exist, if not for the future, then at least as a past for the present. It is in terms of a future made possible by the present that possibility is an illusion that Bergson consistently condemns. The error concerning our notion of the possible is here said to arise when we think that the possible is less than the real and that the real is its fulfilment, or, in other words, when we use the possible as a synonym for the future. The real unforeseeable future wrongly becomes the 'future anterior', the future anticipated.[45] In terms of a present made possible by the past, the possible does appear to have a truth to it for Bergson.[46]

It is not incidental that the title of the introductory essay in *CM* that began our discussion of possibility is 'Retrograde Movement of the True Growth of Truth'. Gilles Deleuze brings out clearly this point of the ontological status of possibility: 'The *retrograde movement* of the true is not merely an illusion *about* the true, but belongs *to* the true itself'.[47] Bergson himself says that it is not we who put the possible in the past but that 'the possible may put itself there'.[48] It would therefore be inappropriate to specify whether possibility is a real or illusory metaphysical entity. Simply because the explanation of the present with the possible is born in part through a retroactive agency, it does not follow that it is wholly unreal. Actions are prior to the things that act. Hence, Bergson can argue that the self, for instance, is a construct – a 'creation of self by self' – but that that is precisely what makes it real.[49] Bergson's 'constructivism', if we can still call it that, has a positive ontological basis rather than a negative one reliant on scepticism, that is, a construct is a reality simply because it is a construct. But note that it is *a* reality; it is not the whole truth, but a part of the truth: no purported alternative truth is ever excluded in Bergson's thought. To see why, we should turn to what he says about truth itself.

TRUTH AND PROCESS

According to Deleuze, 'If we take the history of thought, we see that time has always put the notion of truth into crisis'.[50] Attention to time is an attention to the mobility of reality, to the particularity and novelty of each situation, and hence to the superficiality of eternal truth. So what does Bergson, foremost of the time-philosophers, say about truth? Certainly, the notion of an eternal truth awaiting its discovery by the mind is rejected.[51] Like the pragmatists, Bergson sees truth as '*an invention*' that comes 'little by little into being'.[52] Most often he uses the word 'truth' synonymously with 'reality'.[53] What is true is not what statement corresponds with a reality so much as what is more or less real.[54] So if reality itself is mutable, the truth of every reality is provisional. What starts out as merely a 'refractory' representation can become a given truth, clear and intelligible, simply in virtue of our historical acquaintance with the concept. A true affirmation can thus have a 'retroactive' or 'retrograde' movement: 'the paradox of today is often only the truth of tomorrow'.[55] Truth *grows* on us. But if familiarity breeds belief, this is not to say that truth is arbitrary, for not every notion becomes familiar to the same degree: only those which 'push their roots deepest into reality', says Bergson, gain the continual usage required for eventual admittance into fuller credulity.[56] The organic imagery and evolutionary understanding of Bergson's epistemology is blatant.

We usually suppose objectivists to believe that there are enough true and false descriptions to justify the substantial nature of truth; relativists, on the other hand, appear to believe that there are many equally valid descriptions and so no truth. If truth existed, it would have to be absolute and singular. The Bergsonian view is no less licentious, tolerating an ever-increasing plurality of interpretations. But from this multiplicity it goes on to draw the alternative conclusion that there must be something peculiar about descriptions rather than something wrong with truth. If we give up on truth, it is only because we have a false conception of what truth should be, 'in virtue of the principle deep-rooted in our intellect, that all truth is eternal. If the judgement is true now, it seems to us it must always have been so'.[57] But it is truth which is multiple for Bergson because it is an emergent process: 'the true growth of truth'.

If reality is mutable then the idea that it can be described by eternally true laws is also made a nonsense. Certainly, Bergson made it clear that no such laws could be found in the life sciences: 'There is no universal biological law that applies precisely and automatically to every living thing.

There are only *directions* in which life throws out species in general'.[58] But he also made the same point for the natural sciences, in fact. In particular, he feels that the supposedly necessitating nature of scientific law is actually a product of an anthropomorphic understanding of physical reality. Bergson parodies the conception of an objectively necessary set of natural laws thus:

> There is a certain order of nature which finds expression in laws: facts are presumed to 'obey' these laws so as to conform with that order. The scientist himself can hardly help believing that the law 'governs' facts and consequently is prior to them, like the Platonic Idea on which all things had to model themselves. The higher he rises in the scale of generalizations the more he tends, willy-nilly, to endow the law with this imperative character; it requires a very real struggle against our own prepossessions to imagine the principles of mechanics otherwise than as inscribed from all eternity on the transcendent tables that modern science has apparently fetched down from another Sinai.[59]

This is an important point: too easily we regard laws as eternal edicts which precede observed facts and even oblige the facts to obey them, much as our conventional social laws precede the behaviour they codify. For Bergson, a law is always subsequent and subordinate to the facts: the facts may tend to give it the impression of necessity – otherwise we would not call it a 'law' at all – but it is certainly not eternal nor antecedent to the facts.[60] Nicholas Rescher describes the process philosopher's approach as follows: 'The laws of nature, too, are merely transitory stabilities that emerge at one phase of cosmic history only to lapse from creation and give way to variant modes of operation in the fullness of time'.[61]

Nevertheless, Bergson's process view of truth is not without its own problems. We were told that the emergence of truth is not arbitrary, for not all notions 'push their roots' deep into 'reality', which begs the question as to the meaning of this penetration and this reality. To examine these issues we must turn again to what Bergson says about the origin of mental content.

INTELLECT AND IMMOBILITY

A defender of immutable truth might say that the addition of indexical markers to a statement will fix its truth-value in perpetuity, as for example if one were to say, 'I thought that the sky was blue at 1p.m. on the 5th of June 1970 in *x*' (*x* being a complete description of one's situation). But then we face the issue of whether conceptualisations of context such as indexicals really can give a complete account of context. It is sometimes thought that a statement's meaning regains its fullness when reconnected to the pragmatic context of the person uttering it in his or her situation at the time of its utterance. But how could any analysis, description or account of meaning effect this without travelling back in time to *be* the sentence, person and situation? How can one represent a previous context when an essential part of that context is its as yet unrepresented state?[62] One could retort that whatever there was in the situation left out *de jure* by description will in any case be quite peripheral to requirements. Yet, this is the whole point under debate. Anthropologists like Gregory Bateson, artificial intelligence designers like Terry Winograd and even some philosophers have warned us of the danger of contextual representation.[63] Context is not a separate variable upon which the meaning 'within' the context is dependent or independent according to one's theoretical stance: the meaning is a part of the context. Meaning does not reside *in* the environment, it emerges *as* it.

In Bergsonian philosophy, the problem of context translates into the problem of specificity. The major difficulty Bergson sees for philosophy is that of 'finding a place for personality' and 'of admitting real individualities' in the world as science presents it. In the light of this, the fundamental purpose of philosophy, he claims, 'is to speculate, that is to say, to see'. In an expanded, that is, a redeemed perception, 'No aspect of the real would be substituted for the rest ostensibly to explain it'. Turned in the normal, utilitarian direction of mind, however, perception and intellect are eliminative and impoverishing. We isolate a moving object from its supposedly static context or world by disregarding the specific moment that individuates that world as the one belonging exclusively to the object. Indeed, prior to our inattention, there was no 'object plus world' at all. For the purely pragmatic need to control, we cut the 'object' out as a figure against a disconnected background. It is precisely when we abstract (or extract) our regard from 'them' in favour of an overview that the two are separated: 'The concept generalizes at the same time that it abstracts'.[64] By immobilising inhabitant and place, one ignores what is specific to both at each moment, and so they dissociate into a relation of container and contained.

The figure of containment has been ubiquitous in Bergson's work. Be it the 'empty container' of homogeneous space, the condensation of material *durée* worked by perception, the consumption of others by our body or the confinement of individuals within closed society, the inside–outside dichotomy is basic.[65] The formalism of intellect is said to represent a frame in which an infinity of objects can be manipulated, the relation of 'content to container' being one of the fundamental schemes it uses to interpret reality.[66] Therewith, the intimacy between context and content is broken by immobilising the context as a rigid container and projecting all novelty into the quantitative motion of the object it supposedly contains. Inside and outside are created by a discriminating apportionment of change. Wherever we are given a '*moving continuity*', we dissociate it into 'two terms, permanence and change, and then represent permanence by *bodies* and change by *homogeneous movements* in space'.[67] But this is less an illusion so much as a generated reality begun by the movement of matter itself and completed by intellect. Or rather, matter and intellect are both phases of a process of productive repetition locked in a struggle with difference as its other side. Intellect is one product of this genesis: it is produced as a content in two senses, as logical content *qua* meaning and as psychological content *qua* consciousness within the body. But thinking of logical content as immobilisation and spatial content is not a metaphorical mapping: the spatiality and content of mind are rightly confused, both being engendered by a temporal phenomenon.[68] As an aspect of process reality, logic is physical in origin and actuality.

With these ideas of regard and disregard for the *durée* of the world, Bergson can build a value-system: 'True superiority [is]...a greater force of attention'.[69] In answer to our question earlier, a greater truth, one which pushes its roots deeper into reality, is what gives greater attention towards the singularity of the other, a justice to that alterity. But again, without wishing to retread old ground, this is as much an ethical statement concerning values of superiority and inferiority as it is an empirical and metaphysical one concerning perception. Ultimately, there is a metaphilosophical question subtending this mix of ethics and empirics.

METAPHILOSOPHICAL DUALISATION

Some may balk at the notion of metaphilosophy we have been using throughout this study. What is 'metaphilosophy' after all? If philosophy is the higher-order discipline *par excellence*, perpetually driven to reflect on extraneous first-order content – nature, mind, justice, beauty and so on – then such metaphilosophy could be nothing other than simply more philosophy rather than something standing over and above philosophy itself.[70] The prefix 'meta', of course, is ambiguous, pointing to a practice of second-order reflection on whatever discipline it is adjoined to – as in meta-ethics or metapolitics, for instance – as well as the fundamental principles which condition that discipline. Metaphilosophy can also forward itself as the history, sociology or analysis of philosophical positions as they are located in any set of such positions, actual or potential. But, if this were the case, we would have to concede that metaphilosophy is really just an interdisciplinary alloy – philosophy mixed with history, sociology or whatever – rather than a heightened level of abstraction taking philosophical content *per se* as its object.

Yet a rationale for this term is evident in the real distinction between philosophical monism (the only position deemed possible in many contemporary circles) and metaphilosophical dualism or dualisation, which is Bergson's own peculiar view. What he writes about reductionism in the specific areas of biology, psychology or physics, he also regards as valid for metaphilosophy. Totalising philosophies lack explanatory power, for in claiming that everything is (directly or indirectly) x, y or z (metaphysics reduces to logic, ethics is first philosophy and so on), they lose the ability to account for their opposite, even as a derivative illusion or error. The very *firstness* of a philosophy – be it a branch of philosophy like ethics or a school of philosophy like materialism – inevitably enters it into a relationship of reduction, elimination or separation with its rivals. But in each case, it can be asked whether there is any remainder left of the rival and, if so, of what type. What is at issue here is the self-sufficiency or identity of the monism.[71]

Take the work of Levinas and Deleuze, for instance. Levinas argues that 'ethics is not a moment of being; it is otherwise and better than being, the very possibility of the beyond'.[72] In the course of showing us this primacy of the ethical he explains various phenomena such as conversation, teaching, representation, objectivity, consciousness and time as all ultimately ethical in their significance.[73] Likewise universality, generalisation and language are said to presuppose equally an ethical commerce between a plurality; in effect, 'all the other structures rest' on the primacy of ethical.[74]

Of course, Levinas cannot and does not provide a naturalistic bridging mechanism that would explain how ethics engenders such apparent non-ethical entities as language or generality, for then that mechanism itself would take privilege over the ethical. Ethics simply transcends the empirical realm by *fiat*. At best, Levinas can cite a paradox in order to explain the place of the good 'over every essence': the power of the infinite and ethical is such that it can condescend to become its opposite in the finite. To deny it this power over even logic would be to make it less than infinite.[75] Again though, this power of the infinite cannot be deemed metaphysical in essence, nor can the tenability of Levinas' explanation be on account of the coherence of its understanding of the infinite.[76] He must show that it is wholly ethical why the infinite falls or condescends itself, that is, its trancendency is the higher-order transcendence of a lower-order transcendence into immanence. Nevertheless, we can ask in turn what it is that facilitates such condescension if not the possibility of levels as such, that is, of empirics, ethics and logical orders as modes of reality understood by philosophy. The conditions of possibility for any notion of first philosophy and what therewith becomes second, third or fourth philosophy (and so on) is studied by metaphilosophy itself.

Gilles Deleuze is, in many respects, the inverted image of Levinas: for him, the first philosopher is a naturalist and first philosophy must be naturalism. In a mix of metaphysics and empiricism that he calls 'transcendental empiricism', he describes the project of a new naturalism which refuses to 'devaluate Nature by taking away from it any virtuality or potentiality, any immanent power, any inherent being'.[77] Desire and power are returned to the physical. In this, Deleuze sees himself in that line of naturalists running from Spinoza through Nietzsche and up to the present who are profoundly anticartesian. All duality between the human (*res cogitans*) and the natural (*res extensa*) must be erased, especially that dualism which underlies all others, 'the structure Other' which places us within an archetypal perceptual dyad.[78] Dichotomous identification, arboreal branching, binaries: all such dualisms 'are the enemy, an entirely necessary enemy'.[79] The admission that this enemy is entirely necessary (and so spawning a new metalevel dualism) is enlightening, for even the admirers of Deleuze's work with Félix Guattari in particular have noted the continual use of dualism in their writings.[80] The 'magic formula' they openly seek in their philosophy of desire is 'pluralism = monism', a view that Bergson could have endorsed simply because it stems in part from their reading of Bergson. But it seems that some pluralisms are less plural than others, leaving a place for exclusion when it comes to what Deleuze and Guattari call 'molar' phenomena such as morality, religion, and indeed dualism itself.[81]

The original French title of Bergson's last collection of essays, *The Creative Mind*, is *La Pensée et le mouvant*. 'Thought and Instability' might have been a better choice of translation, for its introduction clearly states the aim of Bergsonism to be a philosophy which 'would follow the undulations of the real'. He argues against all 'artificial unities' in philosophy that attempt to embrace the totality, be the unifying concept ego, will, idea or whatever else. Irrespective of what term is used in triumph, 'It will be emptied of all meaning from the moment it is applied to the totality of things'.[82] Take the philosophy of will, for example:

> To place will everywhere is the same as leaving it nowhere...It makes little difference to me if one says 'Everything is mechanism' or 'Everything is will': in either case everything is identical. In both cases, 'mechanism' and 'will' become synonyms of each other. Therein lies the initial vice of philosophical systems. They think they are telling us something about the absolute by giving it a name...But

the more you increase the extension of the term, the more you diminish comprehension of it. If you include matter within its extension, you empty its comprehension of the positive characteristics by which spontaneity stands out against mechanism and liberty against necessity. When finally the word arrives at the point where it designates everything that exists, it means no more than existence. What advantage is there then in saying that the world is will, instead of simply saying that it is?[83]

In place of the ubiquity of either desire or responsibility (Deleuze or Levinas), Bergson's intuitive philosophy can never impose a 'totality' but remains passive before reality, though such passivity nonetheless requires a great effort.[84] The relative truths of a philosophy of the will or of the ego would not be erased, however, but would belong to a dynamic metaphilosophical truth that never ceases to evolve.

Deleuze and Levinas attempt to aggrandise their own methodology with the status of 'first philosophy'. Either empiricism or ethics is transcendent. Yet, what they separately promote is precisely what Bergson attempts to straddle at a metaphilosophical level. Bergsonism has no ultimate message in terms of either a Manichaeism of good versus evil or a naturalism of active and reactive will. In that both these thinkers were historically indebted to Bergson, one can also regard their separate philosophical trajectories as partial readings of Bergsonian themes: they isolate tensions and tendencies that remain necessarily intertwined in Bergson's thought.

Monisms try to show that 'everything is *x*', but must, in the end, show how some *x* relates to some other *y*, even if this *y* is an illusion – the illusion of dualism, for example. Cartesian dualism in particular may be 'dead in the water' in contemporary philosophical terms, but materialism ought not ignore its own inability to explain away the abundantly vital metaphilosophical duality of materialism and dualism. In addition, having rejected any defensive recourse by materialists to a theory of error or misrepresentation through Bergson's critique of negation, it is this metaphilosophical weakness that can be used to critique all monism.

All the same, Bergson is not simply a dualist in any usual sense of the term. The real crime of monistic philosophy is simply that it is static. Most of the critical examinations of Bergson agree on this: his thought embraces a '*dynamic* monism' allowing for 'qualitative *diversity*'; he is neither a monist nor a dualist alone, they say: the 'infrastructure' of his philosophy is at once 'dualist and unitary'.[85] H. Wildon Carr mentions 'divergent tendencies' in Bergsonism rather than any dualism but, whatever the formulation, in each case it is a question of a process of dualisation over static dualism or monism.[86]

In his own words, what Bergson advocates are dualities according to a 'law of dichotomy'. By this he understands a universal principle of bifurcation which explains how every unity is provisional and practical, being destined to fragment for the simple reason that life, as we learnt, is understood as a reciprocal interpenetration of opposed forces held together in an unstable tension.[87] This constant dichotomisation (without subsequent Hegelian mediation, we must add) is the driving force of reality.

The law of dichotomy or dualisation, however, presents us with the following final dilemma. If every reality must eventually bifurcate for Bergson, can this be true at the metaphilosophical level of dichotomy itself? Could even this philosophy of creativity, as a purportedly absolute depiction, ironically propound an uncreative reality? On the other hand, if we take on board Bergson's view that the laws of nature are mutable entities, surely the law of dichotomy, being subordinate to the changeable facts of reality, can itself be falsified. The law of dichotomy may thus itself dichotomise to its opposite as part of a concrete, empirical and creative process.[88] Therefore, we are left with a paradox on our hands. If this law of creativity is true, then it can create its own untruth; but this falsification of the law would actually prove its own veracity.[89]

W. V. O. Quine has written that paradoxes such as these – which he calls 'antinomies' because they prove their truth only when they are falsified – have had a long tradition in generating 'crises in thought'. While their paradoxical nature stems from their directly or indirectly self-referential character, the crises they inspire are most often resolved by a renovation in thought usually involving the demise of some long-held principle formerly supposed self-evident. Once that principle is removed, the paradox is transformed into a platitude.[90] As Bergson said, 'The paradox of today is often only the truth of tomorrow'.[91] What we must seek in our struggle with the paradox of dichotomy is the principle that needs to be removed to render it a commonplace.

ALL KINDS OF EVERYTHING

Answering this puzzle brings us back to Bergson's plurality of levels of existence and the ontology of images used in *MM* to designate every reality. Bergson's choice of 'image' here might be deemed part of a covert preference for idealism, but it can just as equally be read as a form of 'ultra-externalism', founding mind wholly on matter.[92] What is significant is that it is neither of these, for Bergsonian images are said to pre-exist any bifurcation between inside and outside, subject and object.

Each image within this menagerie can be impoverished to become a percept-image and further again to become a concept-image, as types of image build upon each other into a system of ever more rarefied strata. That is why Bergson describes the concept as an image *of* an image; nevertheless, he never explains the 'of' here in terms of reference, but simply asserts the existence of an imagery from the outset that is subsequently more and more decontextualised.[93] This impoverishment of a given type of image is itself a process, the process of abstraction which is simultaneously the process of inattention to specificity. However, this inattention is described ultimately as a process of immobilisation. Each level of imagery is also a context that can be immobilised to become a container for some 'new' content-meaning. Hence, what novelty the concept has is born from an immobilisation of its context such that the former can stand out as something new against a static background. So, where we spoke earlier of inattention as the agent of abstraction, one should not read that as a psychological process opposed to a physical one.

Now we come back to the puzzle concerning the creation of uncreativity. The first thing to note is that it bears many of the hallmarks of Bertrand Russell's paradox of non-self-membered classes. Quine regards Russell's paradox as a genuine antinomy of the sort that its truth ensures its falsity similar to the way in which the law of dichotomy ensures its own refutation.[94] In addition, Bergson's paradox might also be resolved with something akin to Russell's answer to the class problem, namely his theory of types.[95] Russell reduces his paradox to a confusion between different types of propositional function, from first-order, object-related language, upwards to increasingly higher-order languages. Whenever a paradox of self-reference is generated, one's explanatory scheme must be stratified into a hierarchy of what Russell would call logical types.

In Bergson's case, the confusion would be between different orders of immobilisation-abstraction. Bergson, though, places his pluralism foursquare in the cosmic realm: it is a matter of bifurcating realities rather than logic or language alone.[96] The stratification of levels in his thought intentionally con-fuses a logical 'meta-form', so to speak, with the supposedly mere first-order realities of time, biology, ethics or psychology. The list of these metaforms in Bergson's work is as long as the list of paradoxes connected with it. In Chapter One we touched on the paradox of the A-theory of time which involved a temporal process that would itself require a time in which to proceed, leading us on to an infinite regress. If the present is a moving entity, according to what measure of temporality does it move? A second-level temporality or super-time seems necessary. But this is exactly what Bergson's theory of the planes of *durée* offers us: time is a hierarchy of temporal rhythms running at different rates, each a condensation of other rhythms, of others' *durée*. The pulsations of one being subsume within themselves those of another in a nested order of ever more contractile *durées*.[97] Time is not a single unilinear succession but a multistoried range of differentiation. Alongside time, freedom too was understood in *TFW* as potentially self-referential: we are free both to retain our freedom and to lose it in self-mechanisation (a paradox that would animate most of Sartre's existential writings). As for *CE*, we also examined biological evolution as a movement with a self-referential teleology; that is, it evolves towards the ideal of perpetual evolution. Yet, in making evolution itself the 'issue' of life (in the logical and productive senses of that term), *CE* also incorporates the possibility of evolving to another *ideal*: that of a non-evolving state. Both the processes of organic life and of death are immanent to the *élan*. Vitalisation and materialisation. Bergson's is as much a theory of 'metabiology' as it is a theory of 'biology', though in a fuller sense of that term than George Bernard Shaw intended when he used it in *Back to Methuselah*. Though there are others (such as the relativisation of relativity in *DS* for instance), the last metaform we should mention is the proposal in *MM* that perception itself, though not fully self-referential, is still a 'realized contradiction' in that it compounds the sameness of self with the alterity of reality while not reducing either.[98] In a letter from Bergson to John Dewey in 1913, he responds to a recent critical essay by Dewey on his work by describing his position, not as a full-relativism this time, but inversely as a 'partial realism':

> In general, I believe that the explanation for all these criticisms, and the point of departure for all my replies, is your implicit refusal to accept the *partial realism* of the doctrine I set out. As I say in the introduction to *Matter and Memory*, I place myself in a position midway between realism and idealism, but in a certain measure I am realist.[99]

No less than a full-relativism establishes a higher-order absolute, the midpoint between realism and idealism is a higher-order realism. In this, Bergson accords with pragmatism's refutation of any strict division between the synthetic (factual) and the analytic (logical): every type of reality is imbued with 'referential' powers: reality itself is in principle a set of neutralised images. Therefore, there is no solid, first-order brute reality upon which a hierarchy of abstraction can elevate itself: abstraction exists at every level such that the hierarchy in question is not logical *in toto* but multifaceted, with psychology, biology, ethics and logic providing different names for, and modes of, this stratification.

Another of these facets is metaphilosophy itself, or the perpetual renovation of philosophy into new philosophy. A stated ambition of *MM* was to substitute a higher-order duality for the lower-order dualism of mind and matter: 'Because we have pushed dualism to an extreme, our analysis has perhaps dissociated its contradictory elements'.[100] Bergson's point is less that we should supersede dualism *per se* so much as what he calls 'ordinary dualism'. Dissociation replaces this dualism by working on the theme of dualism itself and pushing it to an extreme. By taking a lower-order dualism to the limit, it is replaced by the dualism of this dualism and its opposite.

Of final significance in what Bergson says about the different levels of reality is his explanation of philosophical illusion in terms of a confusion between these levels. Too often, he believes, philosophers fall into bewilderment by taking what is true only at a particular level of reality and predicating it of 'all of reality' – if this last phrase is at all meaningful any more. Similarly, Russell's theory of types has been said to '[lay] down the principle that the meaning of a propositional function is not specified until we specify the range of objects which are candidates for satisfying it'.[101] It has also been claimed that Russell's paradoxes in general (the paradox of non-self-membered classes is only one of them), 'pin-point questions about the limits of meaningfulness, and...seem to imply that we cannot talk unrestrictedly about *everything* there is'. In other words, we cannot talk indiscriminately about all entities, 'only about entities of a *given* type'.[102]

Now type theory had a strong influence on the Logical Positivists' attack against metaphysics. Yet, despite Bergson being targeted by both Russell and the Positivists in this, his own metaphysics actually leads him to a similar position regarding totalisation: 'What really matters to philosophy is to know *what* unity, *what* multiplicity, *what* reality [is] superior to the abstract one and the abstract multiple'.[103] To say anything of everything, be it negative or affirmative, is to say nothing at all. For Russell, 'all' is an empty term. But in Bergson's temporalised version of this idea, 'al-ways' is equally empty.

In Bergson's most famous work, *CE*, he asserts that 'It is no longer then of the universe in its totality that we must speak...for the universe is not made, but is being made continually'. The point here is not a quantitative one concerning an expanding, condensing or dying universe, but deals with the emergence of unforeseeable novelty. And this novelty also concerns our thoughts in and about philosophy. In philosophy, because Bergson believes that the way to remedy our overly rigid thinking is by thinking 'in' *durée*, and with that he commends the use of fluid concepts and permanently mutating philosophical schemes: metaphysics, he writes, must be perpetually 'remodelling' itself on the processes of reality. Yet, then this enterprise begins to merge with the process even of philosophy as such, where fundamental principles proceed to dichotomise into new, apparently opposed forms.[104] The highest-order descriptions must themselves transform, these alterations being one more example of a process. However, even the 'must' here is not a necessity, however nonsensical this must sound. Just as we are about fall into nonsense, into paradox, a new level is engendered where the certainties and 'always' at one level, become partial and transient. Reality, says Bergson, is neither finite nor infinite but 'indefinite': 'action on the move', we recall, 'creates its own route, creates to a very great extent the conditions under which it is to be fullfilled, and thus baffles all calculation'. In a genuinely creative universe there is the incessant production, not only of what is real, but also of what can be possible, such that 'What is absurd in our eyes is not necessarily so in the eyes of nature'.[105]

Be it described in terms of *durée*, dichotomy, dissociation or *élan*, Bergsonism is a profoundly unstable philosophy. The first half of this book sought the basis of Bergson's dualism in several of these descriptions as they occur in *TFW* and his other books up to *TSMR*. Now we have learnt that not one of these terms is the key, because this dualism should really be read as a metaphilosophical dualisation: the perpetual reflection of philosophy upon itself; a self-reference which must first engender paradox and, then, not a fall into relativism or a rejection of metaphysics, but a new level of philosophical vocabulary. Philosophy in evolution. Remember that Bergson advises that his own concepts such as *durée* and qualitative multiplicity must eventually be superseded. Such linguistic supersession is not simply a question of avoiding a fall into platitudes and rigid associations; rather, it is essential, he says, that we continually create new concepts instead of simply new names for old concepts. For Bergson, philosophy is not about discovering the right expression to represent reality, be that reality a process one or not: the absolute is not comprehended simply 'by giving it a name'.[106] On the contrary, because logical essences themselves mutate, philosophy is about *creating* the right expression. To understand how and why Bergson's pluralist discourse is engendered one must restore priority to the metaphilosophy of change at the heart of his work: this is not the 'abandonment of rigorous critical standards' Isaiah Berlin thought it to be, but the production of something quite rare, a living philosophy.

NOTES

1. *CM*, p. 206 [*OE*, p. 1438].
2. *CM*, pp. 207–8, 207, 206 [*OE*, pp. 1439, 1438, 1437–8].
3. *TFW*, p. 219 [*OE*, pp. 143–4].
4. *ME*, p. 7 [*OE*, p. 818].
5. *CE*, pp. 89, 90, 111–12 [*OE*, pp. 567, 568, 586].
6. *CM*, p. 34 [*OE*, p. 1274].
7. For the 'things in general' and 'past in general', see *M*, pp. 411, 1062.
8. *CM*, p. 200 [*OE*, p. 1432].
9. Paradis 1991, pp. 17, 19; see also *CM*, p. 40.
10. *MM*, p. 1 [*OE*, p. 169].
11. *CM*, p. 26 [*OE*, p. 1268].
12. *CE*, p. 380 [*OE*, p. 799]. See for examples *CE*, p. 224 [*OE*, p. 675]: 'Deduction succeeds in things moral only metaphorically' and *TFW*, p. 58 [*OE*, p. 41]: 'It is only by a metaphor that a sensation can be said to be an equal distance from two others'.
13. *M*, p. 1064. This brings Bergson closer here to Wittgenstein's plea for 'perspicuity' as opposed to Carnap's 'model of clarity by explication'; see Hart 1990, p. 215.
14. On simplicity: see *TFW*, p. 141 [*OE*, pp. 93–4]; on unity and multiplicity: *TFW*, pp. 80, 83, 87 [*OE*, pp. 54–5, 56–7, 59]; on same and other: *TFW*, pp. 121–2 [*OE*, pp. 80–1]. See also *CE*, pp. 239–40 [*OE*, p. 688] on types of 'likeness' or *MM* pp. 208–10 [*OE*, pp. 300–11] on types of 'similarity'. *CM*, pp. 35–6 [*OE*, p. 1276] adds further to types of clarity and *TFW*, pp. 75–6n [*OE*, p. 52n] provides two senses of the verb 'to distinguish'.
15. *CM*, p. 53 [*OE*, p. 1295].
16. *TSMR*, pp. 116, 161 [*OE*, pp. 1073, 1112].
17. *CE*, p. 169 [*OE*, p. 631].
18. Bergson 1970, pp. 34–5: commends the Pythagoreans for having the first insight into the relations between number and space.
19. Čapek 1971, p. 176.
20. This use of qualitative multiplicity belongs to the early phase in his thought when he simply opposed it to quantity rather than allowing it to subtend both quantity and quality as in his later work.
21. *TFW*, pp. 121, 85–7, 121–3, 127–8 [*OE*, pp. 81, 58–9, 80–2, 84–5]. That there is a difference in kind between quality and quantity is a token of the fact that this theory of number in *TFW* represents Bergson's earliest understanding of qualitative multiplicity, and so has yet to reach its more sophisticated rendering in *CM*.
22. Russell 1914, p. 14.
23. *TFW*, p. 95 [*OE*, p. 64].
24. Carr 1914, p. 28.
25. Čapek 1971, p. 182.
26. Brouwer 1975b, p. 492; see also Reichenbach 1959, pp. 189–90.
27. See Wittgenstein 1974 at 1.13, 2.11, 2.202, 3.4, 3.42, 4.463; see also Pariente 1969, pp. 198–9.
28. Čapek 1971, p. 76.
29. See Frege 1972, p. 330. The second and third reefs were accounting for the numbers zero and one, and accounting for large numbers. As we know from Chapter Six, for Bergson, zero would be less a number than an erroneous concept, namely

that of nothingness which has behind it an act of negation inspired by desire and regret. As for the number one, if Milič Čapek is right and Bergson does strongly resemble that other intuitionist philosopher of number, L. E. J. Brouwer (see Čapek 1971, pp. 183–4), then Brouwer's notion of 'two-ity' (Brouwer 1975d, p. 523) or 'two-oneness' (Čapek 1971, p. 184) would provide the strategy for accounting for the number one. Brouwer also provides the answer to Frege's last reef concerning the inability of any psychologism to account for the existence of large numbers. All such numbers only come into existence when they are known to exist: we create them (see Brouwer 1975b, p. 482).

30. This strategy is all the more justified when we consider that Frege's account of this *Frege* problem for psychologism can be found in his review of Husserl's 1891 *Philosophy of Arithmetic* and its theory of the 'genuine apprehension of a plurality' which, as Aron Gurwitsch has pointed out (see Gurwitsch 1964, p. 140n127), bears considerable comparison with Bergson's concept of qualitative multiplicity in *TFW*.

31. *TFW*, pp. 75–9 [*OE*, pp. 51–4].

32. Frege 1972, p. 330.

33. See *TFW*, pp. 97, 138 [*OE*, pp. 65–6, 91].

34. *CE*, pp. 11, 221–2 [*OE*, pp. 502, 673].

35. We are leaving aside the issue of whether Frege should have posited this supersensuous realm at all if there is already enough in his other ideas to obviate its necessity; see on this Dummett 1991, pp. 249–62.

36. See Brouwer 1975c, p. 508.

37. See *DS*, p. 134 [*M*, p. 189].

38. *CE*, pp. 223, 231–2 [*OE*, pp. 674, 681].

39. *CM*, pp. 21, 23–4 [*OE*, pp. 1262, 1265].

40. Other examples he gives include how a work of genius only becomes such a 'work of genius' retrospectively by bringing with it 'a conception of art and an artistic atmosphere which brings it within our comprehension' (*TSMR*, p. 75 [*OE*, p. 1308]). Equally, historical actions, defying all calculation, nonetheless create their 'own route' or 'the conditions under which…[they are] to be fulfilled' (*TSMR*, p. 296 [*OE*, p. 1227]); in other words, they prepare the structural forces – economic, ideological and so on – that will become their own explanation.

41. See *CM*, pp. 25–6 [*OE*, pp. 1266–7].

42. See *TSMR*, p. 294 [*OE*, p. 1225] and Lacey 1989, p. 184.

43. We take this list from Blackburn 1984, p. 213.

44. When he does deny it, he describes any notion of possibility as merely 'the mirage of the present in the past' (*CM*, p. 101 [*OE*, p. 1341]).

45. See Jankélévitch 1959, pp. 21, 61.

46. Once created, a possible work of art, for instance, 'will then be real, and by that very fact it becomes retrospectively or retroactively possible' (*CM*, p. 100 [*OE*, p. 1340]).

47. Deleuze 1988, p. 34.

48. *CM*, p. 101 [*OE*, p. 1340].

49. *CE*, p. 7 [*OE*, p. 500].

50. Deleuze 1989, p. 130.

51. See *CM*, p. 22 [*OE*, p. 1263].

52. *CM*, pp. 215, 216 [*OE*, p. 1447]. A. R. Lacey points to Bergson's 'affinity with

[William] James' and 'the strong pragmatist element in Bergson' (1989, p. 92; see also p. 131).

53. Though Bergson does make a distinction between truth and reality in one instance of correspondence with William James: see *M*, p. 727.

54. Certain theorists are of the opinion that truth must not only pertain exclusively to language, but must pertain to one type of linguistic entity alone, statements (see, for instance, Goodman 1978, p. 19: 'Finally, for nonverbal versions [of the world] and even for verbal versions without statements, truth is irrelevant'). Bergson, on the contrary, would see perception, art and belief being just as open to the category of truthfulness as is language. See for some useful comments on this geneal issue Tallis 1988, p. 248: 'Truth may be variously seen as residing in the relation between: perception and reality; belief and reality; knowledge and reality; thought and reali-ty...and so on. It may even be argued that truth resides in reality itself...Why, then, choose the relations between *statements* and reality as the privileged repository of truth?'

55. *M*, p. 1092.

56. See *CM*, p. 217 [*OE*, p. 1449]; *CE*, pp. 164, 226 [*OE*, pp. 627, 677].

57. *CM*, p. 22 [*OE*, p. 1263].

58. *CE*, p. 17 [*OE*, p. 508].

59. *TSMR* p. 12 [*OE*, p. 984].

60. Nor should we forget that the facts themselves, that is, particular observations, can be more or less theory-laden.

61. Rescher 1996, p. 91.

62. This is a corollary of Bergson's view that Paul cannot fully represent Peter without being Peter, one condition of which is that one is not representing Peter.

63. Bateson 1972, p. 338; Winograd and Flores 1986, p. 43n7; Derrida 1982.

64. *M*, p. 1052; *CE*, p. 207 [*OE*, p. 661]; *CM*, pp. 134, 196 [*OE*, pp. 1370, 1400].

65. Significant research has been done to show what hold the image of containment has on our thought, in terms of how we think of both our body and the world, and our abstract reasoning; see Johnson 1987, pp. 20–40. In particular he states that 'Whether in one, two, or three dimensions, the physical *in-out* orientation involves separation, differentiation, and enclosure, which implies restriction and limitation' (p. 22). He also lists five 'entailments' of containment: protection from/resistance to external forces; limitation; fixity of location; in/accessibility to view; and transitivity.

66. See *CE*, pp. 156–8 [*OE*, pp. 620–2].

67. *MM*, p. 260 [*OE*, p. 333].

68. It is noteworthy that in Gregory Bateson's model for the genesis of higher symbolic functioning in organisms, the assumption must be made that the context in which a potential sign is being produced never changes, otherwise a second-order learning, an image of an image (which is one of Bergson's descriptions of an idea – see *CE*, pp. 167–8 [*OE*, p. 630]), can never be generated. See Bateson 1972, p. 288.

69. *CM*, p. 84 [*OE*, p. 1384].

70. See Hylton 1984, p. 394: 'Philosophy is a subject for which the meaningfulness of its terms and the correctness of its procedures is always an issue; the distinction between philosophy and metaphilosophy is therefore not a useful one, because meta-level issues constantly arise, within the practice of the subject'.

71. We are ignoring the possibility of taking 'first philosophy' as a mere principle of methodological inquiry which remains agnostic regarding ontological questions: in

our view, the normative significance of a first philosophy must also entail an ontological heirarchy incompatible with non-monistic philosophies.

72. Levinas 1987a, p. 165.
73. Levinas 1969, pp. 51, 172, 210, 281.
74. Ibid. p. 73.
75. See ibid. 1969, p. 103: 'The Place of the Good above every essence is the most profound teaching...of philosophy. The paradox of an Infinity admitting a being outside of itself which it does not encompass, and accomplishing its very infinitude by virtue of this proximity of a separated being – in a word, the paradox of creation – thenceforth loses something of its audacity'.
76. In his works after *Totality and Infinity*, especially *Otherwise than Being or Beyond Essence*, what comes to the fore is the issue of Levinas' enunciation of his philosophy and how it must also operate as an ethical 'saying' too.
77. Deleuze 1990b, p. 278; Deleuze 1990a, p. 227.
78. See Deleuze 1990b, pp. 308–9.
79. Deleuze 1987, pp. 20–1.
80. See Deleuze and Parnet 1987, pp. 33–4.
81. See Mullarkey 1997 for a critique of Deleuze's materialistic reduction of molar entities.
82. *CM*, pp. 31, 48 [*OE*, pp. 1272, 1290–1].
83. *CM*, pp. 48–9 [*OE*, p. 1291].
84. *CM*, p. 31 [*OE*, p. 1272].
85. Čapek 1971, p. 193; Čapek 1987, p. 132; Mourélos 1964, p. 90.
86. Carr 1975, p. vii.
87. See *TSMR*, pp. 296ff [*OE*, pp. 1227ff].
88. Nicholas Rescher (1996, p. 151), however, seems less concerned with a similar issue to this in his own presentation of process metatheory: 'No matter what law may be at issue, we can ask questions about it that demand an answer in lawful terms. Given such as unending exfoliation of law levels, new metadisciplines can in theory always spring up to relate old disciplines. A fundamental principle is at work here. Since laws take the hypothetical form "If such-and-such possibilities were realized, such-and-such results would ensue", the finitude of the manifold of actuality does not entail the finitude of the diversity of laws'. In response to this optimism, we might still ask: how 'fundamental' is this principle? As just one more metatheory, surely it too can 'exfoliate'?
89. It is also amazing that Bergson should deem the law of dichotomy a fundamental reality, calling it the 'workings of nature' (*TSMR*, p. 297 [*OE*, p. 1228].), when Zeno's first paradox – which is closely associated with the Achilles paradox (emblematic of all Bergson opposes) – is also called 'the dichotomy' (Bergson calls it that, for instance, at *M*, p. 757). Here we see Bergson's duplicitous attitude even to the term 'dichotomy' itself.
90. Quine 1976, pp. 7, 5, 12.
91. *M*, p. 1092.
92. See Moore 1996, pp. 31–2.
93. See *CE*, pp. 167–8 [*OE*, pp. 629–30].
94. Quine 1976, p. 12.
95. See Russell 1956, pp. 59–102.

96.   Russell eventually adopted a linguistic interpretation of the theory of types: a differ-
      ent type equals a different syntactical function rather than different type of entity.
97.   See Smith 1994b, who argues that this regress can be infinite and benign.
98.   *MM*, p. 270 [*OE*, p. 339]. We might add ourselves that the notions of difference
      and repetition pulsating at the heart of *durée* can both be metaforms too: when the
      property of self-identity inheres in some entity it also inheres in its own inherence
      in that thing, for the inherence of self-identity in the entity is the same as the inher-
      ence of self-identity in the thing. And when one entity is different from another,
      the inherence of this difference in the first is also different from its inherence in the
      second, as is the inherence of difference in the inherence of difference in the first,
      and so on to infinity; see Smith 1994b, pp. 192–3. Smith adds that these regresses
      are benign in that each regress has a complete *analysans*, namely, a sentence which
      explicitly refers to all stages of the regress by means of a phrase like 'and so on to
      infinity'.
99.   See Bergson 1999, p. 86.
100. *MM*, p. 236 [*OE*, p. 318].
101. Ayer 1972, p. 49. See also Russell 1956, p. 62: 'Whatever we suppose to be the
      totality of propositions, statements about this totality generate new propositions
      which, on pain of contradiction, must lie outside the totality . . . Hence there must
      be no totality of propositions, and "all propositions" must be a meaningless phrase.'
102. Skorupski 1993, pp. 165–7.
103. *CM*, p. 176 [*OE*, p. 1409].
104. *CE*, pp. 254–5 [*OE*, pp. 669–70]; *CM*, p. 34 [*OE*, p. 1275]; *ME*, p. 77 [*OE*, p.
      862]. Therewith, the impression that metaphilosophy is simply more philosophy is
      given some credibility; only some, though, because there is still an inside and an
      outside to philosophy such that a reflection on philosophy can remain non-philoso-
      phy, if only momentarily. What must be admitted, however, is that the inside –
      outside dichotomy is real but also dynamic, so that what may begin on the outside
      (meta-philosophy), may eventually be incorporated into an inside.
105. *CM*, p. 211 [*OE*, p. 1442]; *TSMR*, p. 296 [*OE*, p. 1227]; *CM*, pp. 21, 206 [*OE*,
      pp. 1262, 1438].
106. *CM*, p. 49 [*OE*, p. 1291].

Bibliography

Wherever a translation or later edition of a book or article is cited in the bibliography, the original year of publication (where available) will be in square brackets after the title of the work. Where two works by an author have the same year of publication there is an additional letter (a, b, c, and so on) following the year, to distinguish their abbreviated forms in the endnotes.

Alexander, Ian W. (1957), *Bergson: Philosopher of Reflection*, London: Bowes and Bowes.

Alexander, Samuel (1966), *Space, Time and Deity* [1922], two volumes, London: Macmillan.

American Psychiatric Association (1994), *Diagnostic and Statistical Manual of Mental Disorders, Fourth Edition*, Washington, D.C.: American Psychiatric Association.

Ayer, A. J. (1972), *Russell*, London: Fontana.

Bachelard, Gaston (1963), *Dialectique de la Durée* [1936], Paris: Presses Universitaires de France.

Balibar, Etienne (1991), 'Citizen Subject', in Cadava et al. 1991, pp. 33–57.

Barron, Frank (1987), 'Bergson and the Modern Psychology of Creativity', in Papanicolaou and Gunter 1987, pp. 205–22.

Barthelemy-Madaule, Madeleine (1966), *Bergson, adversaire de Kant: Etude Critique de la Conception Bergsonienne du Kantisme*, Paris: Presses Universitaires de France.

Bateson, Gregory (1972), *Steps to an Ecology of Mind*, New York: Ballantine Books.

Beckner, Morton (1972), 'Vitalism', in *The Encyclopedia of Philosophy*, Vol. VIII, New York: Macmillan and The Free Press, pp. 253–6.

Béguin, Albert, and Pierre Thévanez (eds.) (1943), *Henri Bergson: Essais et Témoignages*, Neuchâtel: Editions de la Baconnière.

Bell, David, and Neil Cooper (1990), *The Analytic Tradition: Meaning, Thought and Knowledge*, Oxford: Blackwell.

Benjamin, Andrew, and Peter Osborne (eds) (1991), *Thinking Art: Beyond Traditional Aesthetics*, London: Philosophical Forum/Institute of Contemporary Arts.

Benjamin, Walter (1992), *Illuminations*, edited by Hanna Arendt, London: Fontana.

Bergson, Henri (1969a), 'Fictitious Times and Real Times' [1924], translated by P. A. Y. Gunter, in Gunter 1969, pp. 168–86.

——(1969b), 'Henri Bergson, Albert Einstein and Henri Piéron: Remarks concerning Relativity Theory', in Gunter 1969, pp. 123–35.

——(1970), 'Aristotle's Concept of Place' [1889], translated by John K. Ryan, in *Ancients and Moderns: Studies in Philosophy and the History of Philosophy*, vol. XV, Washington, D.C.: Catholic University of America Press, pp. 20–72.

——(1999) 'A Letter from Bergson to John Dewey', in Mullarkey 1999, pp. 84–7.

Bidney, D. (ed.) (1963), *The Concept of Freedom in Anthropology*, The Hague: Mouton.

Blackburn, Simon (1984), *Spreading the Word: Groundings in the Philosophy of Language*, Oxford: Clarendon Press.

Blanché, Robert (1969), 'The Psychology of Duration and the Physics of Fields' [1951], translated by P. A. Y. Gunter, in Gunter 1969, pp. 106–20.

Borch-Jacobsen, Mikkel (1991), 'The Freudian Subject, from Politics to Ethics', in Cadava et al. 1991, pp. 61–78.

Borst, C. V. (1970), 'Introduction', in Borst (ed.) *The Mind/Brain Identity Theory*, London: Macmillan, pp. 13–29.

Boundas, Constantin V. (1996), 'Deleuze-Bergson: An Ontology of the Virtual', in Patton 1996, pp. 81–106.

Brooks, Daniel R., and E. O. Wiley (1988), *Evolution as Entropy: Toward a Unified Biology* [1986], Chicago and London: University of Chicago Press.

Brouwer, L. E. J. (1975a), *Collected Works: Volume One: Philosophy and Foundations of Mathematics*, edited by A. Heyting, Amsterdam: North-Holland.

——(1975b), 'Consciousness, Philosophy, and Mathematics' [1948], in Brouwer 1975a, pp. 480–94.

——(1975c), 'Historical Background, Principles and Methods of Intuitionism' [1952], in Brouwer 1975a, pp. 508–15.

——(1975d), 'Points and Spaces' [1954], in Brouwer 1975a, pp. 522–38.

Burwick, Frederick, and Paul Douglass (eds.) (1992), *The Crisis in Modernism: Bergson and the Vitalist Controversy*, Cambridge: Cambridge University Press.

Cadava, Eduardo, Peter Connor, and Jean-Luc Nancy (eds.) (1991), *Who Comes After the Subject?*, London: Routledge.

Canguilhem, Georges (1943), 'Commentaire au troisième chapitre de *L'Evolution créatrice*', in *Bulletin de la faculté des lettres de Strasbourg*, vol. XXI, nos. 5–6, pp. 126–43 and no. 8, pp. 199–214.

Čapek Milič (1952), 'La Genèse idéale de la matière chez Bergson', in *Revue de métaphysique et de morale*, vol. LVII, pp. 325–48.

——(1971), *Bergson and Modern Physics: A Reinterpretation and Re-evaluation*, Dordrecht: D. Reidel.

——(1987), 'Bergson's Theory of the Mind-Brain Relation', in Papanicolaou and Gunter 1987, pp. 129–48.

Cariou, Marie (1990), *Lectures Bergsoniennes*, Paris: Presses Universitaires de France.

——(1999), 'Bergson: The Keyboards of Forgetting', in Mullarkey 1999, pp. 99–117.

Carr, H. W. (1914), 'On Mr. Russell's Reasons for Supposing that Bergson's Philosophy is not True', in Russell 1914, pp. 26–32.

——(1919), *Henri Bergson: The Philosophy of Change*, London and Edinburgh: T. C. and E. C. Jack.

——(1975), 'Translator's Preface', in *ME*, pp. v–viii.

Casey, Edward S. (1984), 'Habitual Body and Memory in Merleau-Ponty', in *Man and World*, vol. XVII, pp. 279–97.

——(1987), *Remembering: A Phenomenological Study*, Bloomington: Indiana University Press.

Casey, Gerard (1992), 'Minds and Machines', in *American Catholic Philosophical Quarterly*, vol. LXVI, pp. 57–80.

Chalier, Catherine, and Miguel Abensour (eds.) (1991), *Emmanuel Lévinas*, Paris: Editions de l'Herne.

Churchland, Paul M. (1979), *Scientific Realism and the Plasticity of Mind*, Cambridge: Cambridge University Press.

——(1988), *Matter and Consciousness: A Contemporary Introduction to the Philosophy of Mind* [1984], Cambridge, MA: MIT Press.

——(1990), 'Eliminative Materialism and the Propositional Attitudes' [1981], in Lycan 1990, pp. 206–23.

——(1995) *The Engine of Reason, the Seat of the Soul: A Philosophical Journey into the Brain*, London and Cambridge, MA: Bradford Books.

Clarke, Paul A. B., and Andrew Linzey (eds.) (1990), *Political Theory and Animal Rights*, London: Pluto Press.

Clarke, Simon (1981), *The Foundations of Structuralism: A Critique of Lévi-Strauss and the Structuralist Movement*, Sussex: Harvester Press.

Cohen, Gillian, Michael W. Eysenck and Martin E. Le Voi (1986), *Memory: A Cognitive Approach*, Milton Keynes: Open University Press.

Cohen, Jack, and Ian Stewart (1994), *The Collapse of Chaos: Discovering Simplicity in a Complex World*, London: Viking.

Cohen, Richard A. (1987), 'Translator's Introduction', in Levinas 1987b, pp. 1–28.

Coveney, Peter, and Roger Highfield (1991), *The Arrow of Time: The Quest to Solve Science's Greatest Mystery*, London: Flamingo.

Crane, Tim, and D. H. Mellor (1990), 'There is No Question of Physicalism', in *Mind*, vol. XCIX, pp. 185–206.

Critchley, Simon (1992), *The Ethics of Deconstruction: Derrida and Levinas*, Oxford and Cambridge MA: Blackwell.

Danto, Arthur, and Sidney Morgenbesser (1960), *Philosophy of Science*, New York: World Publishing.

Davidson, Donald (1980), *Essays on Actions and Events*, Oxford: Clarendon.

Davies, Paul, and John Gribbin (1991), *The Matter Myth: Towards 21st-century Science*, London: Viking.

Dawkins, Richard (1982), *The Extended Phenotype: The Gene as the Unit of Selection*, Oxford and San Francisco: W. H. Freeman.

——(1986), *The Blind Watchmaker*, Harlow, Essex: Longman Scientific and Technical.

——(1989), *The Selfish Gene* [1976], Oxford: Oxford University Press.

Deleuze, Gilles (1956), 'La Conception de la Différence chez Bergson', in *Les Etudes Bergsoniennes*, vol. IV, pp. 77–112.

——(1972), *Proust and Signs* [1964], translated by Richard Howard, London: Allen Lane.

——(1986), *Cinema 1: The Movement-Image* [1983], translated by Hugh Tomlinson and Barbara Habberjam, London: Athlone Press.

——(1988), *Bergsonism* [1966], translated by Hugh Tomlinson and Barbara Habberjam, New York: Zone Books.

——(1989), *Cinema 2: The Time-Image* [1985], translated by Hugh Tomlinson and Robert Galeta, London: Athlone Press.

——(1990a), *Expressionism in Philosophy: Spinoza* [1968], translated by Martin Joughin, New York: Zone Books.

——(1990b), *The Logic of Sense* [1969], translated by Mark Lester with Charles Stivale, edited by Constantin V. Boundas, New York: Columbia University Press.

——(1994), *Difference and Repetition* [1968], translated by Paul Patton, London: Athlone Press.

——(1995), *Negotiations, 1972–1990* [1990], translated by Martin Joughin, New York: Columbia University Press.

——and Félix Guattari (1987), *A Thousand Plateaus* [1980], translated by Brian Massumi, London: Athlone Press.

——and Claire Parnet (1987), *Dialogues* [1977] translated by Hugh Tomlinson and Barbara Habberjam, London: Athlone Press.

Delhomme, Jeanne (1954), *Vie et conscience de la Vie: Essais sur Bergson*, Paris: Presses Universitaires de France.

——(1960), 'Nietzsche et Bergson: La Representation de la Vérité', in *Les Etudes Bergsoniennes*, vol. V, pp. 37–62.

Dennett, Daniel C. (1979), *Brainstorms: Philosophical Essays on Mind and Psychology* [1978], Sussex: Harvester Press.

——(1991), *Consciousness Explained*, London: Allen Lane.

Derrida, Jacques (1982), 'Signature, Event, Context' [1972], in Derrida *Margins of Philosophy*, translated by Alan Bass, Sussex: Harvester Press, pp. 307–30.

Descombes, Vincent (1979), *Modern French Philosophy* [1979], translated by L. Scott-Fox and J. M. Harding, Cambridge: Cambridge University Press.

Dingle, Herbert (1965), 'Introduction', in *DS*, pp. xv–lxii.

Dobzhansky, T., F. J. Ayala, G. L. Stebbins, and J. W. Valentine (1977), *Evolution*, San Francisco: W. H. Freeman.

Douglass, Paul (1992), 'Deleuze's Bergson: Bergson Redux', in Burwick and Douglass 1992, pp. 368–88.

Dretske, Fred (1990), 'Misrepresentation', in Lycan 1990, pp. 129–43.

Dummett, Michael (1991), 'Frege's Myth of the Third Realm' [1981], in Dummett, *Frege and Other Philosophers*, Oxford: Clarendon Press, pp. 249–62.

Edelman, Gerald (1992), *Bright Air, Brilliant Fire: On the Matter of Mind*, London: Penguin.

Eigen, Manfred (1992), *Steps Towards Life: A Perspective on Evolution* [1987], translated by Paul Woolley, Oxford: Oxford University Press.

Eldridge, Niles (1995), *Reinventing Darwin: The Great Debate at the High Table of Evolutinary Theory*, New York: John Wiley & Sons.

Fabre-Luce de Gruson, Françoise (1959), 'Sens Commun et Bon Sens chez Bergson', in *Revue Internationale de Philosophie*, vol. XIII, pp. 187–200.

Fodor, Jerry A. (1987), *Psychosemantics: The Problem of Meaning in the Philosophy of Mind*, Cambridge, MA, and London: Bradford.

Frank, Simon (1943), 'L'Intuition Fondamentale de Bergson', in Béguin and Thévanez 1943, pp. 187–95.

Frege, Gottlob (1972), 'Review of Dr. E. Husserl's *Philosophy of Arithmetic*' [1894], translated by E. W. Kluge, in *Mind*, vol. LXXXI, pp. 321–37.

Gale, R. M. (1973–74), 'Bergson's Analysis of the Concept of Nothing', in *The Modern Schoolman*, vol. LI, pp. 269–300.

Gallagher, Idealla J. (1970), *Morality in Evolution: The Moral Philosophy of Henri Bergson*, The Hague: Martinus Nijhoff.

Gallois, Philippe, and Gérard Forzy (eds) (1997), *Bergson et les neurosciences: Actes du colloque international de neuro-philosophie*, Le Plessis-Robinson: Institut Synthélabo.

Game, Ann (1991), *Undoing the Social: Towards a Deconstructive Sociology*, Milton Keynes: Open University Press.

Gilson, Bernard (1978), *L'Individualité dans la philosophie de Bergson*, Paris: Librairie Philosophique J. Vrin.

Giroux, Laurent (1971), *Durée Pure et Temporalité: Bergson et Heidegger*, Montreal: Ballarmin.

Globus, Gordon G. (1995), *The Postmodern Brain*, Amsterdam and Philadelphia: John Benjamins.

Goodman, Nelson (1978), *Ways of Worldmaking*, Sussex: Harvester Press.

Goodwin, Brian (1994), *How the Leopard Changed its Spots: The Evolution of Complexity*, London: Weidenfeld and Nicholson.

Gouhier, Henri (1972), '*Avant-propos*', in *M*, pp. vii–xxiii.

——(1987), *Bergson et le Christ des évangiles* [1961], Paris: Vrin.

Gould, Stephen Jay, and Niles Eldridge (1972), 'Punctuated Equilbria: an Alternative to Phyletic Gradualism', in Schopf 1972, pp. 82–115.

——and Richard C. Lewontin (1994), 'The Spandrels of San Marco and the Panglossian Paradigm: A Critique of the Adaptationist Programme' [1978], in Sober 1994, pp. 73–90.

Gregory, R. L. (ed.) (1987), *The Oxford Companion to the Mind*, Oxford: Oxford University Press.

Griffin, David Ray, John B. Cobb Jr., Marcus P. Ford, Pete A. Y. Gunter, (1993), *Founders of Constructive Postmodern Philosophy: Pierce, James, Bergson, Whitehead, and Hartshorne*, Albany: SUNY Press.

Grogin, R. C. (1988), *The Bergsonian Controversy in France, 1900–1914*, Calgary: The University of Calgary Press.

Gross, David (1985), 'Bergson, Proust and the Re-evaluation of Memory', in *International Philosophical Quarterly*, vol. XXV, pp. 369–80.

Gunter, P. A. Y. (ed.) (1969), *Bergson and the Evolution of Physics*, Knoxville: University of Tennessee Press.

——(1971), 'Bergson's Theory of Matter and Modern Cosmology', in *Journal of the History of Idéas*, vol. XXXII, pp. 525–42.

——(1983), 'Introduction to the UPA Edition', in UPA editon of *Creative Evolution*, pp. xvii–li, Washington, D.C.: University Press of America.

——(ed.) (1986), *Henri Bergson: A Bibliography* [1974], Bowling Green, OH: Philosophy Documentation Center, Bowling Green State University.

——(1992), 'Bergson and Sartre: The Rise of French Existentialism', in Burwick and Douglass 1992, pp. 230–44.

——(1993), 'Henri Bergson', in Griffin et al. 1993, pp. 133–63.

——(1995), 'Bergson's Philosophy of Education', *Educational Theory*, vol. XLV, pp. 379–94.

Gurwitsch, Aron (1964), *The Field of Consciousness*, Pittsburgh: Duquesne University Press.

Hand, Séan (ed.) (1989), *The Levinas Reader*, Oxford: Blackwell.

Hanna, Thomas (1962), 'The Bergsonian Heritage', in Hanna (ed.) *The Bergsonian Heritage*, New York and London: Columbia University Press, pp. 1–31.

de la Harpe, Jean (1943), 'Souvenirs Personnels d'un Entretien avec Bergson', in Béguin and Thévanez 1943, pp. 357–64.

Hart, W. D. (1990), 'Clarity', in Bell and Cooper 1990, pp. 197–222.

Hartshorne, Charles (1987), 'Bergson's Aesthetic Creationism Compared to Whitehead's', in Papanicolaou and Gunter 1987, pp. 369–82.

Hausman, Carl R. (1975), *A Discourse on Novelty and Creation*, Albany: State University of New York Press.

Heidsieck, François (1957), *Henri Bergson et la notion d'Espace*, Paris: Le Circle du Livre.

Herman, Daniel J. (1980), *The Philosophy of Henri Bergson*, Washington, D.C.: University Press of America.

Hude, Henri (1989–90), *Bergson I et II*, Paris: Editions Universitaires.

Husson, Léon (1959), 'La Portée Lointaine de la Psychologie Bergsonienne', in *Actes du Xe Congrès des Sociétés de Philosophie de Langue Française*, Paris: Armand Colin (henceforth '*Actes*'), pp. 157–62.

Hylton, Peter (1984), 'The Nature of the Proposition and the Revolt Against Idealism', in Rorty, Schneewind, and Skinner 1984, pp. 375–97.

Hyppolite, Jean (1991a), 'Aspects Diverses de la Mémoire' [1949], in Hyppolite, *Jean Hyppolite: Figures de la pensée philosophique*, Paris: Presses Universitaires de France, two volumes, vol. one, pp. 468–88.

——(1991b), 'Du Bergsonisme à l'Existentialisme' [1949], in Hyppolite, *Jean Hyppolite: Figures de la Pensée Philosophique*, two volumes, vol. one, Paris: Presses Universitaires de France, pp. 443–58.

Ingold, Tom (1995), 'Swept Away by the Current, Review of *River out of Eden*', in *Times Higher Educational Supplement*, 16 June, no. 1180, p. 28.

Jankélévitch, Vladimir (1959), *Henri Bergson*, Paris: Presses Universitaires de France.

Johnson, Mark (1987), *The Body in the Mind: The Bodily Basis of Meaning, Imagination, and Reason*, Chicago and London: The University of Chicago Press.

Kearney, Richard (1984), *Dialogues with Contemporary Continental Thinkers: The Phenomenological Heritage*, Manchester: Manchester University Press.

Kemp-Smith, Norman (1947–8), 'Bergson's Manner of Approach to Moral and Social Questions', in *Proceedings of the Aristotelian Society*, vol. XLVIII, pp. 1–18.

Kim, Jaegwon (1994), 'The Myth of Nonreductive Materialism' [1989], in Warner and Szubka 1994, pp. 242–60.

Lacey, A. R. (1989), *Bergson*, London: Routledge.

de Lattre, Alain (1990), *Bergson: Une Ontologie de la Perplexité*, Paris: Presses Universitaires de France.

Lecercle, Jean-Jacques (1991), 'Berkeley: Bishop or Busby? Deleuze on Cinema', in Benjamin and Osborne 1991, pp. 193–206.

Levinas, Emmanuel (1969), *Totality and Infinity: An Essay on Exteriority* [1961], translated by Alphonso Lingis, The Hague: Nijhoff.

——(1981), *Otherwise Than Being or Beyond Essence* [1978], translated by Alphonso Lingis, The Hague: Nijhoff.

——(1985), *Ethics and Infinity* [1982], translated by Richard A. Cohen, Pittsburgh: Duquesne University Press.

——(1987a), *Collected Philosophical Papers*, translated by Alphonso Lingis, The Hague: Nijhoff.

——(1987b), *Time and the Other* [1983], translated by Richard A. Cohen, Pittsburgh: Duquesne University Press.

——(1989), 'Ethics as First Philosophy' [1984], translated by Séan Hand and Michael Temple, in Hand 1989, pp. 75–87.

Lewin, Roger (1992), *Complexity: Life at the Edge of Chaos*, New York: Macmillan.

Lewis, David (1990), 'What Experience Teaches' [1988], in Lycan 1990, pp. 499–519.

Liedloff, Jean (1986), *The Continuum Concept* [1975], London: Penguin.

Llewelyn, John (1995), *Emmanuel Levinas: The Genealogy of Ethics*, London and New York: Routledge.

Loveday, T. (1908), 'Review of *L'Evolution créatrice*', in *Mind*, vol. XVII, pp. 402–8.

Lycan, William G. (1990), 'The Continuity of Levels of Nature' [1987], in Lycan, *Mind and Cognition: A Reader*, Oxford: Blackwell, pp. 77–96.

Lyons, Joseph (1987), *Ecology of the Body: Styles of Behaviour in Human Life*, Durham, NC: Duke University Press.

Maritain, Jacques (1968), *Bergsonian Philosophy and Thomism* [1948], translated by Mabelle L. Andison and J. Gordon Andison, New York: Greenwood Press.

May, William E. (1970), 'The Reality of Matter in the Metaphysics of Bergson', in *International Philosophical Quarterly*, vol. X, pp. 611–42.

McLure, Roger (1982), 'Original and Psychic Temporality (A Study in Ontological Meaning and Foundation)', in Wood and Bernasconi 1982, pp. 161–97.

McTaggart, J. M. E. (1908), 'The Unreality of Time', in *Mind*, vol. XVII, pp. 457–74.

Mellor, Hugh (1981), *Real Time*, Cambridge: Cambridge University Press.

Merleau-Ponty, Maurice (1960), *Elogie de la philosophie et Autres Essais*, Paris: Gallimard.

——(1962), *Phenomenology of Perception* [1945], translated by Colin Smith, London: Routledge and Kegan Paul.

Midgley, Mary (1980), *Beast and Man: The Roots of Human Nature*, London: Methuen.

Minski, Marvin (1988), *The Society of Mind*, New York: Touchstone.

Miquel, Paul (1994), 'Animalité et humanité dans *L'Evolution créatrice* de Bergson', in Niderst 1994, pp. 201–11.

Missa, Jean-Noël (1993), *L'Esprit-cerveau: La philosophie de l'esprit à la lumière des neurosciences*, Paris: Vrin.

Monod, Jacques (1972), *Chance and Necessity: An Essay on the Natural Philosophy of Modern Biology* [1970], translated by Austryn Wainhouse, London: Collins.

Moore, F. C. T. (1996), *Bergson, Thinking Backwards*, Cambridge: Cambridge University Press.

Morot-Sir, Edouard (1962), 'What Bergson Means to Us Today', in Hanna 1962, pp. 35–53.

Mourélos, Georges (1964), *Bergson et les Niveaux de Réalité*, Paris: Presses Universitaires de France.

Mullarkey, John (1994–5), 'Duplicity in the Flesh: Bergson and Current Philosophy of the Body', in *Philosophy Today*, vol. XXXVIII, pp. 339–55.

——(1997), 'Deleuze and Materialism: One or Many Matters?' in *South Atlantic Quarterly*, vol. XCVI, pp. 439–63.

——(ed.) (1999), *The New Bergson*, Manchester: Manchester University Press.

Nagel, Thomas (1979), 'What is it Like to be a Bat?' [1974], in Nagel, *Mortal Questions*, Cambridge: Cambridge University Press, pp. 165–80.

——(1986), *The View from Nowhere*, Oxford: Oxford University Press.

Nemirow, Lawrence (1990), 'Physicalism and the Cognitive Role of Acquaintance', in Lycan 1990, pp. 490–9.

Newton, Isaac (1960), '*Scholium* to the definitions', in Danto and Morgenbesser 1960, pp. 322–9.

Newton-Smith, W. H. (1980), *The Structure of Time*, London: Routledge and Kegan Paul.

Niderst, Alain (ed.) (1994), *L'Animalité: Hommes et animaux dans la littérature française*, Tübingen: Gunter Narr Verlag.

Nowottny, W. (1965), *The Language Poets Use*, London: Athlone Press.

Oaklander, L. Nathan, and Quentin Smith (eds.) (1994), *The New Theory of Time*, New Haven and London: Yale University Press.

Ortony, Andrew (ed.) (1979), *Metaphor and Thought*, Cambridge: Cambridge University Press.

Papanicolaou, A. C., and P. A. Y. Gunter (eds.) (1987), *Bergson and Modern Thought: Towards a Unified Science*, Chur, Switzerland: Harwood Academic Press.

Paradis, Bruno (1991), 'Indétermination et mouvements de birfurcation chez Bergson', in *Philosophie*, no. 32, pp. 11–40.

Pariente, J. C. (1969), 'Bergson et Wittgenstein', in *Revue Internationale de Philosophie*, vol. XXIII, pp. 183–200.

Patton, Paul (ed.) (1996), *Deleuze: A Critical Reader*, Oxford: Blackwell.

Peacocke, Christopher (1989), 'No Resting Place: A Critical Notice of *The View from Nowhere* by Thomas Nagel', in *The Philosophical Review*, vol. XCVIII, pp. 65–82.

Pilkington, A. E. (1976), *Bergson and his Influence: A Reassessment*, Cambridge: Cambridge University Press.

Popper, Karl R. (1966), *The Open Society and its Enemies*, two volumes [1945], London: Routledge and Kegan Paul.

Quine, W. V. O. (1976), *The Ways of Paradox and Other Essays* [1966], Cambridge, MA, and London: Harvard University Press.

Rachels, James (1991), *Created from Animals: The Moral Implications of Darwinism*, Oxford and New York: Oxford University Press.

Ray, Christopher (1991), *Time, Space, and Philosophy*, London and New York: Routledge.

Reichenbach, Hans (1959), *The Rise of Scientific Philosophy*, Berkeley, University of California Press.

Rescher, Nicholas (1996), *Process Metaphysics: An Introduction to Process Philosophy*, Albany: SUNY Press.

Robinet, André (1965), *Bergson et les métamorphoses de la durée*, Paris: Editions Seghers.

Rorty, Richard (1982), 'Comments on Dennett', in *Synthese*, vol. LIII, pp. 181–7.

J. B. Schneewind and Quentin Skinner (eds.) (1984), *Philosophy in History: Essays on the Historiography of Philosophy*, Cambridge: Cambridge University Press.

Rose, Gillian (1984), *Dialectic of Nihilism: Post-Structuralism and Law*, Oxford: Basil Blackwell.

Rose, Steven (1987), 'Memory: Biological Basis', in Gregory 1987, pp. 456–60.

Russell, Bertrand (1908), 'Mathematical Logic as Based on the Theory of Types', in *American Journal of Mathematics*, vol. XXX, pp. 222–62, reprinted in Russell 1956, pp. 59–102.

——(1914), *The Philosophy of Bergson*, London: Macmillan.

——(1956), *Logic and Knowledge*, London: Allen & Unwin.

Rycroft, Charles (1987), 'Dissociation of the Personality', in Gregory 1987, pp. 197–8.

Ryle, Gilbert (1971), 'The Thinker of Thoughts: What is 'Le Penseur' Doing?' [1968], in Ryle, *Collected Papers*, two volumes, vol. two, London: Hutchinson, pp. 480–96.

Sacks, Sheldon (ed.) (1979), *On Metaphor*, London and Chicago: The University of Chicago Press.

Santoro, Liberato (1993), 'Aristotle's Concept of Mimesis', in Santoro, *The Tortoise and the Lyre: Aesthetic Reconstructions*, Dublin: Irish Academic Press, pp. 38–46.

Scharfstein, Ben-Ami (1943), *Roots of Bergson's Philosophy*, New York: Columbia University Press.

Schlesinger, George (1994), 'Temporal Becoming', in Oaklander and Smith 1994, pp. 214–20.

Schopf, Thomas J. M. (1972), *Models in Paleobiology*, San Francisco: Freeman Cooper.

Schwartz, Sandford (1992), 'Bergson and the Politics of Vitalism', in Burwick and Douglass 1992, pp. 272–305.

Searle, John (1992), *The Rediscovery of the Mind*, Cambridge, MA, and London: MIT Press.

Serres, Michel (1977), *Hermes IV: La Distribution*, Paris: Éditions de Minuit.

Sherry, David M. (1988), 'Zeno's Metrical Paradox Revisited', in *Philosophy of Science*, vol. LV, pp. 58–73.

Singer, Peter (1981), *The Expanding Circle: Ethics and Sociobiology*, Oxford: Clarendon Press.

Sipfle, David A. (1969), 'Henri Bergson and the Epochal Theory of Time', in Gunter 1969, pp. 275–94.

Skorupski, John (1993), *English-Language Philosophy 1750–1945*, Oxford: Oxford University Press.

Smart, J. J. C. (1970), 'Sensations and Brain Processes' [1959], in Borst 1970, pp. 52–66.

Smith, Quentin (1994a), 'General Introduction: The Implications of the Tensed and Tenseless Theories of Time', in Oaklander and Smith 1994, pp. 1–14.

(1994b), 'The Infinite Regress of Temporal Attributions', in Oaklander and Smith 1994, pp. 180–94.

Smolin, Lee, (1997), *The Life of the Cosmos*, London: Weidenfeld and Nicholas.

Sober, Elliot (1993), *The Philosophy of Biology*, Oxford: Oxford University Press.

——(ed.) (1994), *Conceptual Issues in Evolutionary Biology*, Cambridge, MA, and London: Bradford.

Soulez, Philippe (1984), 'Bergson ou la littérature déniee?', in *L'Homme et la société*, nos. 73–4 (July–December), pp. 197–208.

Sperber, Dan (1996), *Explaining Culture: A Naturalistic Approach*, Oxford: Blackwell.

Sperry, Roger (1983), *Science and Moral Priority: Merging Mind, Brain, and Human Values*, Oxford: Blackwell.

Sprigge, T. L. S. (1988), *The Rational Foundation of Ethics*, London: Routledge and Kegan Paul.

Squire, Larry R. (1986), 'Mechanisms of Memory', in *Science*, vol. CCXXXII, pp. 1612–19.

Stephen, Karen (1922), *The Misuse of Mind: A Study of Bergson's Attack On Intellectualism*, London: Kegan Paul, Trench, Trubner.

Sterelny, Kim (1995), 'Understanding Life: Recent Work in Philosophy of Biology', in *British Journal of the Philosophy of Science*, vol. XLVI, pp. 155–83.

Stevenson, J. T. (1970), 'Sensations and Brain Processes: A Reply to J. J. C. Smart' [1960], in Borst 1970, pp. 87–92.

Tallis, Raymond (1988), *Not Saussure: A Critique of Post-Saussurean Literary Theory*, Basingstoke: Macmillan.

——(1991), *The Explicit Animal: A Defence of Human Consciousness*, Basingstoke: Macmillan.

Tallon, Andrew (1973), 'Memory and Man's Composite Nature According to Bergson', in *New Scholasticism*, vol. XLVII, pp. 483–9.

Teichman, Jenny (1988), *Philosophy and the Mind*, Oxford: Blackwell.

Thom, René (1975), *Structural Stability and Morphogenesis: an Outline of a General Theory of Models*, translated by D. H. Fowler, Reading, MA: W. A. Benjamin.

Trotignon, Pierre (1991), 'Autre Voie, Même Voix: Lévinas et Bergson', in Chalier and Abensour, 1991, pp. 287–93.

Wagner, Helmut. R. (1983), *Alfred Schutz: An Intellectual Biography*, Chicago and London: University of Chicago Press.

Wagner, Steven J. (1994), 'Supervenience, Recognition, and Consciousness', in Warner and Szubka 1994, pp. 87–98.

Warner, Richard, and Tadeusz Szubka (1994), *The Mind – Body Problem: A Guide to the Current Debate*, Oxford: Blackwell.

Williams, Clifford (1998), 'A Bergsonian Approach to A- and B-Time', in *Philosophy*, vol. LXXIII, pp. 379–93.

Winograd, Terry, and Fernando Flores (1986), *Understanding Computers and Cognition*, New Jersey: Ablex.

Wittgenstein, Ludwig (1974), *Tractatus Logico-Philosophicus*, London: Routledge and Kegan Paul.

Wolff, Edgar (1957), 'La Théorie de la Mémoire chez Bergson', in *Archives de Philosophie*, vol. XX, pp. 42–77.

——(1959), 'Mémoire et Durée', in *Actes*, pp. 333–7.

Wolsky, Marie de Issekutz, and Alexander A. Wolsky (1992), 'Bergson's Vitalism in the Light of Modern Biology', in Burwick and Douglass 1992, pp. 153–70.

Wood, David (1989), *The Deconstruction of Time*, Atlantic Highlands, N.J.: Humanities Press.

——and Robert Bernasconi (eds) (1982), *Time and Metaphysics*, Warwick: Parousia Press.

Worms, Frédéric (1997a), *Introduction à* Matiére et mémoire *de Bergson*, Paris: Presses Universitaires de France.

(1997b) 'La Théorie bergsonienne des plans de conscience: genèse, structure et signification de *Matière et mémoire*', in Gallois and Forzy 1997, pp. 85–108.

Wright, Larry, 'Functions' [1973], in Sober 1994, pp. 27–47.

Zaner, Richard M. (1971), *The Problem of Embodiment: Some Contributions to a Phenomenology of the Body*, The Hague: Martinus Nijhoff.

Index